Praise for Oola for Women

"*Oola for Women* is the success formula for a new generation. When you're stress-free, inspired, and reaching for your dreams, there's so much you can do . . . for yourself, for your family, for others. Together with women everywhere, Dave Braun and Troy Amdahl will change the world with Oola."

—JACK CANFIELD
Co-Creator of the *Chicken Soup for the Soul*®
book series and international bestselling
author of *The Success Principles*

"The good news about *Oola for Women* is that it doesn't preach or guilt-trip women into fulfilling some pre-defined image of success. We get to be ourselves and choose the ultimate dream life we want. That right there is some serious breathing space. What a blessing! Thank you, Dave and Troy."

—IYANLA VANZANT
Author and host of *Iyanla: Fix My Life*
(Oprah Winfrey Network)

"With *Oola for Women* as their guide, our wives and daughters can step into their power and enjoy their lives more."

—JOHN GRAY
Bestselling author of *Men Are From Mars, Women Are
From Venus* and *Beyond Mars and Venus*

"How did our modern-day lives get so scattered and complicated? *Oola for Women* cuts through life's craziness in favor of simplicity, balance, and focus, and the stories of women on the road to Oola make you feel like there's a vast sisterhood of women on the journey with you. I loved it."

—JJ VIRGIN
Celebrity health expert and four-time
New York Times bestselling author

"Once in a while, a revolutionary book comes along that not only changes the way women think, but that also gives them permission to start living in a whole new gear. *Oola for Women* is that kind of game-changer."

—PATTY AUBERY
#1 *New York Times* bestselling coauthor of twelve
Chicken Soup for the Soul books for women, Christians and teens,
and past president of Chicken Soup for the Soul Enterprises, Inc.

"As women today continue to stress themselves out over trying to achieve the perfect work-life balance, finally there is *Oola for Women* providing a lifeline of hope and pathway for every woman to achieve One Big Life of OOLA!"

—SHARON LECHTER, CPA CGMA
Author of *Think and Grow Rich for Women*, Co-author of *Outwitting the Devil*, *Three Feet From Gold*, *Rich Dad Poor Dad* and 14 other Rich Dad books

"Braun and Amdahl have done it again. In *Oola for Women*, they explain the simple formula for creating a life that's awesome in every way. From great relationships to stress-free finances to superb health and a group of friends who support you, get ready for a great ride . . . and a great read."

—MARCI SHIMOFF
Bestselling author of *Happy for No Reason*

"As much as I loved the first book, I love this one even more. The principles are simple and the stories are relatable. I love what Oola stands for and strive for it daily."

—CARRIE TOLLEFSON
Wife, mother of three, professional broadcaster, and Olympic middle-distance runner

"Living in bliss is something every woman wants, but getting there can be a struggle. Now, *Oola for Women* has come along to give you the roadmap and put gas in your tank! Grab your BFF's, decide what you want, and get started on that marvelous road trip to happiness."

—LISA NICHOLS
New York Times bestselling author of *No Matter What!* and *Abundance Now*, and featured teacher in *The Secret*

"A lot of authors say 'This book is a movement,' but it's really not. The Oola team is different. The books they write aren't just books, they invite us all to bigger, bolder lives. Don't miss the invitation. Don't miss this book."

—JON ACUFF
New York Times Bestselling author of *Do Over*

"The OolaGuys put on paper what I hope to relay in my music, a message of grace, hope and God's amazing plan for each of us. This is a must-read for all the influential women in my life."

—DANNY GOKEY
#1 Recording Artist and Dove Award Recipient

Oola
FOR
WOMEN

FIND BALANCE
IN AN UNBALANCED WORLD

*How to Balance the 7 Key Areas of Life to Have Less Stress,
More Purpose, and Reveal the Greatness Within You*

DAVE BRAUN and TROY AMDAHL
*with Janet Switzer
and 42 Incredibly Inspiring Women*

Health Communications, Inc.
Deerfield Beach, Florida

www.hcibooks.com
www.oolalife.com

Library of Congress Cataloging-in-Publication Data
is available through the Library of Congress

ISBN-13: 978-07573-1984-6 (Paperback)
ISBN-10: 07573-1984-X (Paperback)
ISBN-13: 978-07573-1985-3 (ePub)
ISBN-10: 07573-1985-8 (ePub)

Publisher: Health Communications, Inc.
          3201 S.W. 15th Street
          Deerfield Beach, FL 33442–8190

For information, please address the authors at *support@oolalife.com*.

Cover design by Svetlana Uscumlic
Cover graphics by Max Amdahl
Cover photo by Ryan Longnecker
Interior design and formatting by Lawna Patterson Oldfield

Mom, thank you for forming me into the man I am today—
even if it took wooden spoons and
kneeling in the corner at times . . . I love you.

To my four sisters, Dawn, Deanne, Denette,
and Danielle, you are my rock.
Thank you for always listening to me and loving me.

To my ex-wife, Michelle, thank you for being a great mom
and taking care of our "precious cargo" on this
crazy journey we call our life.

To my four daughters, Ashelyn, Tamaryn, Tiandra,
and Brynnae, you are my "why."

I am forever grateful that God chose me to be your dad . . .

I love you more than dirt.

—Dave Braun

To my wife, Kris,
my daughters, Joelle and Alea,
my mom, Charlotte,
and my sisters, Tammy and Teresa,
and to all the other women in my life
who have influenced me and inspired me
to be a better man.

—Troy Amdahl

CONTENTS

Section One:
INTRODUCTION TO **OOLA**

Get ready to live the life of your dreams,
even if things are "messy" right now.

Section Two:
THE 7 F'S OF **OOLA**

Lower your stress level and find your life purpose
by balancing these 7 areas of life.

What is fitness the Oola way?
Larger Than Life by Melissa Cairns
Fighting Forward by Gabriele Grunewald
　Keep It Simple

Section Three:
OOLABLOCKERS

Overcome the 7 key traits that block you
from living the life of your dreams.

Section Four:
OOLAACCELERATORS

Want to get the life of your dreams faster?
Ignite your journey with these positive behaviors and habits.

Section Five:
3 **SIMPLE** STEPS TO THE **OOLA**LIFE
Your daily action plan for living the life of your dreams.

OOLA PERMISSIONS

INTRODUCTION

O *oh la la . . .* that's what life feels like when you're happy, growing, and looking forward to what the world has in store for you.

It's the feeling you get when you've landed that better job, grown a bigger business, or watched your kids succeed at something they're passionate about. It's what you tell yourself when you've bought that dream house, saved your first $1,000, or paid off the last of your debts. It's the confidence you feel being fit and date-night ready for the first time in years—or the sense of wonder and enchantment you feel on your first trip to Paris with the girls.

Whatever rocks it for you, Oola means living life firing on all cylinders—joyful, wholehearted, and ready to take advantage whenever good times and opportunity appear.

THE **HISTORY** OF **OOLA**

Since the first copy of the original *Oola* book rolled off the presses a few years ago, the Oola lifestyle has become a phenomenon with readers seeking balance in an unbalanced world. Over 100,000 copies of the book have been sold, without a publisher, out of the back of our 1970 VW Surf Bus—while tens of thousands more people have handwritten their dreams on stickers and stuck them to the sides of the OolaBus. Many others have even gotten Oola tattoos to remind them to "Live Oola" and pursue their dreams. And our OolaPalooza live events have been routinely sold out since the day we started them. The Oola message has taken us to countless cities across America and (via the nearly one million Oola fans on social media) to every major city in the world.

So who are the majority of *Oola* book readers, event attendees, and social media followers? Who are the people embracing the Oola message and incorporating these simple life-changing principles into their daily lives?

Women.

When we realized this trend, it made perfect sense. While a circus performer might spin seven plates in a single show, women spin seven plates (figuratively) every day. They juggle work, kids, family, and home life—hoping there's room left in there somewhere for "me time." And if you own a small business or have a demanding career (as many of our readers do), you also juggle customers, clients, sales, marketing, professional events, and so many related activities that it's truly mind-boggling how much you pack into a twenty-four-hour day.

We think you're awesome. And we want to help transform the juggling act you do every day into a dream lifestyle of simplicity, tranquility, abundance, and opportunity. That's what "living Oola" means—and for you, it's not only an attainable goal, but a well-deserved reward.

LET'S REVISIT: **THE 7 F'S OF OOLA**

In the first *Oola* book, we said that to create a balanced life—one that's extraordinary and linked to your unique purpose and future goals—there are seven areas to focus on: fitness, finance, family, field (career), faith, friends, and fun. *Oola for Women* tackles these same seven areas of life—helping you create a vibrant, but manageable lifestyle that supports your goals and helps you live your best and highest purpose.

In the seven chapters of Section Two, we'll help you do what's necessary to feel good, look good, and have enough energy to pursue your OolaLife—instead of constantly yo-yoing with diet products and exercise programs that actually do harm. You'll learn to forget what the rest of the world believes about money and investing—and instead, simplify your life by taking control of your debt, spending, earning, giving, and investing. We'll show you how to nurture the loving relationships and establish proper boundaries around the toxic ones—from your core family to your distant relatives, and others.

If you're not in your dream job now, we'll help you decide what you'd truly like to do, figure out how to get paid for it—then create a plan to transition. We'll help you discover your true purpose in life, accessing faith in your own path to Oola through a relationship with God. Along the way, we want to help you cultivate a support structure of friends who "get you" and unconditionally love and support you. And finally, we want to make sure you plan fun adventures—from mini-breaks in your own backyard to "bucket list" getaways around the world—as the most enjoyable perks of living the Oola lifestyle.

OOLABLOCKERS
AND **OOLA**ACCELERATORS

Of course, as you're creating balance in the seven areas above, sometimes internal dialog and old habits get in the way. They block you from creating the life you want. In the opposite way, there are certain habits and actions that will accelerate the process—helping you get to a "state of Oola" faster than you thought possible.

We call these influencers Blockers and Accelerators, and you'll discover these in Sections Three and Four. From eliminating fear to learning how to erase guilt, anger, shame—and even overcoming laziness—you'll discover how to banish self-sabotage and focus on your future.

Once you're past these blocks, it's time to change the way you roll—with accelerators like gratitude, love, discipline, passion, and wisdom. We'll show you how to find those things you love that will ignite your journey and make the OolaLife that much more enjoyable.

OOLA IN ACTION

The Oola formula is simple. Once you read about it, it's time to develop some concrete plans for getting there. In Section Five, the real work begins of defining where you are today, where you want to go, and how you're going to get there. We'll help you hone in on what's working right now—and what you need to *start working on* first.

With simple life hacks like writing your must-do's on a 3x5 card, assembling your go-to crew of supporters, and doing the worst first (plus many more), we've got a way to help you fast-track yourself to the OolaLife.

START LIVING THE **OOLA**LIFE TODAY

Along the way, we'll share the stories of women from all walks of life who have many of the same dreams, goals, desires—and down-falls—as you might have. Many of them are women we've met at Oola events. Others are women we met as they wrote their dreams on stickers for the OolaBus. Still others have shared their story with us on social media. These women are inspiring *because* they're ordinary women doing extraordinary things.

Some of them are facing challenges or awkwardly learning the ropes or caught up in a "season" they're working through. These women are *Seeking Oola,* while others whose stories you'll read have mastered the OolaLife—they're *Living Oola* and have wisdom, insights and lessons to impart.

Wherever you are and whatever your goals, *Oola for Women* is here to be your guide, your playbook, and your go-to resource for getting from where you are now to where you want to be.

Master the 7 F's of Oola, get solid on the Accelerators, crush the Blockers, and follow the 3 Simple Steps to the OolaLife—and you'll be on your way to living the deepest desires of your heart.

INTRODUCTION TO **OOLA**

"*Don't be afraid to be awesome.*"

— Jacqueline Macinnes Wood | @jacquelinemwood
Actress and talk-show host

Oo´• la \ *n. adj.* \ **1 a** : *a state of awesomeness* **b** : *a life that is balanced and growing in the key areas of health, finances, career, relationships, and well-being* **c** : *a destination (i.e., getting to Oola)* **2 a** : *describing actions, insights and goals that lead to a balanced life (ex: That's so Oola.)* **3 a** : *the ultimate plan for achieving balance in an unbalanced world.*

Oola is that place we all shoot for. It's the place where the major areas of our life—finances, health, family, career—are balanced, strong, and growing. We're achieving what we want to achieve. And we're moving forward from where we are to where we want to be.

7

Oola is that ultimate destination where everything just *works*. Life is manageable, fun, fulfilling, and stress-free.

But more than just a positive state of being, Oola is also the euphoria you feel when you celebrate a success, visit an exotic place, or hear your baby laugh for the first time. *I want more of this,* you smile to yourself—reveling in the sheer joy and wonder of the moment.

That's Oola.

And in this first section of *Oola for Women,* we'll show you more of what it's like to be "in Oola." But, most importantly, we'll reveal how it's possible to start with almost identical beliefs, passion, goals, and dreams as the next person—but, years later, end up in two very different places.

CHAPTER 1

WHAT IS **OOLA?**

"What does a crazy-busy career woman do when
she's about to lose her mind?
She buys a goat."

— Jennifer Warren
Organic farmer

A s the OolaBus pulled into the parking lot along the Northern California coast, we could just make out in the distance the random collection of surfers, sunbathers, and families who'd decided to hit the beach that day. It was the third stop on our first Oola road trip—a dude-inspired trek that had us rambling up Pacific Coast Highway in an old Volkswagen Surf Bus, amply supplied with coffee, donuts, and two sons for good measure.

We had no idea how the Oola message would be received. But we were inspired to meet people, share Oola, and help them reconnect with their dreams. We hit on the idea of passing out stickers and Sharpie pens so anyone who wanted to could write down their most heartfelt desire and plaster it on the side of the bus.

As a small crowd began to form and we began to talk about the OolaLife, we could see hope begin to replace worry and resignation in the eyes of the people around us. Some were there to learn more about our mission. Others were looking for weed. And some were merely curious.

But one woman will forever stand out in our minds.

We saw her immediately—a classy, effervescent, beautiful thirty-five-year-old who was there with her husband and kids taking photos in the surf at sunset. What we thought were typical family portraits were actually something far different. They were memories in the making. Photos meant to record a life. And meant to last a lifetime.

The woman, we learned, had Stage IV cancer. She knew what the future held, but that day at the beach she was upbeat, smiling, and self-assured as she wrote her own Oola sticker:

Be strong enough through my cancer
to see my girls become women.

Instead of focusing on her own worries, she—like so many women we've met—had simplified her priorities to the one thing that truly mattered to her: watching her girls grow up.

That's when Oola got real for us. That's when we realized that it *is possible* to strip away the clutter of everyday life and truly live the authentic desires of your heart as if nothing else matters.

As we got into the bus to leave the beach that day, we fell silent for a time. That story—and so many others just like it—stayed with us. And stayed. And stayed.

WHY IN THE WORLD WE TOOK THIS ON

Unlike the woman on the beach, far too many of the women we've met during our Oola travels have lost the connection to their goals and dreams. They're so busy tending to the day-to-day details of life that they've lost themselves in the process.

But when we hand a woman a Sharpie and a handful of stickers, then ask, *What are your dreams for your life?*—something magical happens. Her eyes light up, the stress of the moment falls away, and she begins to reconnect to the true, authentic desires of her heart— tentatively at first, then joyfully as she begins writing what only she can say.

Tens of thousands of stickers later, the stories from women we've met have molded us as men. We've learned from *you*. We took on this mission as an honor and a privilege—not to tell you what to do—but because we want women everywhere to rediscover *their* true purpose and passion. We want our daughters to grow up in a world where they're empowered, understood, and fulfilled.

WHAT IS **OOLA**?

For these women, for our daughters, and for the hundreds of thousands of women we've met worldwide, Oola is a state of awesomeness. It's when your life is balanced and growing in the 7 key areas of life: fitness, finance, family, field (career), faith, friends, and fun.

It's living an inspired life—one that *you* define.

In fact, we hope you'll discover that, when it comes to defining a perfectly balanced and exceptional life, *your* opinion is the only one that matters. What the world says you should want, pursue, have or own makes no difference. It's *what you want* that matters most.

And what's even more exciting is that, in the pursuit of Oola, you'll likely become a different person. The process will change you into someone who is more authentic and more honoring of your own needs—versus constantly suppressing who you are and what you want because it doesn't fit the world's definition of who you should be.

The planet would be a very boring place if everyone were the same. Don't be like *anyone* else on Earth. Stay true to your own self instead.

What does that kind of authenticity look like? One of our favorite examples of staying true is the story of Jennifer (you'll meet her later) who bought her husband a goat for Christmas and ended up transforming their unhealthy, overworked and overscheduled suburban life into a back-to-the-land organic farming experience that's fulfilling and enjoyable for all—including their 10 dairy cows, 4 pigs, 100 chickens, 16 geese, 5 ducks, 12 dairy goats, and 26 rabbits.

Now that's different.

NOT JUST FOR WOMEN WHO ARE STRUGGLING

Of course, lots of women are already crushing it in every area of life. They've got successful businesses, beautiful families, marriages that rock, and lots of stress-free fun time with friends, family, and mentors.

Yet even with a life that's working on every level, there's still something more they want to accomplish or fix or change.

Maybe you're doing great, too, but want to take life to the next level. You're more capable than you realize. You want to take on a new project or bigger challenge. Perhaps the world's problems are calling to you. Or maybe you want to transition from a stable life to an exciting new adventure.

Oola is for you, too.

CHAPTER 2

GOING THROUGH A SEASON ON THE WAY TO **OOLA**

"A woman is like a tea bag. You never know how strong
she is until she gets in hot water."

— Eleanor Roosevelt
Longest-serving First Lady of the
United States, diplomat, and activist

As we said, everyone is different. Which also means there's more than one path to Oola. Sometimes though, you'll find yourself in a season of difficulty. Whether it's financial trouble, divorce, unemployment, a health crisis, or a family member whose train-wreck existence is impacting your life, that's your season to work through—emerging on the other side both wiser and better equipped to resume your path.

Oola came about after one such season. In fact, looking at the root cause of strife is what led us to hone and refine the Oola formula—eventually writing the first book about it.

HOW DID I GET HERE?

by Dave Braun

I t's hard to believe it was just three years ago I made The Call.

The image in my mind is as clear today as it was then. Earlier that night, I was sound asleep in my uncomfortable bed at a discount motel. I wasn't on vacation—this was my home. I didn't pay by the night—I paid by the month.

The sound was loud and abrupt. I thought someone was breaking into my room. Startled, I jumped up to see what was happening. I looked out the window and saw the police with a battering ram, breaking into the adjoining room.

This was surreal and deeply humbling at the same time. All I can remember thinking is, "How did I get here?" Just a few short years earlier, I had it all. I was a married man with five beautiful kids. I had seven years of college, a net worth of over $2 million, and a $1.4 million house in the foothills of the mountains.

How did this happen? How did I end up in this crap motel where most residents paid by the hour?

At that moment, I knew I needed to reach out to someone. I reflected on all the relationships in my past for just the right resource. I was embarrassed, and wasn't looking to be judged but rather nudged in the right direction. As dark as everything felt around me, I always maintained a sense that "things are going to be okay." In my core, I just knew I needed to get back on the path that I had strayed from some time ago.

I thought back to my internship fifteen years earlier and a guy I knew back then. You probably know a guy like him. I remember one of our mutual friends tossing him a gold horseshoe about the size of a half dollar and telling him to stick it up his ass so he could have a matching set. You know the guy—lucky with zeroes on the end.

Everything he touched seemed to turn to gold. He was just lucky . . . or so I thought. During my internship, as I spent time talking with him and learning from him, I realized it wasn't simply luck. He worked hard at keeping his life in balance. He made a conscious effort to grow in the important areas in his life. This reflection reconnected me to the path, the pursuit of Oola. I knew whom I needed to call.

I walked outside and looked at my neighbor's door, which was dented from the battering ram. I remember thinking that the door looked like how I felt. I walked through the rhythm of the lights from the police car reflecting off the buildings around me and made my way to an alley protected from the wind. I remember it was cold outside, but I was not cold. I was humbled, ashamed, and oddly optimistic all at the same time.

I had the phone in my hand, hoping to gain the courage to make that call. I knew this was the call I needed to make. I felt it. With vulnerability, I called the OolaGuru.

THE **OOLA**GURU

The call was exactly the one I needed to make at exactly the time I needed to make it. I hadn't spoken with the OolaGuru in quite a while. Miles and months had come between us, and this one phone call revealed how our paths had diverged. At one time we were almost of one mind. We had similar dreams, goals, and aspirations. But while my life hit rock bottom, the OolaGuru seemed to have it all.

The OolaGuru is a very private guy. He's far from shy, but his anonymity is based in humility. He listens more than he talks. And, let's just say that he has what most of the world wants. He has always been the guy in the group we looked to when we wanted to up our game, in any category of life.

He was completely debt free by the age of forty, he has been married to the same gal (whom he met in kindergarten, by the way) for more than twenty-six years, he formally retired at forty-two, and now does what he wants, when he wants.

I remember when he couldn't run a mile. He then set his mind to it, began running marathons, and even completed an Ironman. He spends a ton of time with his kids and works on his faith, dare I say, faithfully.

His personal passion is travel, and he has been to over fifty countries and counting. Sounds like fiction, but he is the OolaGuru.

When I called him, he was at his winter home in Arizona. I did most of the talking, and he did most of the listening. I needed to talk, and he was good at listening. After an hour of dumping my problems on him, all I can remember him saying was, "Well, I think you have found the bottom. The good news is it's only up from here."

He then told me a story about how they design a car so you can see both in front of you and behind you. They provide a rearview mirror, which is small but adequate. The front windshield is large and unobstructed. It's designed so you can easily see what's ahead. He pointed out how the views ahead and behind are designed to scale. You do need to look behind you from time to time, but only briefly. The majority of your energy and focus, however, should be on the windshield in front of you.

In that moment, I learned that my life is the same way. I do need to look at my past, but only briefly from time to time, and only to learn from it. The majority of my time should be spent looking forward, planning where I am going.

◎ ◎ ◎ ◎

JUST LIKE THE **OOLA**SEEKER, YOU MAY BE GOING THROUGH A **SEASON**, TOO

If life has you feeling battered but hopeful, realize that where you are right now is simply where you are, not *who you are*. You are designed for greatness. Your challenges don't define you. It's just a season you're going through.

And like the OolaSeeker, the majority of your time should be spent looking forward—planning where you're going next.

So let's get started.

SECTION TWO

THE 7 F'S OF
OOLA

*"If everything was perfect, you would never learn
and you would never grow."*

— Beyonce Knowles-Carter | @beyonce
Most nominated woman singer in the history
of the Grammy Awards, philanthropist, and
founder of House of Deréon women's fashion line

Welcome to the heart of the book. Over the next seven chapters, you'll discover the Oola basics—the areas you've gotta get right to enjoy a more inspired, exceptional, and unworried life.

These are the areas that are worthy of your attention—with each F representing a key category: fitness, finance, family, field, faith, friends, and fun. Here's where you'll make your major goals. Here's where you'll decide what you want. It's your life.

And while countless books have been written about each one independently, we want to present them as part of a complete life. We'll familiarize you briefly with each category, then give you a few tips to master that F quicker and easier. We'll share insights we've gleaned from thousands of Oola event attendees. Plus, we'll share stories of women—some who have gotten things right and are *Living Oola*, and others who are still working on mastery . . . they're *Seeking Oola*.

As you read through these categories, begin the process of self-assessment. In which F's are you Oola strong? Where are you weak? Are you balanced? By starting to answer these questions now, you'll be better prepared for the back of the book where we outline *3 Simple Steps to the OolaLife*.

Let's get started on the 7 F's with the first chapter: OolaFitness.

OOLAFITNESS

"I've always believed fitness is an entry point to help you build that happier, healthier life. When your health is strong, you're capable of taking risks. You'll feel more confident to ask for the promotion. You'll have more energy to be a better mom. You'll feel more deserving of love."

— Jillian Michaels | @jillianmichaels
Fitness expert, life coach, and television personality

Pursuing your OolaLife takes energy, focus, and stamina. In dude-talk, it requires a full-court press to clean up the messes, handle the garbage, make new plans, and pursue new paths. You may spend a lot of mental time outside your comfort zone—and you'll probably spend extra physical energy on making the changes you want—so your body needs to show up fully to support you in this effort. Not only that, but you'll want to be fit to fully enjoy the OolaLife once you get there.

But what is fitness the Oola way, exactly?

OolaFitness isn't just going to a gym or drinking a green smoothie. It's your overall health, both physical and mental. It's what you put in your body and what you get out of your body. It's how your body feels and functions. Do you feel sore and fatigued when you roll out of bed in the morning? Do you routinely feel foggy and tired throughout the day and go to bed exhausted?

What kind of fuel do you put into your body? Mainly whole foods and natural options—or processed and "would you like fries with that" options?

How about your thoughts? Are you feeding your mind healthy thoughts that breed confidence and worth, or are you planting seeds of fear, doubt, worry, and regret?

OolaFitness is all about becoming the best physical and mental version of you—all while keeping a healthy level of balance along the way. On social media, you'll often see us seeking out the best donut and coffee shops in the cities we roll through on the OolaBus. Why? Well, because we love donuts and great coffee! But again, this is the exception not the rule. It's all about balance. What you might not see is that we work out six days a week and eat healthy 80 percent (well, maybe 70 percent) of the time, saving the 20 percent for family dinners, new restaurants and experiencing local food, and the intermittent indulgences.

OolaFitness is striving to do better.

No matter where your starting point—whether couch potato or seasoned triathlete—the point is to work out harder, eat less crap, and choose more nutrient-rich foods. It's not only putting healthy food in your belly, but also putting healthy thoughts in your mind.

In fact, mental and emotional health is also a big part of OolaFitness. Depression, anxiety, and other conditions can get in the way of an awesome life. While they can generally be helped by daily exercise, good nutrition, meditation, and a healthier lifestyle, sometimes these conditions need to be addressed head on—by a professional—as part of your Oola journey.

Most importantly, however, be *consistent* in pursuing your goals, be patient with yourself, and cut yourself some slack if you fall away from your plan. Just hop back on and go get it.

Pretty simple, right? Yeah, but not easy.

What complicates "fitness" for most people is the overabundance of fad science and food hacks that tell us that pills, trendy exercises, unhealthy diets, and other wacky ideas are the solution—all pitched to us at 3:00 AM on an infomercial while we're sitting on the couch destroying a quart of double-chocolate chunk ice cream. Gimmicks and quick fixes are not legitimate substitutes for common sense, good nutrition, and regular physical activity.

We're all at different points on our fitness journey. Some are training for a PR in their next marathon, others are in a health crisis. The goal, regardless of where you are, is progress. If you're struggling, there is hope and it starts with a simple action. That's how Melissa started, as we'll see in her "larger than life" story.

LARGER THAN LIFE
by Melissa Cairns

I come from a family of food-lovers. My mom baked fresh muffins, breads, and cookies several times a week. We were comforted with food. It's how we expressed love. It's how we felt connected.

Food made me feel good. By the time I was a teenager, I was secretly self-medicating my crazy adolescent emotions and life with food. I would eat upstairs in my room and hide the wrappers. I would sneak food out of the pantry and into my school bag. My parents were so busy with life that they hardly noticed. Day by day, month by month, year by year, the weight came on.

When I reflect on the past twenty years of my life, the list of things I couldn't do far exceeded the list of things I could. I couldn't go on rides at theme parks because I couldn't fit in the seats. Going out to eat should be a treat, but I sat through most meals in misery. I was either pinched in pain because I couldn't fit in the booth, or worried that the chair wouldn't hold me. I couldn't fly in an airplane without raising my hand for a seatbelt extender and squashing the person next to me. I couldn't have a "normal" pregnancy, with the risks of gestational diabetes being too great. I couldn't even relax in social situations, in anticipation of snide comments or judgmental stares. I couldn't ride a bike. I couldn't get into bed without pain and I couldn't get out of bed in the morning without extra time and incredible effort. I couldn't sit on the floor and play dolls with my daughters and I couldn't even think about playing in the backyard.

It seemed as if every day a random kid would approach and innocently ask, "Why are you so big?" I never knew how to respond.

People talk about living "larger than life"—and I was, in the worst of ways. I was living a life too large to fit into the world happening around me.

My youngest daughter's third birthday was the day that I decided enough was enough.

My oldest daughter had missed out on so much because she had an obese mom. I didn't want my youngest to have the same experience. I wanted to be an active, fun, and involved mom. I wanted to be an example and not an embarrassment. I wanted to be there for my husband, too. I needed to be healthy for *them*, to care for my family, and most importantly, I needed to be there for *me*. I deserve more than to be in pain every day. I deserve more than to miss out on the adventures of life because of my obesity. *I am worth not living in the world of "Oh, I couldn't,"* I said to myself. Then and there, I decided I wanted to live in the world of *"I can."* It was time to get real about where I was—with my health and my weight—then get real about where I wanted to go.

I walked up to the bathroom scale. I stood there and thought, *What should my ideal weight be?*

I decided that I wanted to weigh 160 pounds. Then I did what I'd been afraid to do countless times before: I stepped on the scale. Wow! To hit my goal weight, I needed to lose 229 pounds.

A month later, I was well into my weight-loss journey and already down eleven pounds. We were on vacation and I decided to take some time for myself and listen to a good book. I downloaded *Oola: Find Balance in an Unbalanced World* on a recommendation from a friend. As I listened, the authors told stories about their lives and frequently referenced the 7 key areas of life I needed to balance and grow in order to live the OolaLife. I wanted that. I wanted to live fully in the 7 key areas.

As I listened, it became obvious to me that Fitness was my thing to conquer. I felt relieved that I had already started taking action there.

I continued to listen and I realized that, in my life, all 7 F's were suffering because of my weight. My weight created stress on my Finances and my Field because of my lack of energy. The things I "couldn't" do in my life affected my family and prevented me from having fun. A poor body image from my weight affected relationships with friends.

Oh my gosh, I thought. *I'm all F'd up!*

Instead of being discouraged, however, I used Oola as a catalyst to keep going. I used it to keep walking every day and to keep logging my food intake . . . to keep smiling when I wanted to cry and to keep going when I wanted to die. Oola never *told* me how—I *knew* how— but it brought clarity and passion to my "why."

Today, I have lost 139 pounds. I only have 90 pounds to go to hit my goal of 160. This weight-loss journey has been filled with blood, sweat, and tears—literally! But most importantly, it's been filled with words like "I can" and "I could." I could dance for hours at my baby sister's wedding without pain in my body. I could take a Zumba class with my eleven-year-old daughter with just normal muscle soreness the next day. I can be a Girl Scout leader and keep up with those young girls on a camping and hiking trip in East Hampton. I can feel the burn in my quads as I pedal uphill. And I can feel the wind in my hair as I coast down the hill for the first time in years.

Losing weight has also resulted in a domino effect of positive change in the other key areas of life. My relationships are stronger, my business has grown, my finances have drastically improved, and my family is active and more connected. I even started a couch-to-5K program and am running now. I am super excited about that!

With all the amazing things that are happening to me, the best part has been breaking the legacy of obesity in my family and inspiring others to be healthier and better versions of themselves. The Oola-Guys say that *together, we can change the world with a word . . . Oola. By simply making ourselves the best versions of us, we will inspire those around us.*

I have seen this firsthand with my family and friends.

If you had told me twenty years ago, ten years ago, even two years ago, that I would get to where I am today, I wouldn't have believed it. Every day I'm simply amazed and excited about what this life has to offer. I truly feel that I'm living larger than life . . . in a good way.

The OolaBus is plastered with tens of thousands of dreams from people we've met along the road. Many of the goals are written on red stickers—which are the fitness stickers. And many of those people are women wanting to lose weight.

Melissa taught us that it starts with a simple step: a healthy level of disgust. *I'm better than this. I deserve more than this. And this changes today!*

Of course, the side benefit isn't only what Melissa lost. It's what she gained: the other six F's of Oola began to improve in her life, she gained confidence and worth, and most importantly, she broke the legacy of obesity in her family.

But what if your OolaFitness gets rocked by something out of your control? How does one push through when it feels as though life just keeps pushing back?

FIGHTING FORWARD

by Gabriele Grunewald

grew up in the rural, lakes country town of Perham, Minnesota, population 3,087. I fell in love with running as a kid. My mind felt clear, my body strong, and my soul free. I loved the simplicity of the act of running. No equipment, no rules, no set time, no confinement . . . just a pair of shoes and an open country road. I was hooked.

Early mornings, late nights. Missing parties and dances . . . all for laps and miles. Through strains and fractures, wins and losses. I was determined to make my mark. It turns out I was good at it.

Although I loved to compete, I ran for how it made me feel. Running challenged me to push myself. To grow. To test my limits. I wanted to be great.

While running for the University of Minnesota, and preparing for my 1500-meter race at the Sun Angel Classic in Tempe, Arizona, my cell phone rang. It was Good Friday in April of 2009, and I was with my teammates in the hotel lobby. I answered. It was my doctor from Minnesota. He had something important to tell me.

I had cancer.

A small bump on the left side of my neck, just beneath my ear, had been bothering me for a couple months. I sought advice from the University of Minnesota athletic trainers. "A swollen lymph node," they thought; nothing too concerning for an otherwise very healthy twenty-two-year-old. To be sure, they encouraged me to see an ear, nose, and throat specialist. I did so, and my diagnosis ended up being a rare salivary gland cancer: adenoid cystic carcinoma. The final track season, the one that was supposed to be "the one," was over. Surgery to remove the salivary gland and local lymph nodes was scheduled for the following Thursday; radiation therapy on deck after my recovery from surgery.

Shock. Disbelief. Fear. But I still wanted to run my race the next day. I was certain I was in the best shape of my life. And cancer couldn't take that away, at least not for a few more days.

I was right. I ran the fifth fastest time in school history on the day after I was diagnosed with cancer. But now, my season was over.

There was much uncertainty in the next few days, weeks, and months. Running fell to the periphery as I recovered from a delicate six-hour surgery to remove the cancerous tumor. The burns from radiation therapy left my skin red, raw, and caused permanent hair loss.

During this time I ran very little. From time to time I would escape my medical reality for a 5K run to stay connected to the sport I loved. It was in those moments, with my feet moving and mind clear, I began to let go of what could have been, and looked forward to what was possible. I became deeply motivated to test the human body and the human heart. Running became not only a distraction from my current reality, it made my life feel normal again. Running became my motivation to beat cancer. Running became my motivation to live fully; to test what is possible.

At first I ran slowly and not very far, but I gradually got stronger. I pictured myself in a University of Minnesota uniform again.

It wasn't long before I was able to return to competition. I won my first event, an indoor 3000-meter race. As my strength returned, so did the speed. I made my first appearance at a national championship—the

2010 USA Indoor Track and Field Championships just ten months after that call from my doctor.

The 2010 outdoor track season turned my dreams into reality. I fought against the limiting belief that my body was fatigued from fighting cancer. I kept reassuring myself that the battle strengthened me, not weakened me. I revisited my goals. I found the courage to aim higher than just getting back on the track and racing again. I didn't simply want to compete. I wanted to win.

My success on the track resulted in an invitation to join Team USA Minnesota in June of 2010, and I lowered my personal best one more time, to 4:12, in Belgium that July. I signed with Brooks Running in August. I was officially a "Pro Runner" and as they say, the rest is history. Or so I thought.

I was finally done with cancer, but cancer wasn't done with me.

Just months later, arms still raised in triumph from my comeback, I faced another cancer diagnosis. This time it was my thyroid. I didn't know what else to do but fight and run. Not run away from the cancer, but through it, and punching it in the face on the way by. I beat thyroid cancer, and kept running.

And now, as cancer visits for a third time (this time in my liver), I look at the thirteen-inch incision scar on my abdomen and do what I know how to do: I clear my mind, I move my feet, and I run hard. I don't give up.

I realize that I am in the middle of my story. And with the Olympics less than four years away, my dreams are more alive now than ever.

My life, like many others, has hard parts. Regardless, I wake up every day, put my shoes on, move my feet, and keep pushing. I do this for me and for everyone who faces a challenge and is brave enough to fight forward.

◎ ◎ ◎ ◎

Whether you're battling health challenges like Gabriele and Melissa, or simply need to improve your stamina, get more sleep, eat right, conquer depression, or overcome anxiety, you have the power within you to master OolaFitness. We've got some strategies that work *and* that keep it real.

KEEP IT SIMPLE. Fitness isn't rocket science. Most people know the basics: eat less than you burn or burn more than you eat. It's also common sense that getting adequate sleep and regular exercise not only improves your mood, it boosts your energy, enhances your confidence, and keeps your body goal-jeans ready. When you look good, you feel good—and that kind of sparkle is hard to resist.

You don't need "advanced science" or quick fixes to help you get fit. Those methods aren't sustainable and they definitely aren't Oola. So, don't get paralyzed in the analysis of what so-called "experts" say. Be authentic and choose the right solution for you, and stick to it. You may go through a season of sacrifice and hard work to get there, but committing to a healthy lifestyle will keep you fit.

WORK HARDER. As our bodies adapt to exercise—or as we get older—it seems harder and harder to stay in shape. Metabolism slows and the same three miles you've been walking for years suddenly don't deliver the same benefits as they did before. That's why you have to continually up your game. Eat a little smarter, move a little faster, walk a little farther, add a new activity like swimming, resistance training, or hot yoga. Mix it up and your body will respond again.

EAT SMARTER. It's so easy to get empty calories today. Since 1980, the amount of sugar *added* to foods has increased by 30 percent. It's in things you wouldn't necessarily expect, like low-fat salad dressings, flavored waters, energy drinks, and in most processed foods labeled "fat free." That's not only unbalanced, it's just crazy. To add to the problem, today's portion sizes are completely out of control. A 64-ounce soda at a convenience store contains a week's supply of sugar. And a single pasta dish at most Italian restaurants can feed a family of four.

Of course, once the food industry created more obese people than ever before, scientists and fitness "experts" over-complicated the fix with packaged diet foods and expensive workout equipment. News stories report every medical opinion—and studies are released almost daily that seem to contradict each other. Who can keep track of it all?

The truth is, you already *know* how to stay fit and healthy.

Cut down on sugar, bad fats, and excessive breads and grains. Eat whole foods prepared from scratch instead of packaged, over-processed fare. Get regular exercise you can maintain over time. Drink plain filtered water. And eat less than you burn.

But don't pretend that you don't know what to do. Make it a goal to change one thing at a time. Keep your fitness routine simple and authentic to you. Don't get so caught up in the *how*. Instead, focus on *why* improvement in this area is important to you. Think of Melissa doing this for her kids . . . *that* is how change happens.

OOLAFINANCE

"While there's a talent for making money,
it takes real talent to know how to spend it."

— Candace Bushnell | @candacebushnell
Author of *Sex in the City* later adapted
into the popular television show

When we ask our audiences, "Who out there writes a monthly budget?" fewer than 5 percent of people raise their hands. We get that there's nothing sexy about sitting over a spreadsheet crunching numbers, but this is not cool. Trying to manage your financial life—not to mention creating an abundant financial future for yourself—is impossible if you're not tracking your spending and sticking with a pre-determined plan.

It's why so many people have virtually nothing left to invest or save for emergencies—they never budgeted to set aside that money in the first place. Money comes in, money goes out, but nothing sticks.

What's even more crazy is out-of-control spending—a problem we see everywhere. *We want it and we want it now!* And credit makes it so easy to buy stuff we don't need—usually with high interest rates and hidden fees (and usually overpriced). Of course, retailers can overprice things because they know we aren't worried about the price. We're so excited to buy that we're only concerned with the payment. They even tell you it's "smart" to buy on credit in order to build your credit; what they don't tell you is that this can keep you in debt indefinitely if you're not careful. Since everyone else seems to be doing it, most people never consider paying cash or curbing their consumption altogether. It's so socially prevalent that debt now seems normal.

The reality is, however, if you spend your life serving payments, you can't live your purpose.

YOU **CAN'T** BE HAPPY WHEN YOU'RE STRESSED

Heavy debt and financial stress (made even worse by the Great Recession of 2008) is one of the leading causes of marital stress. It's also the #1 reason why people lose their purpose and passion. Debt and financial burdens smother your options, bury your dreams, and take away your ability to make plans and move forward. You can't think, feel, or find happiness with the weight of unrelenting financial stress. That's no life. And it certainly isn't Oola.

We meet many women who are financial wizards. However, we talk to many more who are completely unplugged on the subject of money. They say, "Oh, my husband takes care of that." Or, "I'm not good with numbers." Or that, as a couple, they have *separate* finances. What?! Is this 1950? That's messed up. You don't have to be a Nobel economist, but every woman should know the family and household finances just as well as her spouse. At a minimum, you should know every dollar coming into your household every month, as well as every dollar going out. In marriage, it's not "your money" and "my money"—it's "our money." Pay attention to what is going on with "our money."

If you don't know, start asking questions.

Do you both have a will? Do you have proper insurance? How about an emergency fund? Are you planning for a debt-free future that's comfortable in retirement? There are tons of checklists and resources online to help you create a plan and start investigating. Educate yourself. You don't need to become an expert, but you do need to get involved.

This is critically important if you're a *single woman* homeowner— the fastest growing class of homeownership. Today, single women are buying homes at nearly twice the rate of single men and now own more than 18 million properties. They account for 23 percent of first-time buyers and 16 percent of repeat buyers, according to a National Association of Realtors study.* If this describes you, then you've got a significant number of financial obligations to manage,

---

* As reported in *USA Today.*

from mortgage payments to home maintenance, financial planning, retirement investing, long-term care insurance, and saving for your kids' college. It's endless.

If you're a young woman hoping to buy a house or get married, putting your finances in order is one of the most important things you can do. And if you're in your forties (or older), you've got retirement planning and estate planning to deal with, too. Don't sweep this stuff under the rug and ignore it. Take control of your finances before they take control of you.

GOING TINY TO LIVE BIG

by Christian Axness

I started working when I was young, but it wasn't until I was eighteen that I landed a "real job" in the apartment industry. I began in the leasing office, worked my way up, and by the time I was twenty-three, I had over 1,200 units in the portfolio that I managed for investors.

As for my husband, Nate, he followed his dream and became a firefighter. The money was flowing. My husband and I were partying, and our "American Dream" was happening. In 2011, when the housing market finally bottomed-out, Nate and I decided that we were going to become "real" adults and buy our first home. We bought what we considered a fixer-upper and the perfect investment property. It was at the top end of our budget. The following month, I found out I was pregnant with our first baby. Many of the projects that we had planned for the house suddenly took a back seat when Ella arrived in our lives in July 2012.

This is when life got real.

After promises of time off from my company went unfulfilled, I was forced to make some difficult choices. I knew I wanted to be with my young daughter but had no clue what that scenario might look like. So, six months after my daughter was born, I resigned from my full-time job to open my own retail business. I opened a baby store where I could work my own hours, keep my daughter with me, and live life by my design.

Oh, how wrong I was.

Turns out when you own your own business, it's twice the work with no time off—and, oh, by the way, you make little to no money. So, there we were with a home in disrepair, strapped for cash, and saddled with a failing business.

It was on the two-year anniversary of the business when I finally realized it was over. My business was failing and our fixer-upper was falling apart. I was physically sick from the stress, and even though I'm one of the most optimistic people you'll ever meet, at this point in the journey I had no hope. We were in pre-foreclosure on our house with penalties mounting. As our second child was about to arrive, our water was due to be shut-off and our business landlord was literally screaming for his money.

I just couldn't do it anymore.

We abruptly closed the doors on our retail business, and I went home with my tail between my legs. I was hurt, I felt like a failure, and I was clueless on what to do next. The worst part for me was hearing my husband leave the house at 4:00 AM to walk around the block because he, too, was sleepless and losing hope.

Not knowing where to turn, a friend helped me start a business from home. It wasn't much at first, but I earned enough to pay the past-due water bill. I loved the freedom that working from home provided, and over time the income improved. A year later, I was covering all our monthly expenses. Even with that, for some reason we still had more month left at the end of the money. Then we realized the problem was *us*.

It was time to get on a budget and fix our spending habits. We built up a small emergency savings fund and we were beginning to pay down debt. On the path to financial freedom, we were continuing to grow our business, mitigating house disasters with our small emergency fund, and beginning to see the light at the end of the tunnel. After digging ourselves out of the hole, we were finally able to begin dreaming again and talking about the future.

Have you ever been there? So stressed and exhausted that you just fall into a routine of survival and you can't even dream?

Here is where things get good . . .

After fully committing to an ultra-strict budget, we finally made the last payment on our credit card. The only debt remaining was our mortgage. We had become so obsessed with the idea of living debt-free that the idea of a bank owning our home got under our skin. We were at IKEA buying some home furnishings when we decided to call a Realtor instead. At the end of the phone call, we left our shopping cart full of junk in the store and drove home. The next day our house was on the market. Two months later, the house and everything in it was sold. We took our tiny surplus and bought a tiny home (plus a big-ass truck to tow it), and put the rest into a fully funded emergency savings fund.

The whole idea of the minimalist lifestyle really spoke to us.

We had already experienced the American Dream—credit card payments, endless home repairs, car payments, vacations we couldn't afford, keeping up with the Joneses—and we were done with all of it.

Today we are debt-free, living simply, and growing our business. We owe nobody. Because of this, at thirty-two years old, Nate was able to put in his two-week notice to retire from his firefighter job. Our children are looking forward to not saying good-bye to their dad for days at a time. Our family is on the path to a balanced OolaLife. We are ridding ourselves of the things that rob us, and investing in the things that grow us. In fact, we are heading out on a one-year cross-country family trip with our tiny home and our big-ass truck.

Some may call it the adventure of a lifetime. We call it freedom!

◎ ◎ ◎ ◎

Your OolaLife is your OolaLife. The financial goals and dreams you have for your life are unique to you. Maybe you want to live simply—or *maybe* you want to crush it . . .

FROM BREAD BAKER TO BREADWINNER

by Debra Raybern

It was a beautiful Monday morning—a day spent homeschooling our twelve-year-old daughter Sharon, preparing meals, a little sewing and crochet, and enjoying being a stay-at-home mom. But this wouldn't turn out to be just any ordinary Monday, for that evening our world would be rocked to its core. After twenty-one years of marriage, my husband Paul suddenly experienced a change of address—to Heaven. By Tuesday morning I was planning a funeral. A great move for him, but one I wouldn't treasure for years to come.

He was the breadwinner, I was the bread baker.

As the days unfolded I began to fully comprehend the gravity of my financial situation. Raising a twelve-year-old daughter alone. Marketable skills for a well-paying job: completely obsolete. And, oh yes, $165,000 in debt. With no backup to rely on, I knew it would be up to me to provide for us. My work ethic was great and my entrepreneurial spirit was alive and well, but where would it take me?

God was about to totally transform our lives and grow me in ways I didn't see coming. I never asked why; somehow I always knew Paul's death would mean life to others but didn't know how that would manifest. My passion for herbs and healthy eating—things I was

43

already sharing on a small scale—were the catalyst for meeting our needs and beyond.

I was already having fun teaching bread-baking and soap-making classes and even some basic herbal workshops out of our home in the country, but even all these were not enough to provide the income necessary to help us dig out of such a deep hole. And that didn't even count the long hours and messy kitchen my daughter and I had to clean up after classes. I tried a couple of homeschool sales-related endeavors, which brought in needed money, but it wasn't where my heart was, nor did I feel it was sustainable in the long run. I was looking for a longer term opportunity that would provide an income for years to come.

I continued to pray and ponder my situation, looking for a better way. One day, we saw a TV commercial that said the average American was $6,000 in debt. My daughter and I high-fived and laughed, "We are so above average!"

Although we laughed, my heart hurt. I knew I needed to do more. I needed to find a way to dig out of this mess.

I loved natural products and had spent a great deal of time learning about them and their applications. I knew there was an opportunity to help others while also helping my family. Certainly, there were other like-minded women, with children at home and a house to take care of, who wanted to earn a few extra dollars sharing what they loved. So I started my own small venture that I could also present as a business opportunity to other women in my shoes. I committed to not turning back until I was 100 percent debt-free and had a steady reliable income for Sharon and me. This took five years. But they were some of the best (and most difficult) years of my life. Our quilting hobby, crocheting, scrapbooking, and bread-baking were shelved for a while, but I knew they would return one day. It was a small sacrifice that would pay off big in the long run.

The journey wasn't easy. There were long hours for me and long car rides for Sharon, who watched movies from the backseat DVD player. Before long, both of us had soon memorized the scripted lines from our favorites. Fresh-ground nut butter and whole-fruit puree sandwiches on whole-wheat bread (aka PB&J) and a thermos of chicken soup served as lunch for most trips. Occasionally, we'd stop at a fast-food restaurant for snacks—only because we were using their bathroom and I felt we needed to buy something. My Safari van saw so many miles the air-conditioning went out and the power windows wouldn't roll down. Thankfully there were signs of success—our debt decreased and we made enough money to buy a new car to drive all over Texas sharing my love of natural wellness.

I remained focused on my plan, yet determined to live life to the fullest because I knew firsthand it could be cut short in an instant. Nearly twelve years later, I can say I'm finally living the dream—*my* dream. I have a big beautiful home, a condo on the beach, a passport used in over twenty countries, and friends around the globe. My daughter is grown and married and has a business of her own that provides a solid foundation that continues to flourish and change lives every day.

I learned that if you have the need (or the dream) of a better life, start now. Don't wait until the what-if's in life force you into drastic change. There was no quitting or turning back for me. I resolved to create and build a business that would more than abundantly supply our needs.

It wasn't always easy, but I believed in what I was doing and I believed in me. Life may throw you a curve ball, something unexpected, something terrible. If it does, lean in. You are stronger and more capable than you know. Of this I am sure.

◎ ◎ ◎ ◎

Whether you're a nineteen-year-old college student, a twenty-three-year-old newlywed, a thirty-year-old single mom, or a fifty-year-old CEO of your own company, there are basic financial tactics that will move you toward the OolaLife. Even later—in your sixties or seventies—it's not too late to take better control of your finances. What do we recommend?

CRUSH DEBT. If there's one thing we see that truly sucks the life out of people, it's debt. In fact, it is so evil that 2,000 years ago, the Bible warned us against going into debt. Today you can finance everything from a $199 juicer to Sea World tickets. What? One of our favorite authors is radio host and financial expert Dave Ramsey, who says the only acceptable debt is a fifteen-year mortgage with 20 percent down, where the monthly payments are no more than 25 percent of your take-home pay.

We agree.

Credit card debt, student loans, second mortgages, leasing a car "because you can deduct the interest," and taking on bigger mortgage payments to get a better tax write-off—none of that makes sense financially. Every dollar you pay in interest is a dollar you do not have. Period. It's a racket—with banks and financial services companies making money once you're heavily in debt. If you eventually want to be sitting on a beach when everyone else is working, that doesn't happen by continually paying interest. Don't listen to people who advise you to go into debt. They're likely making money off of you (or want you to join them so that their *own* debt feels more normal).

In the same way, you shouldn't take financial advice from someone who's trying to sell you something. Car companies who push leases as a "great deal" are really just trying to sell you a car by making it affordable enough to get the paperwork signed and that car off the lot. Furniture companies who promise "easy financing" are trying to sell you furniture you can't afford. Don't fall for these tactics.

If you *are* in debt and wish you had read this advice years ago—if you took out $100,000 in student loans to study for a career that pays $32,000 a year, or if you got clobbered in the last recession and find yourself underemployed with persistent debt—it's not too late to rewrite your story. Pay down your smallest debts first by making the biggest payments you can afford. Then tackle the next biggest debt, then finally your mortgage. Calculate how long it will take to become debt-free and don't deviate from your plan. Be unbalanced temporarily if you have to—take on two more jobs if you need to—but no matter what, *don't take on more debt* while you're trying to pay off what exists now. Sacrifice now to win later.

INCREASE YOUR INCOME. In the same way, you should do everything you can to create surplus money—this will accelerate your ability to pay off debt, build a seven-month emergency fund, and start you on the path to a life of financial abundance. Throw your life out of balance for a season if you need to. Crush that real estate thing, pick up side jobs, grow a network marketing business, build a mutual fund portfolio, or do whatever else to begin to create extra income. Reduce debt and build residual income streams that will take care of your family long-term. This is exactly what the OolaGuru did to retire debt-free at forty-two years old. He apportioned each raise as follows: upgraded lifestyle (travel, daily activities, shopping, charitable giving) using 10 percent; debt-reduction using 45 percent; and increased investments using the remaining 45 percent. For example, if he received a $1,000-per-month raise, he would add $100 per month to lifestyle (probably donuts!), use $450 to reduce debt, and invest $450 in mutual funds.

Staying focused on the goal of financial freedom will help you do three things: take back your life from crushing debt; keep you from making the same mistakes again; and most importantly, keep your focus on the excitement of your purpose and not on the stress of the payments.

GIVE JOYFULLY. If you grew up believing that "money is evil," we love you, but you're wrong. Money is neutral. It is simply an amplifier. Yes, if you are selfish, greedy, and indulgent, more money will make you more of all of these things. But, like most people we meet, if you are kind, responsible, and generous, more money will allow you to be increasingly kind, responsible, and generous.

Giving is very Oola.

Just as you should be a good steward of the money that comes in, learn to become a joyful giver, too. Be responsible and build a surplus, but don't hold onto money with clenched fists—clenched fists are not open to receiving more. Money doesn't benefit the world unless it's flowing through you. Giving a portion of your income away—freely, willingly, and joyfully—not only benefits others, it releases money's control on you.

OOLAFAMILY

"Feelings of worth can flourish only in an
atmosphere where individual differences are appreciated,
mistakes are tolerated, communication is open, and
rules are flexible — the kind of atmosphere
that is found in a nurturing family."

— Virginia Satir
Family therapy pioneer

Once you start the journey to a balanced life, you'll discover that family relationships can either help you up—or trip you up.

While some women have won the domestic lottery and enjoy supportive, kind, and loving families, *way too many others* have toxic parents, checked-out teenagers, and marriages that are on life support. So where should you focus *your* energy in order to grow in this category?

It's complicated.

Parents, siblings, spouses, children, extended relatives—not to mention "co-this" and "step-that"—are all bound to us by blood, marriage, or adoption. That's the definition of family. But unlike blocking toxic friends on Facebook, you can't always unfriend family members. Or can you?

To start the process of dealing with family issues, present and future, we recommend grouping family relationships into ever-widening circles—from your closest loved ones at the center of your life to arm's-length family relationships in the furthest circle.

YOUR **INNER** CIRCLE

Your inner circle consists of the family members who you spend the most time with—most likely your spouse and kids if you're married; if you're single, maybe your ex-husband, step-kids, parents, and siblings. If you have a grandparent, aunt, or "second mom" you grew up with and are still close to, you might include them in this core group. These inner-circle family relationships deserve your highest commitment and should be your top priority.

Hopefully, they've got your back and they unconditionally love you and are always there for you. Ideally, life with your inner circle family is full of good times, great advice, and nonstop applause of your growing accomplishments. Done right, these family members help you progress on your journey to Oola.

Unfortunately, we find that the inner circle is a common place for toxicity. Instead of cheering you on, sometimes these family members hold you back—telling you in passive-aggressive, negative, or down-right abusive ways what you can't do or are not capable of. Instead of loving you unconditionally, they love you on *their* terms—with conditions—which, in reality, isn't love at all.

This inner circle is important. Making sure the love in this circle is pure and free of toxicity is important to you living full-out. This area is also where it's best to get real with yourself. Are *you* loving with conditions? Are *you* adding toxicity to your family's inner circle?

IN-LAWS AND OUTLIERS

The next circle should be filled with family members who are further out: in-laws, cousins, aunts, and uncles—as well as parents from whom you're estranged. You keep track of them, but you don't necessarily include them in your everyday communications or decisions. While they can impact your life (negatively or positively)—and especially your marriage and your self-esteem—your job is to keep the drama and personalities from doing any real damage.

YOUR OUTER CIRCLE

The furthest circle out are distant relatives you rarely see or speak to. You don't really know what's going on with them besides what you see on social media. They're your outer circle. Hopefully, they are loving and supportive as well, but if toxicity lives in your outer circle, it should never be allowed to affect your inner circle.

So what's the most important thing to remember as you group your family relationships into circles and think through who's on your A-team?

Powerful emotions tend to drive your responses and decisions the closer someone is to you.

If you had a fight with your teenager this morning, that's major. But if you've just heard that your brother-in-law's ex-aunt is divorcing . . . *meh*, that's not so troubling.

One way to grow toward Oola in this category is to adjust your emotions to fit the event by maturely and lovingly processing the junk that comes up. When confronted with someone else's emotional outbursts, wild demands, or wayward decisions, what's the most loving thing you can do? Have you thought about *their* motivation? Do you have all the facts? How can you support them, guide them, and love them unconditionally even though they just delivered the emotional equivalent of a tsunami?

TOXIC AND **ABUSIVE** FAMILY MEMBERS

Of course, what can really mess women up are *toxic* relationships that are hurtful, manipulative, or abusive—whether it's your spouse, your adult children, your in-laws or someone else. Of course, it's your decision how much longer you'll put up with the disrespect, bullying, financial drain or emotional trauma. But realize that, as long as you fail to act, it's a good chance others are being hurt besides you.

Even toxicity from the past can affect you, whether it was physical abuse or simply a lack of recognition, affection, or love. We've met countless women whose fathers never said to them, "That's my girl!" or "I love you"—so now they struggle with unconditionally loving themselves, their husbands, and children because of something that happened decades ago.

Decide *today* to respond differently to toxic family members. Build healthy boundaries. Demand to be treated better. Be specific about the new behavior you want. And if it's physical abuse that's happening, get some distance . . . now. If you need help, get it. Asking for help is not a sign of weakness but a sign of strength.

IF YOU'RE NOT **WORKING** ON YOUR MARRIAGE, YOU'RE **WORKING** ON YOUR DIVORCE

If you're married, your highest priority in OolaFamily is your spouse. No exceptions. Invest in your marriage. Whether it's date nights, a simple text of appreciation, or an evening walk away from the busyness of life and the kids, be sure to focus quality time and energy on each other.

Yes, the kids need your time, too, but more importantly, they need to see what healthy love looks like in a marriage. Show them. Don't take your marriage for granted and let it become stagnant. Work on your marriage so that, one day, you won't experience the stress of working on your divorce.

NEVER LET **OUTER-CIRCLE** FAMILY MEMBERS AFFECT YOUR HEALTHY **INNER-CIRCLE** RELATIONSHIPS

If you take in your nephew who's addicted to meth because your sister can no longer "manage him," or if you loan out the upstairs room to your aging uncle until he finds a place he can afford, realize that your marriage will probably suffer—not to mention your kids and your own equilibrium. Even becoming your mother-in-law's primary caregiver because your husband asks you to can create disruption that endangers a marriage.

We're not telling you what to do. We're just saying that you need to consider your options if presented with this dilemma—and think through how this will affect your inner circle.

Finding yourself as the primary caregiver for aging parents, often while still raising your kids, is a huge issue for women in their forties and fifties. Realize, however, that there *are* other solutions: senior helpers, assisted living, house sharing with a friend. While moving in with you might be the easiest decision, make sure this change is healthy for you and your family. Don't let your core family members fall victim to others who pull you away. Trying to be all things to all people is not sustainable. Take care of yourself and those you love the most so you're better able to tend to the needs of others.

BRIGHT LIGHTS AND BIG DREAMS

by Jami

My knees were shaking. I could feel the tears welling up in my eyes. I had sweat beading up on my forehead. In front of me was a microphone. I looked in the audience searching for a friendly face to calm my nerves, only to be blinded by the stage lights looking back at me. I attempted to speak but nothing came out.

What was I thinking? I said to myself. *Why did you volunteer to come up on stage?*

I glanced down. I was holding the key to my OolaLife and it terrified me. The little orange sticker read, *My children need to move out*—written in my own handwriting.

The process that led me to that moment on stage had started a couple days before. A close friend invited me to attend Oola-Palooza. I didn't know what to expect, except that my friend said it was life-changing and I desperately needed some changes in my life. With nervous anticipation, for two days I sat, listened, and wrote. My struggle began when Dr. Troy and Dr. Dave talked about dreaming big in the 7 key areas of life. I remember my mom saying, "If you don't dream, you won't be disappointed." I lived most of my life with that limiting mind-set.

Rooted by the negative seeds planted so long ago, it was a challenge that weekend to dream at all. Dreaming of what I wanted for my family was especially difficult. Struggling, I asked Dr. Troy for help. I said to him, "I have two adult children living at home," and before I finished my sentence he looked me in the eyes and asked, "Is that good for you? Is that good for them?" Then he walked away. Of course, I knew the answers before he made me confront them: *No and no.*

I knew that, in order to have the family life of my dreams, I needed my adult children to move out. At twenty-eight and twenty-nine, I knew it was time for my children to take control of their own lives and they couldn't do that living with me. I cried the rest of the weekend.

Although I knew it was the right thing for me, my kids, and my marriage, I felt like I was committing relationship suicide. My daughter and her four kids had been with us for three years. In many ways, I felt like I needed them as much as they needed me. My son, on the other hand, had been through an unexpected divorce and was now living with us—still recovering. He has two children. I worried they would both be so angry when I asked them to move out, that I wouldn't see them or my grandkids again. But our house was overfull and it was affecting my marriage.

We dreaded having the conversation with them—it was all I could think about. One day, I decided that today is the day. I sat my kids down and apologized for allowing them to stay with me for as long as I had. I explained that I was enabling them and keeping them from the true purpose of their lives. I took a deep breath and told them they had to move out by the first of the year. My son told me exactly how he felt and stormed out of the room. My daughter said nothing, which was almost more painful. The next few days and weeks—honestly, months—were difficult.

My son found a place to live right away, with a stranger. It wasn't the best situation, but he was on his own. He was working two jobs, spending time with his kids, and sleeping when he could. He ended up in the hospital for a week because of an infection that was made worse by his diabetes being out of control. As a caring mom, I felt terribly guilty. I felt like it was my fault that he was living like this. It was my fault his diabetes was out of control. On and on, I beat myself up and questioned my decision. Because he was in the hospital, he lost pay from both jobs, and his life began to spiral out of control. He lost his car. He was kicked out of his apartment. I hated watching him go through all of this. He spent countless nights sleeping at friends' homes and showering at the gym. Many times he fell asleep at the gym, waking up hours later because he was so exhausted. It was months before he could get a place of his own and start getting his life back on track.

My daughter made plans to move out the first of the year. She rallied to finish college while living with us. She became focused—applying for jobs and looking for a place to live. Shortly after moving out, she and her husband reconciled. A year later they welcomed their fifth child. They now live 700 miles away from us. Although heart-wrenching at times, she is happy, and that makes me happy. After getting settled into her new life, my daughter told me that I had done the right thing. She just needed that extra push to reconnect to her purpose for her life.

In April, I had the chance to take my son to OolaPalooza. He set goals and dreams for his life. I've watched him take steps toward reaching his goals and learn new things about himself. It's not perfect but it's progress. I know he feels better about himself. He has an apartment now with his name on the lease, and it's a safe place for him and his kids. He is working three jobs right now so he can reach the goals he set at OolaPalooza. I'm proud of him.

It's been just over a year since standing on that stage with the dream for my family held tightly in my hand. It hasn't all been easy, but it's been worth it. Through it all, my letting go and my children finding their path, we are still a family. Although the challenges keep coming, we keep fighting. My mom was wrong; dreams can come true, and I won't be disappointed.

Every day you'll be faced with decisions and challenges that will affect the future of your family. Deciding to love your family well is one decision you can make today and every day. Choose now to love those in your inner circle in a way that empowers—not enables.

But what if your family life is different than what you planned?

MY FAIRY-TALE LIFE

by Marcie Lyons

As a little girl, I loved the story of Cinderella and other princess fairy tales full of tragedy and love. I would often dream about my Prince Charming. I even went as far as planning our magical wedding, our big beautiful house, our perfect children . . . and our happily ever after.

Then at age seventeen, out of nowhere, I found my Prince Charming. It was at the "Last Day of School" party and he was the good-looking guy in charge of the music. I had seen him before but we had never talked.

It wasn't long before we were inseparable teenage sweethearts. We dated all through our senior year of high school, went to all of the dances together, and got married after our first year of college. My fairytale dreams were becoming my reality. Soon, we were welcoming the first of our "perfect" children. As time went on and before I knew it, we were welcoming number six.

But soon, the threads of our fairy-tale life started to unravel.

My husband, JC, was diagnosed with diabetes, lost his business, and was depressed. Financial stress started to consume us, and after years of trying to hold it together, we had to sell our beautiful home. We moved into a more affordable house, and while we thought that would fix our problems, the stress followed us.

This weighed heavily on our marriage and JC's depression grew worse. I found myself having to lift his spirits daily. I kept thinking that although life is not perfect, we will be okay.

But one hot summer day, JC went hiking. He didn't come home. Terror struck me as I thought, *Is he hurt? Does he have enough water? Did something happen to his car?* After three days of searching, rescuers found his lifeless body at the bottom of a cliff.

I had just turned forty years old and I was a widow. My fairy-tale was over. My dreams were crushed. I was now living a nightmare.

Three weeks after the funeral my life entered an all-time low. I found a note that JC had left. It was a suicide note. I was utterly heartbroken. I was a single mom surrounded by six mournful children and a head full of secrets and unanswered questions. I felt more alone than ever before in my life.

Lonely and lost, I went about my life. A few months later, my ten-year-old daughter told me that she and a boy at school wanted to plan a time to get together with our families. He had recently lost his mother to cancer. I told her that would be fun and felt that I should offer support, but didn't know how to get a hold of the boy's dad to make arrangements.

Since I knew where they lived, I'd drive by their house as part of my daily routine. Taking my kids to and from school, I would always look to see if he was outside; he wasn't.

As the weeks turned into months, one day, there he was in his driveway. I didn't want to lose my chance of meeting him, so I pulled over with the kids in the car. "They said, Mom, what are you doing? We are going to be late!"

Matt was in his baseball hat and had just sent his kids to school. I walked up, as he looked at me confused, and said, "Hi, I'm Marcie. We have never met, but. . ."

After a brief conversation, he said we should get our families together sometime. I gave him my phone number and ran back to the car.

Laughing, I said, "His name is Matt."

My son gave me a funny look and said, "Mom, you're crazy!"

We started hanging out as families and understood what each other was going through. Our kids had so much fun together and Matt became my new best friend. We talked about our lives before the funerals. We laughed about kids, dating again, and how tired he was of chicken nuggets. I taught him the real reason all his clothes were turning pink, and he taught me about the noises I was hearing with my car.

When Valentine's Day rolled around, I was on a date with another guy when Matt texted me. He was out of town and wanted to wish me well. I couldn't stop thinking about Matt in a whole new way that night. I realized that my best friend Matt had become my Prince Charming. That same weekend, he figured it out, too. We broke off all other dates and started spending every minute together. He was my miracle. Our kids didn't seem as surprised as Matt and I that we had fallen in love.

Matt proposed to me during summer vacation in Newport Beach, California. It was the best day of my life. No . . . the wedding day was. It was magical. Our girls were our bridesmaids and our boys were our groomsmen. It was like a fairytale ending.

Matt and I never thought that blending our two families would be a big deal; all nine of our kids got along great. We bought a house and moved both our households into it. We had more furniture than we knew what to do with. We had more of *everything* than we knew what to do with! Eighteen curling irons, three kitchen tables, four sets of dinnerware, six TV's, nine shovels, six couches, and twelve bikes later, we were a family.

Matt's children were athletic and mine were musical and artsy. In my previous life, Saturdays were deep-cleaning day. In Matt's,

Saturday was family soccer day. I cooked a lot and Matt's kids were used to going out to eat. Matt laughed each time my kids asked, "What's Panda? What's Sbarro? What's a food court?"

It has been a few years now and we are adjusting to our new blended family.

This journey has been soul-stretching. I opened my heart to love more people. Hearts are funny that way—you can always fit in one more to love. I love all nine of my kids. I'm crazy about Matt. I love him more each day. Maybe my life has been a fairy tale after all.

◎　◎　◎　◎

Families come in all shapes, sizes, configurations, and colors. Regardless of what your family looks like, your family is your family, and getting your family relationships solid and free of toxicity will make your journey to Oola easier and more enjoyable. When your closest and most emotion-driven relationships are stable, life just *works*.

Here are three tips to help you navigate these complex bonds and interactions.

LOVE WELL. In the many roles you may play—as a wife, a mom, sister, grandmother, and daughter—you'll be called to love your family members in many different ways: unconditional love, romantic love, tough love and even loving someone enough to make them stand on their own two feet. The key is to love well. Be smart about how you respond. Break any negative patterns from your own past so you can be free to love your family in ways that empower and uplift them.

SUIT UP. If you go to a family event or other gathering knowing a toxic, poisonous relative will be there, you can plan ahead to limit your exposure. Emergency responders put on hazmat suits before going into toxic environments and spill sites. You can do the same.

Just like the pros do when exposed to a poison, get in and get out as fast as possible. Arrive late. Leave early. And stay on the opposite side of the room.

Before you even enter the room, take a deep breath and visualize putting on your protective gear. Picture your hazmat suit deflecting the hurtful words, the painful memories, or simply that passive-aggressive glance of disgust. Reaffirm to yourself in advance that you are strong and created for greatness. Let the words and looks bounce off of you. Don't let any negativity stick.

When you leave, practice grace for those who just tried to harm you. While forgiving them doesn't condone their behavior, it *does* draw a line in the sand that says, *I'm not going to let this past hurt affect me anymore.* Whether the hurt is from a painful memory or harsh words across the Thanksgiving dinner table, practice the gift of grace. By putting the pain behind you, you'll be free to reach for the awesome future that's in front of you.

COMMIT. As we said before, if you're not working on your marriage, you're working on your divorce. Don't let family members outside your inner circle affect the relationship you have with your husband and children. But more importantly, as you set goals for your life, make sure you're bringing your inner circle along with you. Don't let your business or your job or your dream life alienate your immediate family—they should be part of the journey and part of your ultimate Oola lifestyle.

If you're single or divorced, decide today who is part of your inner circle—children, parents, siblings, a favorite niece—then protect them and don't let toxic people disrupt these relationships. Have some crucial conversations if you must. Refuse to be taken advantage of. Require others to stand on their own feet. But either way, stay committed to your core family and show up for them first before anyone else.

OOLAFIELD

"What would you do if you weren't afraid?"

— Sheryl Sandberg | @sherylsandberg
Chief Operating Officer of Facebook
and founder of LeanIn.org

W hat do we mean by *field*? It's your career, your calling, it's what you dedicate your life to.

Women wear so many hats—wife, mother, career professional, student, business owner—that it's often tough to say, *Yeah, I dedicate eight hours a day to this one thing.* But whether you're the leader of a company, a homeschooling parent or working your way up the ladder in a job you love, you've got a vocation that occupies a big chunk of your life.

Getting it right is what will get you closer to Oola.

DREAM JOB VS. **DAY** JOB

If money were no object and you didn't have to earn a living, what would you do with your day? Have you ever thought about what your dream job would be? In today's world, most people are torn between paying the bills and working in a career they enjoy. They've never really thought about what would inspire and empower them. They've never matched their unique skills and passion with work that can pay off financially.

But defining your dream job is one of the most important things you can do—whether it's a change of job within your current field or transitioning into another line of work altogether.

Think about those specific aspects of your job that you like. What's the most fun for you? What makes the day fly by? What activities just don't feel like work? Alternatively, what other jobs in your field look appealing? Make a list. Talk to people further up the ladder. Take someone to lunch who has the job you think you'd like to do. And if nothing about your current industry sounds all that cool, consider other jobs, hobbies, and activities you could spend the whole day doing—and have fun doing it.

The next most important step is to figure out a way to get paid for doing the fun stuff. But before you say, *That's impossible*, recognize that people get paid for doing yoga, taking photographs, arranging flowers, planning parties, working with kids, even doing hair and make-up. There are countless stories of bloggers who started writing about their dream life, then ended up selling a line of products or getting paid to write a book or making money in a licensing deal. *Junk Gypsies* was a television show about two women executives who traded big-city life for a vintage decorating business in rural Texas. And Airbnb has transformed thousands of private homes in out-of-the-way places into part-time hotels that pay the bills.

Once you decide what kind of work is going to make you happy, make a plan to transition into that work—even if it's leaving formal employment altogether to stay at home and raise your kids or turning a hobby into a career. Too many women quit the day job to pursue their dream job, only to find out it took longer and was more expensive than they thought. Have a plan to bridge the gap—whether you stay an extra year at your paid job, take a second job to create a rainy-day fund, scale down your expenses . . . or all three. You can't get to Oola if you're financially strapped and under stress. Quitting without a plan *is a very bad plan.*

◎ ◎ ◎ ◎

MY INNER VOICE WAS
WAITING FOR ME TO LISTEN

by Julie Carrier

"You should be a veterinarian," was all I heard growing up. As a child who loved animals, even I saw a future as a vet. I loved animals, I would eventually need a job . . . it made sense. "You'll be great at it," they'd say. "That's what you should do."

The well-loved quote, *Dog is man's best friend*, was clearly too limiting for me as a twelve-year-old since my definition of "best friend" expanded as I grew up to include several stray cats, a twenty-pound rescue rabbit named Thumper, injured birds, abandoned baby squirrels, and a whole host of furry, feathered, or six-legged friends—yes, even including a Madagascar hissing cockroach named Peabody.

But the well-intentioned opinions—shared so often by so many people (and for such a long time)—in my young mind secretly began to shift from a vote of encouragement to an iron-clad expectation.

And so, I was off to Ohio State University to become a vet.

But was this really what I wanted to do? Was this "dream career" in veterinary medicine *my* dream or was it the dream of those other voices charting my path?

When a scholarship allowed me to spend my senior year studying in England—away from family and pressures back home—the distance also separated me from the confusing noise of other people's opinions. I had more time in England for contemplation, which allowed me to question my path that had been predetermined by those around me.

The dreary spring weather in Manchester reflected my mood.

I remember sitting at my desk, surrounded by science books. It's almost as if they were challenging me: *Is this really what you want? Do you want a life of science, procedures, and diagnoses?*

With my heart heavy and full of fear, doubt, anger, and worry, I shouted in my mind the truth, *I'm completely miserable! What am I doing with my life? Just because I love animals doesn't mean I want to be a vet.*

I felt oddly calm—peaceful, actually. For a moment, I was free from the conflict between *what I truly wanted* and the opinions of others.

This peace gave me the ability to ponder and reflect—to hear a question that I was too busy to ask before: *What is a job that I would love so much, that I'd actually do it for free?*

My answer was instant. I saw a flash of memories: of the grateful faces of so many young people I had helped at student leadership camps and conferences; of heartwarming mentoring moments helping young women navigate the challenges of life; of engaging team-building moments; of speaking in front of the groups I went out of my way to volunteer at every summer.

I thought, *Oh, how could I have been so stupid?*

Here I was in my fourth year of school, just now realizing I was on the wrong path when the right path had been in front of me all along! I just never gave myself the opportunity to acknowledge my inner voice and to truly listen to myself—until now.

While some people were not supportive of my decision and a few were actively shocked that a straight-A college senior would completely change her degree program with just a few courses left to graduate, I realized that—as I shared my news—those who loved me were cautiously excited about my new venture. They cared more about me ultimately being happy than my fitting into a perfect "career box."

With newfound energy, I invested the second half of my year in England taking courses in communications, public speaking, and media performance. When I returned to Ohio State, I convinced the administration to let me create my own degree program in "leadership studies." After graduation, I became a management consultant in leadership training and development for the Pentagon. I also won the title of Miss Virginia USA, which let me spend much of the year speaking to kids all across Virginia—as well as helping me launch a national speaking career.

Because I had the courage to pursue my path, to date, I've been blessed to reach over a million girls, teens, and young women. I've appeared on NBC's *Today* show, on Fox News, and as a young women's success coach on MTV—and I was even nominated for an Emmy Award!

Years ago, I changed my major and my life. While I still love animals, I have since exchanged my posse of furred, feathered, and six-legged friends for a single puppy named Floppy-Wonderdog. And although I value the opinion of trusted love ones around me, I continue to listen to my inner voice and boldly pursue my unique path. Does it make life easy and predictable? No. Does it make for an awesome an exciting OolaLife? Absolutely!

◎ ◎ ◎ ◎

When looking at your OolaField, start with one word: authentic. Are you living authentically or at least pursuing your dream job for your OolaField? If your answer is yes, congrats. If your answer is no, it's time to change course. It's time to be real with what you want to dedicate your life to and start taking action toward that. Once you know what you want to do, the next step may be as simple as writing it down.

SECRETARY TO CEO

by *Patty Aubery*

T he early years of my adult life were an unfocused blur. I was twenty-four years old and although I was married, I felt lost, alone, and scared. I was an L.A. girl married to a Jersey guy—trying to live a champagne lifestyle on a beer budget with absolutely no plan on how to get from where I was to where I wanted to be.

How on Earth had this happened to me?

My husband and I were miserable and broke. So we did what every twenty-four-year-old couple should do: we moved in with Mom and Dad.

Not an Oola move.

In fact, once we realized this wasn't a stellar life plan, we quickly wanted out of the house. So I did something I'd never done before: I set a goal. I was so committed, I wrote it down. My goal was simple: *Make $25,000 per year.* In 1989, that was a huge increase over my current pay of $14,900.

We both began looking for better jobs. While laying on my mom's overstuffed couch one weekend, circling help-wanted ads in the *Los Angeles Times*, I spotted what looked like a good bet: $25K a year—Secretary Wanted. It was the best (and the worst) ad I had ever seen. But at least it offered $25,000 a year. I took it as a sign.

In those days, my biggest nightmare was to be a secretary. I'm not

sure why, but the thought of doing clerical work, getting coffee, and taking dictation—with one of those steno pads ever-present on my desk—
horrified me. While I knew my dad had several secretaries (and many
heads of government agencies are called Mr. or Madam Secretary),
in the late 1980's, that term was fast becoming sexist and demeaning.

But still . . . I thought to myself, *Call me what you want as long
you pay me what I want.*

So, that Monday morning, I left several messages on the number
listed in the paper. I think I called it two or three times a day but no
one answered. I was persistent and left repeated messages. Then came
the return phone call. It was an older woman with a very sweet voice.
She asked me to come in for an interview.

The day of the interview I pulled up to the curb of a small development in Pacific Palisades in my Dodge Colt—and made my way to
the three-story town house listed as the job's address.

Odd place for an office, I thought.

As the door opened, there stood a nice soft-spoken woman and a
man who seemed ageless and unpretentious to me. They had funky
hippie furniture, red shag carpet, and potpourri in all of the bath-
rooms. There were books and papers everywhere.

Their "meeting room" was in the kitchen. We sat around a small
table for three—me with my blonde bob and shoulder pads, and
they in their relaxed all-cotton clothes. I was very nervous, but they
seemed nice. We talked for about thirty minutes, then they handed
me a packet of materials and said they would call me.

When I got home, I laid everything out on my bed and looked at
the brochures and pamphlets. Honestly, I had no idea what they did
for a living. I just knew the name of the company was Self-Esteem
Seminars. The guy on the brochure cover—the one I'd met with—was
a professional speaker who talked about how to build self-esteem,
which I was sure was only for losers.

Within the next few days, I went to dinner with some friends and told them about my interview. They had actually heard of this guy, said he was amazing, and hoped I got the job. Now of course, I was secretly hoping I did, too.

But then came the phone call: "Hello, Patty? Hi, hey, it's Jack Canfield. Look, it was really nice meeting you, but we've decided to go with someone who has more experience in the hotel industry and is a bit more mature." (*Mature?* Really? . . . Lawsuit!)

I hung up the phone and continued my search—soon afterward landing another job. It was a long commute from home, completely boring, and paid well short of my goal of $25,000 a year. It wasn't even a nice place to work. But it was a job.

I settled in—and I do mean "settled" because, well, isn't that what you do at a job you hate? Work was just a four-letter word, and I did what I had to do to pay the bills.

Then, three months later, I got a phone call. It was that man again. Jack Canfield.

"Let's talk," he said. "Something tells me we're meant to work together."

Meeting him again around the little metal-and-Formica table in his kitchen, this time I asked for $30,000. He said, "Yes."

I said, "I'm in."

What I'd just accomplished was sinking in fast. A mere five months after setting my goal—a concept foreign to me—I had not only achieved the income I wanted, I had exceeded it. For years, I thought it had been a bold move, but now I know it was fate, luck, and the Universe inviting me to be my best self.

I could have easily told him, "No, thank you, I'm fine where I am."

After all, in the three months I'd been working at the other job, I had already been promoted (literally the week before). But there was this little voice inside me saying, *Well, if he's willing to offer $30,000* *now, what would he be willing to do in a few years? Go, see, trust.*

Today, I'm grateful I was so young and less opinionated. I didn't judge him for passing me up the first time (although it did cost him!). I was open to something totally new and completely foreign to my world. As an eighties girl with long red nails, the furthest thing from my reality was a hippie—twenty years my senior—who'd graduated from Harvard and just wanted to transform the world. He was an author with a simple message of hope, a big heart, and a deep desire to change people's lives. Turns out, he was also into my newfound love for goal-setting.

With the two of us working together, our goals would not be denied.

We weren't even discouraged when 133 publishers told us "no" and rejected the manuscript for a little book he wanted to write called *Chicken Soup for the Soul*. After we finally got a yes, I would literally go door-to-door with the newly published paperback and ask everyone from bagel shops to nail salons to buy a stack for their customers. I was never "too good" to do anything that we thought would build the business.

I continued to set goals and took action toward them every day—even through all of the rejection, disappointment, and challenges. That kind of hustle eventually moved me from secretary to CEO. And with over 200 *Chicken Soup* titles, multiple *New York Times* bestsellers, and over 500 million copies in print in over 40 languages, *Chicken Soup for the Soul* became one of the top-selling non-fiction book series of all time.

I am so glad I put a pen to paper at twenty-four and wrote down that goal. This whole crazy ride—creating a book series, building a brand, transforming millions of people around the world—all started with one goal, and one goal only. In some ways, its simplicity made it less confusing, less overwhelming, and more attainable. All I had to do was focus on making $25,000 a year—nothing more, nothing less.

Just that. It was enough to get me unstuck, out of my parents' house, and moving forward—goal by goal—to the life I had always wanted.

◎ ◎ ◎ ◎

Never underestimate the power within you or the power of listening to your heart and following your dreams. You are more capable than you can ever imagine. But nothing happens without serious hustle and persistence. Whether you're running a business, growing your professional career, or creating a rockin' home environment for your family, what can you do to create more Oola in your *field?*

LOVE IT OR LEAVE IT. Studies show that 70 percent of people hate their jobs[†] and between 40 and 50 percent of marriages in the United States end in divorce. So going to a job you hate, then coming home to a spouse you can't stand—repeating that every day, over and over—isn't a life. It's a prison sentence . . . and it is definitely unOola. Clearly, investing eight hours a day at a job you hate is not only toxic for you, it negatively affects others when you bring home that resentment to everyone else.

If you can't love your work, have a plan to leave it. Create a bridge between your current employment and your dream job so your financial responsibilities are handled. You can do anything for a fixed amount of time if you know there's something better on the horizon. If it's your season to dig in as you're transitioning, work honorably and be sure to provide value and service while you're looking for something more connected to your purpose.

STAY RELEVANT. Famed hockey player Wayne Gretzky once said: *Skate to where the puck is going, not where it has been.* If your

---

† Gallup, January 15, 2017: *www.gallup.com/poll/180404/gallup-daily-employee-engagement.aspx*

career skills are outdated or uninspiring to your employer—or if your business could benefit from being at the forefront of your industry in some way—our advice is to upgrade your skillset so you stay relevant in your field. Start investigating new technology, find different ways to use social media, look for benefits in world events, and anticipate economic trends.

And if you're a stay-at-home mom or a homeschooling mom? That's an amazing calling on your life, but it also demands that you stay relevant in order to raise incredible kids who excel in life. What are some new parenting ideas you can try? How can you create a healthy, stress-free home that helps your kids do better in school and other activities? Think boldly but be authentic.

ALWAYS SEEK TO SERVE. One of our favorite stories is about three stonecutters who, in the 1700's, were working on building St. Paul's Cathedral.‡ The first said, "I am earning sixpence a day." The second said, "I'm cutting this stone true and square." And the third said, "I am helping Sir Christopher Wren build this cathedral where lives will be transformed."

What's the lesson here for all of us? You can: (1) make a living; (2) do your best work; or (3) be of service to a goal that's bigger than yourself. If you're just there for a paycheck, why not *instead* consider the benefits of giving it your best shot and working tirelessly to build something awesome. Your self-confidence would grow—and so would your value to your employer.

Always seek to be of service in your field—whether it's on the job or off the clock. Put in a good day's work. Go the extra mile. Lose the attitude that most people have when they're asked to do something outside their job description.

---

‡ Originally told by business author Peter F. Drucker in his 1954 book, *The Practice of Management*.

Having an attitude of service—and working alongside others to achieve a greater goal—not only keeps you psyched about your own skills, it can also help you identify a new area of career interest and even get you promoted.

OOLAFAITH

"God will give us the strength to be able to handle
things. I mean, you can try to do it on your own, and
sometimes you can pull off some stuff, but in the long
run, it's much easier with Him by our side."

— Bethany Hamilton | @bethanyhamilton
Professional surfer, shark-attack survivor,
author, and mom

Have you ever wondered what your life purpose is? Do you know why you were put on this Earth?

While most people float through life unaware of the bigger picture, the truth is that you are here for a purpose. There's a unique calling on your life that requires your attention, and one of the easiest ways to discover your unique purpose is through a connection with God—our true source of love and wisdom.

In Oola, we don't tell you what to believe or who to believe, but we do know that you can't have the OolaLife without having a higher purpose for your life and without working on your faith. Getting plugged into God and faith is very Oola.

Whether you feel strong in your faith, or your faith is non-existent —whether you're considering a walk of faith for the first time or even just getting reconnected to faith—realize that this connection is where you'll discover your special mission. It's where you can say, "Hey, if this is what I'm supposed to be doing, then smooth my path and keep showing me the next steps."

It's also where you'll find explanations for the crazy stuff that comes up. Lots of people are searching for *why*—especially when things go bad. If you've ever asked yourself, *What's the meaning here? What am I supposed to learn from this?*—faith is the answer when logic alone doesn't explain what just happened.

Of course, not every church, religion, or spiritual community will be a good fit for you. While we're Christians and are open to talking about that with our readers, we also advocate checking out various churches and doctrines to see what feels right for you. Again, your beliefs are your beliefs, but the point is to believe in something bigger than yourself—and to do so boldly.

◎ ◎ ◎ ◎

LEARNING TO LISTEN

by Chaly Jones

I have always felt my biggest contribution in life, and to the world, would be by raising good children—kids who know right from wrong. Children who respect others, show unconditional love, work hard, know God, and understand their purpose in life. Working full time—and as a wife and mother of four, all under age eight—I love my crazy, chaotic, beautiful life. I love all of it. Some days I celebrate, others I simply endure, but in all days I find something to make me smile.

Like the day I found a notecard, worn from the folds and creases of being held by very small hands that read, "Dear Kellen, thank you for being the best brother ever. You love me when I am mean and that is speshiel [special] to me. Love, Kacen."

Or . . . this past Christmas, when proudly hanging on the mantle were embroidered stockings with the names: Drew, Tetyana, Owen, Vanessa, Haley, and Rie. Those aren't our names, we're: Cam, Chaly, Kacen, Kellen, Kamryn, and Kate. I just never found the time to remove the embroidery like I intended when I bought them on sale after last holiday season.

Or . . . the day that, during a run up the mountains, my seven-year-old was getting tired and ready to quit. After some assurance from my husband that the end (and a gorgeous view) was near, my son repeated a phrase I say regularly: "In this family, we do hard things." It made me smile, realizing he understood the significance of these words.

Or . . . the evenings I walk into my son's bedroom and see him on his knees in prayer.

These are the things I celebrate as a mother.

Yet even as there was much to celebrate, and even with the craziness of our lives, I'd been thinking seriously about adoption. Deep down, I felt it was God's plan for our family. As my husband and I discussed the possibility, we were quick to list very logical reasons why it wasn't right. Still, the feelings weighed heavily on my heart. Intellectually, I understood the reasons for pause. Our youngest was five months old. And with very busy boys, our plates were full. We didn't need a baby, we simply needed sleep. But my heart kept calling.

Then I saw a message that Dr. Troy, the OolaGuru, had posted on Facebook. He spoke of his adopted daughter Alea and said, "I wanted to let anyone who is considering adoption know that the answer is an unequivocal *yes*. Yes, you can love an adopted child as your own. Yes, she will feel completely a part of your family. Yes, there will be challenges. And yes, although I don't see my wife's eyes or my nose in Alea, we see God's hand in the process, which makes us know it is right and exactly how He intended it to be."

The feeling that adoption was right for our family was back stronger than ever.

I have attended OolaPalooza countless times, though not as an attendee. I have a unique perspective; I am one of the people in the back making sure the event is running smoothly. It is a great place to be. I love watching people get up on stage and declare with passion the positive changes in their life. It's a powerful moment to witness.

While music was playing and attendees were writing, I noticed Dr. Troy in the back of the room. I approached him and expressed how fear was getting in the way of us pursuing adoption. As we talked, I knew I needed the courage and faith to ask God for help in finding this baby that I felt was meant to be in our family. My twenty seconds of courage was a prayer: if this was to be—if adoption was right— let it be.

Moments afterward, I was caught off guard. I saw my husband go up on the stage. He was going through the event as an attendee, and stood at the microphone to give voice to his major Oola goal. A former wrestler and NCAA Division I athlete, he explained that while the goal in his head was to get into better physical shape, his heart was telling him something different. It was telling him he needed to commit to a family goal.

With tears in his eyes and a nervous tone in his voice, he said, "My goal is to expand our family through adoption."

I didn't know what else to do but to cry and be grateful for this man in my life. My prayer was answered. It was just three months after OolaPalooza that Kate joined our family.

Oola believes together we can change the world with a word. By making ourselves better, we make our families, communities, cities, and the world better. Learning to listen to God's voice and His purpose for my life, our family's life has changed. It has been unexpected, unplanned, and far better than we ever could have imagined.

Listen to that voice—the voice that says life can be better. The voice that says go for it. The voice that says fear is stupid and your dreams are worth it. The voice that says you are stronger than you can ever imagine. Listen to it, and go get it.

There is so much demand for our attention. We're so busy in our heads thinking, planning, and mulling over our day that we often forget to listen to our hearts. People, media, and the world speak to our minds, but God speaks to our hearts. That "feeling" you have is important; listen to it. But what if that feeling is one of pain and anger toward God?

FINDING THE STRENGTH TO WALK THROUGH IT ALL

by Kris Amdahl

S unday mornings were especially sweet. When you are fifteen, it doesn't get much better than letting the dim winter sun wake you up through the curtains, glancing at the clock, then rolling over in heavy quilts because you realize it's the weekend and you can sleep in. However, this Sunday was different.

I woke to my mom sitting at the corner of my bed. This wasn't unusual. I usually required an extra nudge or two to get me out of my comfy quilt cocoon and up for church. What was different were her eyes. Although she tried her best to hide it, they were puffy. It looked as if she had aged ten years over night. As she sat there, all she could do was cry. The only words she could get out were, "It's Mike."

Our family was big, active, and going a thousand miles an hour in eight different directions. I had two sisters and three brothers. Mike was fifteen months older than me. Like most siblings, our relationship consisted of an interesting mix of love and irritation. It seemed like we were either fighting or making up.

The night before we were fighting. Mike wanted $5 from me, and I didn't want to give it to him. It ended with me shouting "no way," slamming a door, and storming away. This wasn't uncommon. What made it hurt was that I quickly realized those were my last two words to him.

He was drinking, they were driving, and he died. And in an instant our family changed. In an instant, I changed. My fifteen-year-old brain couldn't process what had happened. Everyone in my family was so busy dealing with their own grief that they lost track of mine. I went numb.

It is said "time heals," and looking back, it does, but slowly. Winter turned to spring, and my numbness transitioned to anger. I was mad at Mike because he went to the party. I couldn't believe he would drink and drive. I was mad at myself for not giving him $5. But mostly I was mad at God. How could He let this happen?

Before this, I prayed; not as a connection or relationship with God but as a matter of routine. More as an obligation or just something we did as a family, like brushing our teeth or taking off our muddy shoes before entering the house. We said grace at dinner, prayed before bed, and we rarely missed church on Sunday as a family. I believed in God, but church was just something we did. Until this morning, it was not much more.

I know now what my fifteen-year-old brain did not know when I found out my brother died on that cold February morning in Minnesota. When experiencing a great loss there are phases. It's as if I followed the textbook but quit at the last chapter. My emotions seemed to change with the seasons, from anger to questions, and questions to sadness. And then I got stuck. How could I accept that this was God's plan for Mike's life?

I spent a year there . . . in sadness. Learning how to accept condolences, hopping on the school bus without him, his seventeenth birthday, and the first Christmas without his energy and bright smile.

As my adolescent brain processed very adult problems, I finally came to acceptance. And it happened from a simple prayer.

I remember the day I drove to his gravesite. Although I realized he wasn't there, it was the only thing I could think of to feel close to him. I was physically fatigued from the denial, anger, questions, and ongoing sadness. My fatigue opened me to the concept that life will deliver things I will never fully understand. I prayed in a way that I had never done before. Instead of words, like those I would recite but not understand at church every Sunday, I offered my heart. I chose to believe, even in what I didn't understand, and submitted.

"God take over," I voiced.

I didn't ask Him to take over, I *begged* Him to take over. I surrendered my life to Him and His plan. As the tears rolled, the weight lifted. The numbness was gone. I could feel again. I could look forward again. I could let go.

Although the prayer was simple and the relief was real, my decision to submit my life to God and His plan felt under constant attack by this crazy thing called life. It would be challenged when I had kids of my own. When I was in my third trimester, undergoing an emergency appendectomy and being told that my daughter would have a 50 percent chance of surviving the procedure . . . God take over. It would be challenged through the process of international adoption—when holding her picture and not being able to bring her home for nine months and missing her first birthday . . . God take over. It would be challenged in my twenty-six-year marriage to the OolaGuru through seasons of "better and worse," "richer and poorer," and in "sickness and in health" . . . God take over.

With each test, God stepped up. Not always with the outcome I wanted for my life, but with what *He wanted* for my life. And it is His path for my life that I have committed to follow. And this gives my life incredible peace.

Life is beautiful. Life is difficult. And life is everything in between. I know now that I don't have to understand it all, but I can walk through it all . . . with faith.

◎ ◎ ◎ ◎

When we are driving down the road in the OolaBus, we talk about all the amazing things that have happened since the original *Oola* book was released. We often find ourselves on the topic of food, music, cool Oola tattoos that pop up on social media, and believe it or not . . . faith.

It interests us.

We want to believe that, in sharing Oola with the world, we are serving God's purpose for our lives and not our own. We love hearing the many different ways the simple Oola message has transformed lives and families, but we have a special place in our heart for the people who find faith for the first time or give it another shot after being angry with God.

Like a fingerprint, everyone's faith walk is different, but we have found three ways that help you to grow this F of Oola.

DON'T WAIT: FIND THE PATH THAT RESONATES IN YOUR LIFE. Take time now to reconnect to a church or religious group or meditation practice. We're Christians, yes, but you be *you*. Find a message that resonates with you, then lean into this new or renewed walk with God so that it's a regular part of your life. We recommend finding a structured way—ideally a house of worship or small group—where you can connect with others who think like you and who can support you when life gets rough. Be open-minded. Attend at least three times before you decide, *Yeah, this is the place for me . . . or it isn't.*

PLUG IN AND LIVE YOUR FAITH DAILY. Along our journey, we find clarity in reading the Bible where we always seem to find new insights to explain what's going on in our lives and the world (and learn what our response should be).

Daily meditation can also help you get closer to God, as well as get clear on what you should be doing in specific situations. New research says meditation also improves brain function, mood, creativity (and may even counteract loss of brain volume as we age). Hundreds of books and audio meditations exist to help you create a daily meditation habit.

But an even better way to stay connected to God daily is to pray—even if it's a prayer of gratitude, a brief plea for help, or a quick high-five about something good that just happened. That kind of connection starts a relationship with God that's less formal, more connected—kind of like a friend you'd call with good news or bad. Pray with your kids, too, at mealtimes or before they go to sleep at night. Be proactive with your faith every day—don't just show up at church on Sundays for sixty minutes of sermons and sing-alongs with the band.

Faith was a challenge for the OolaSeeker while working his way up from the bottom. He wanted to control everything about his comeback—the pace, the timing, the magnitude. Over time, he came to realize that no matter how hard he pushed, it was ultimately God's timing. While initially this resulted in frustration, over time it has developed into peace.

Work hard, listen to His voice, pray, and keep moving forward.

SERVE OTHERS. Be part of something bigger than yourself by finding a place to give, volunteer, or make a difference—with no expectation of anything in return. Some people do it with money. Others contribute time and abilities.

While the OolaGuru is happy to buy plywood and shingles, it's not in his wheelhouse (or biceps) to build houses in Africa. Actually, we're pretty sure he doesn't know the difference between plywood and shingles. The OolaSeeker, on the other hand, would love to do mission trips. He loves to move stuff around, put it together, and watch the immediate positive impact of his efforts. Use your natural skill sets to benefit others.

Another way to give is to practice simple kindness. As you go through your day, be proactively kind to one another—something we call "random acts of Oola." Whether it's opening the door for a stranger, buying coffee for the person behind you in line, listening to someone who's hurting, or just making eye contact—put a smile on your face and be pleasant to those you meet.

But *never* do good, or give, or volunteer out of guilt. When the OolaSeeker was struggling, the OolaGuru told him, "When you give, make sure it is selfless, feels good, and that it's something you're doing from your heart." Great advice.

OOLAFRIENDS

"*Lots of people want to ride with you in the limo,
but what you want is someone who will
take the bus with you when the
limo breaks down.*"

—*Oprah Winfrey* | *@oprah*
*Billionaire media mogul, talk-show host,
actress, and philanthropist*

O h, the crazy times you can have with friends. While dudes rarely open up about what's on their minds, women have the unique ability to stop what they're doing and focus on nothing else. That's so Oola.

Whether it's a morning text that says all is right with the world . . . or a workday lunch to catch up on the news . . . or a major cryfest to process last night's crisis, friends bring a dimension and sense of security to life that's essential.

Historically, women have developed the instinct to connect. They've survived by forming alliances and staying emotionally close. While guys are doing the hunter-gatherer thing off by themselves, women are on speed dial trying to connect. It's how you survive.

But you gotta get this friends thing right.

Toxic friendships, gossipy friends, needy friends, getting used by others—those situations keep you from living in bliss, pull you away from your purpose, and actually add more stress to your life.

To make sure your friendships are supportive, fun and strong, think of your relationships as a series of circles, just like the family circles in *Chapter 5*.

YOUR **INNER** CIRCLE

First, there's your inner circle of your three to five closest friends— the ones you spend the most time with and the most energy on. These are the friends with whom you share virtually anything. These friend- ships have stood the test of time. You've seen the good (and the bad) from each other and decided to stay friends through it all. These inner-circle friends *must* be encouraging, supportive, and tuned in to what's going on with you. You can trust their advice because they "get you"—they instinctively know what's right for you because they've been your filter, your sounding board, and your cheerleader.

If your inner circle is made up of these types of friends, keep them close and appreciate them. Because you spend the most time with these friends (and call and text them the most), they influence you—and you influence them. As you set goals for the Friends area of your OolaLife, evaluate your inner circle.

Do you have the right people in your inner circle? Do you have toxic friends in your inner circle? The friends who make up your inner circle are vital to your OolaLife . . . choose wisely!

YOUR **CREW**

The next circle of friends is wider. It's made up of people you know well—like those you hang out with at work, your neighbors, or other school moms you see every day. They're usually based on mutual interest or forced interaction, but they can still provide fun times and a sense of connection.

Unfortunately, they also still have the power to cause drama in your life. Once again, invite and nurture the healthy friendships in your crew while fiercely keeping the toxicity and drama out.

YOUR **ACQUAINTANCES**

Lastly, there's the outer circle: your social media connections, workplace buddies, your old high school friends, your husband's tribe. While they may not be major influencers for you, they give life dimension and often provide random opportunities to expand what you're doing in your career or personal life.

How many friends in each circle are enough?

The number doesn't matter. The OolaGuru is pretty private. He's solid with two to three inner-circle friends but doesn't need too many people beyond that. The OolaSeeker, on the other hand, is more social. He gets super jacked connecting with old friends and is always open to meeting new people. Everyone's different. You be *you*.

Of course, what does matter is the *quality* of these friendships. Toxic, jealous, negative, dramatic, gossipy, and manipulative people have no place in your OolaLife. They bring you down and can transfer their own misery and shortcomings onto you. Don't let them in.

TWENTY SECONDS OF COURAGE

by Angela Cardinal

hy am I not happy? I thought to myself as I drove home from work. I had a great husband, a good job, a roof over my head, and food on the table.

My daily commute was an hour each way. I used this time to take inventory of everything that was bad in my life. I needed to find the source of my anxiety and stress.

Could it be my student loans? Was it my job? As a special education teacher, taking care of children with autism and behavioral issues was stressful and at times dangerous. Was that it? As I stared at the bumper-to-bumper traffic in front of me, I smirked as I thought, *Maybe it's this commute!*

That night, as I was getting into bed, I noticed the *Oola* book sitting on my nightstand. While it had been there for six months, I just hadn't found the time to read it.

Maybe the answer is in this book, I thought to myself, picking it up and brushing off the dust. As I started to read, I realized I wanted to learn more. The book simplified this often-unfulfilling thing called life. I even downloaded the audiobook the next morning and listened to it on my commute. I listened to it over and over—hoping to find the answer to how I was feeling.

As the months passed, I felt more moments of peace but the anxiety and stress remained. I started to dig deeper into Oola by watching the OolaGuys on Facebook Live. One day when I was watching, they announced an OolaPalooza in Lexington, Kentucky. In my heart, I knew I needed to go.

That evening, I talked to my husband Jesse about me going to OolaPalooza. We looked at our finances to see if we could make it work. We looked at flights, but they were beyond our budget. I live in Northern Minnesota, and for fun I typed "Lexington, KY" into the maps app on my iPhone. It responded: *14 hours and 36 minutes drive time.* Wow! We figured out that if I drove straight through I wouldn't need a hotel. And if I packed my own drinks and sandwiches in a cooler, I could save money on food. The math worked and I bought my ticket.

I hopped in my 2005 Ford Taurus with 180,000 miles on it and headed south for Kentucky. Next to me in the passenger seat was a cooler packed with tortillas wrapped around bananas and peanut butter, ham and Swiss sandwiches, bottled water, and soda. The budget was tight, the ride bumpy and long, and the food very average—but I was excited!

Over fifteen hours later, I pulled up to my motel on the bad side of town complete with a strip club next door and perfectly timed emergency vehicles with sirens blaring—almost as if to welcome my arrival. I quickly understood why it had been so cheap.

The next day, I found myself sitting nervously front and center at OolaPalooza.

On the afternoon of Day One, the OolaGuys started taking us through the process of writing down dreams and goals for the 7 key areas of life—the 7 F's of Oola. When we got to the sixth F, *Friends,* Dr. Troy asked us to write down our top three to five friends—the people we spend the most head space on. Then he asked us to look at each name and write down our first reaction to that friend.

"When you read each name," he asked, "how do you feel?"

Going through the exercise, I got to the third name on my list: Megan. Right there and then, I simply lost it. I knew immediately that all my stress, my anxiety, my sadness—all of it stemmed from that one name.

I had met Megan six years earlier through a college friend, Drew.[§] Drew was a close friend of my husband and me, and Megan was his new girlfriend. She soon became Drew's wife—and one of my best friends. We were even in each other's weddings. As couples, we did everything together. She was the one friend I talked to every day, and we hung out whenever we could.

So how could this best friend be the source of all my stress and anxiety? How could she be the reason for the tears flooding onto the paper in front of me?

Because she had an affair, left Drew, and created so much pain in the wake of her choices.

I was very angry with her, yet I didn't know how to handle it. When Dr. Dave saw that I was crying, he walked over and asked if he could help.

I told him the whole story. He simply looked at me and suggested that one of my goals for Friends might be to forgive Megan and let her go from my life.

"You don't have to agree with what she did, but you cannot continue to carry this burden and toxicity," he said.

With sadness, I wrote down in my Oola journal:

Forgive Megan and release her as a friend.

---

§ Alternate names used.

Following OolaPalooza, I was exhausted. As I got in my Taurus for the long road trip back to Minnesota, I realized I would have a lot of "windshield time" to reflect on my life. My trip north wasn't filled with excitement and anticipation like the trip south had been; it was filled with fear and worry. How was I going to tell Megan that she hurt me and that I didn't want to be friends anymore? Was she going to be upset? Would I be able to get over this? How would this affect my husband's relationship with Drew? Was it the right thing to do? I was having second thoughts.

When I rolled into Chicago, I pulled over to take a break along Navy Pier. I sat there looking out over Lake Michigan, eating a sandwich from my cooler. On the trails by the lake, I noticed all the people walking in the spring sunshine and hanging out along the water. *They look so happy,* I remember thinking. I wanted to have "happy" in my life again, too. In that moment, I decided not to wait until I got back to Minnesota but to call Megan right away.

During OolaPalooza, the OolaGuys had asked us to identify the one thing that was holding us back from making the necessary changes in our lives; then they challenged us to find "twenty seconds of courage" to handle it, resolve it, or release it. I found my twenty seconds and made the call.

Somewhere during that candid conversation with Megan, I felt the weight lift, the anxiety ease, and my heart open to happiness once again. I hung up the phone and called Drew—her ex-husband—to tell him what I had done. "We're there for you," I said, knowing my husband would have said the same. "We'll help you through this terrible time."

And that is what we did.

Over the next couple of months, as the distance from Megan became greater, our friendship with Drew grew closer. I started to see positive changes in all our lives. Drew forgave Megan and started the process of moving on. By removing a toxic friendship and show-ing forgiveness, I felt happy again. My mind was clear, I was looking forward, and I started to work on my other Oola goals. I got a new job closer to home. We got our debt under control, and—in a moment of pure joy—I found out that I was pregnant with our first child.

With all the positive changes happening, I didn't think life could get any better. But I soon found out what a random gift in the mailbox can do.

As I went outside to collect the mail, like I do every day, I noticed a coral-colored envelope. It was addressed to me, but it didn't have a return address in the corner. I quickly unsealed it and opened up a card, then skipped to the signature to see who had sent it. It was from Drew. He wrote:

> *There is nothing I could ever say that can express how much our friend-ship means to me. It's not much, but I want to let you know that I bought you tickets for the next OolaPalooza. It's a gift, so you can't object. Please accept it as a small token of what you and Jesse have done for me.*
>
> *Love, Drew*

I cried happy tears. Letting go of a toxic friend was one of the hardest things I have ever done. But by letting go, I opened my heart for "happy" again. And it feels good.

Unless you're starring in a reality TV show and you need drama for ratings and the renewal of another season, your life and your time are too valuable to waste in drama-prone and toxic-filled relationships.

The old saying, "You are who you hang out with," is so true. If you see toxicity in your inner circle, start now to clean that up and make room for endearing friendships and mentors who can create a healthy environment for you—as well as lifelong memories.

DON'T GIVE UP THE GIRLS' WEEKENDS

by Angie Frederickson

"I love you, my friends." Somewhere between a smile and tears, I uttered those words and squeezed one last hug from each of them before we parted ways for various terminals at LaGuardia. It was the end of a girls' weekend and we were all headed back to our individual real lives.

The weekend was perfect. Six best friends met in New York City to do what we do best: hang out, laugh, and reminisce. Twenty-plus years ago we met by chance when something drew us to the same college and we crossed paths. The universe must have known that we were perfect complements for each other, because those girls are still my dearest friends today. In fact, we are closer now than when we were in school together.

Getting the six of us together was no small feat. We are spread out all over the globe: Texas, Michigan, Illinois, Virginia, Connecticut, and even across the Atlantic in London. Choosing a weekend is like putting together an intricate puzzle. We have to work around dance recitals and soccer playoffs, kids' birthdays and school fundraisers. After we eliminate all of the dates where responsibility trumps fun, we are maybe left with a Wednesday overnight, eighteen months from now.

Sometimes getting away seems like more trouble than it's worth. Coordinating carpools and hometown logistics practically requires a mathematical algorithm to make it all happen. And then there's the guilt of leaving behind husbands and children to do something for ourselves. Somehow, girls' weekends feel selfish or even indulgent. It's easy to just give up and put it off for another day.

But a girls' weekend with old friends isn't just a vacation. It's a reality check with the people who know us best, and it's what sustains us. We get so caught up in our daily lives at home where playground politics and neighborhood drama somehow seem really important. When you're submerged in a world of suburban self-imposed busyness and keeping up with the Joneses, it's hard to see anything else and there's nothing like an old friend to put it all in perspective.

The six of us finally agreed on a weekend and booked our flights. As we shopped along the Upper East Side and strolled through Central Park, all of the things on our minds flowed effortlessly from our mouths. We retold old stories that still bring back great memories, and we laughed so hard that we feared our post-baby bladders would fail us. We recounted the most ridiculous things we have done, the stuff we stopped short of doing, and the things we really shouldn't admit out loud. But we do, in our safe place where oversharing is the rule.

Manhattan was the backdrop for our time together but it could have been anywhere. It doesn't matter where we go, because we just want to spend time together and channel our inner college girl. Remember her? She's the gal who never let anything get in the way of watching Melrose Place with her roommates, and who knew that a great band playing at the usual bar was a perfectly good reason to blow off studying for an exam. She was only responsible for herself and she didn't take things too seriously.

It's easy to forget that free-spirited girl within, because she gets lost in today's over-scheduling and family chaos. She did a lot more living in the moment, probably because she didn't know any better, but I think she was onto something. That girl is still there; she's just buried beneath maturity, practicality, and a few crow's feet. Spending time with old friends brings her out of hiding and parades her around for a bit, and that's a really good thing.

I cherish our girls' weekends, no matter how infrequent, because they are the only time we get to spend together. Thanks to geography, I don't know their new friends or their favorite restaurants. I don't know my way around their houses, and I only know their children through photos and stories we tell over the phone. Each of us has built an entire life over the past two decades, and we know the highlights but not the specifics. Their new friends and neighbors have taken over as the keepers of their daily information.

But what old friends know is the soul of the true person underneath all of the daily details, and maybe that's the best part to know. Despite our very different adult lives, with careers or lack thereof, and children of different ages and struggles, we are still the same girls we were twenty years ago. We just forget because responsibility landed squarely on each of our shoulders and dug in for the duration. A girls' weekend is the reminder we need.

We were only in New York for forty-eight hours, but for those two days all was right with the world. The laughter and connection picked up right where we left off and reminded us of who we really are. Each of us headed home, armed with the strength to step back into the daily madness feeling a little more grounded.

Wherever your earlier tribe hails from—college, high school, summer camp, former co-workers—find your pre-mom gaggle of girls and embrace them, because they are your connection with a part of yourself you may have lost. Give them a call and start planning your next girls' weekend.

◎ ◎ ◎ ◎

Laughing through road trips. Sharing confidences. Having a BFF who will listen and then set you straight. These are the kinds of friendships that add that special dimension to your OolaLife. But they can only happen when you're *intentional* about the friends you include in your inner circle.

What's our advice to having great friends and being a better friend yourself?

STAY CONNECTED. Technology makes it easy to stay in touch with inner-circle friends (and those in your other circles, too). One woman we know texts TFTDs—*thoughts for the day*—to her closest friends. These are inspiring, reassuring, or funny quotes she finds online that she knows will encourage a friend or make them laugh or just say, *Hey, this is me helping you have a bad-ass kind of day.*

But don't just text or post. Log some genuine, in-person face time with your closest pals. Get together for lunch, meet at the mall, go on a road trip. Being a good friend means you have to invest in your friends even when you're as busy as everyone else.

UNFRIEND, UNFOLLOW, DELETE. One of the most powerful exercises at OolaPalooza is when we ask women to write down their closest three to five friends, then decide whether these people enrich their lives or add to the stress level. Most attendees have a physiological reaction just reading their list—name by name—whether that friend brings a warm, fuzzy feeling or provokes dilated pupils and a cold sweat.

Toxic friends, BFFs who manipulate you, unreliable friends you just can't trust—seriously consider what these people bring to your life, then decide whether to have a crucial conversation, move them to your outer circle, or unfriend them altogether. Getting to Oola takes hard work and focus. True friends want what's best for you. They want to see you win. They are your fans, and you're their cheerleader. Be bold enough to let go of those who are holding you back—and brave enough to seek out new friends who challenge you to be a better you.

We highly encourage *you* to do this same exercise: look at your inner circle of friends and decide if they are life-giving or life-sucking. In addition, look at how *you are* with your closest friends. Are you the toxic one? Do you bring drama to the party? If so, you had better fix this before sharing this book with your girlfriends—and having them unfriend, unfollow, and delete you.

REVERSE ENGINEER THE FRIENDSHIPS YOU WANT. If you know the kind of friends you want in your life—smart, successful, supportive people—why not take a look around and start plugging those people into your life? Look at the areas where you're low. Find mentors for what you want to do. Get out and experience life by getting involved in new activities you're interested in—you'll find people there who can be lifelong friends while mentoring you along the way.

At the same time, be a great friend who other people will *want* to add to their lives. Enrich others. Be a good listener. Bring something to the picnic other than just a common interest.

OOLAFUN

"As hard as it is and as tired as I am,
I force myself to get dinner at least once a week
with my girlfriends, or have a sleepover.
Otherwise, my life is just work."

— Jennifer Lawrence
Actress

Most women don't have enough fun in their lives. They're busy in their careers. They're busy with their kids. They're busy running a household. And they can easily think of twenty-seven better ways to spend the money it would cost for a weekend getaway or that dream vacation to Paris.

Perhaps this describes you.

But what you may not know about is the positive *physiological* effect that fun has on your body, mind, and spirit. Unwinding with friends, laughing through a funny movie, and taking time off for leisure activities or an international trip literally changes your physical and mental state for the better.

First and foremost, it reduces cortisol, the stress hormone—which makes it easier to cope with nerve-wracking situations. But it also boosts serotonin, the brain chemical that regulates mood, memory, and sleep. This reduction in your stress level actually reduces mental strain and the physical drain on your body, too, leaving you more energetic and clear-headed, and with better concentration and focus. Even the American Psychological Association touts the benefits of having fun.

Most important, however, will be the impact on your key relationships. Sharing good times with others helps you form bonds and social connections—one of the fundamental needs of humans.

With all these benefits, the crazy thing is how many women we meet who believe—now that they're adults—they somehow *shouldn't* have fun. Reading a book, soaking in the tub, enjoying a glass of red wine, getting a pedicure—these are easy, everyday fun things you can do to unplug, unwind, and chill out.

WHAT KIND OF **FUN** IS ON YOUR BUCKET LIST?

If you're one of those adult women who has told herself, *Someday I'll have fun . . . like when I'm retired and sixty-five,* be aware that you can still be super-productive and fun-loving—in smaller ways, on a limited budget, and with (or without) your kids in tow.

Guys have mastered this art of disconnecting and having fun. There's Monday Night Football, Saturdays at the golf course, and Tuesday's softball league. While they're having fun, they're *not* taking care of other responsibilities . . . are we right? Waiting until you have the spare time, the kids are grown, and there's enough money in the checking account means you'll probably have forgotten what fun even looks like.

So, a major goal for you on your journey to Oola should be to decide *what you'll do for fun*—on a weekly basis, over occasional weekends, during your annual vacation, and especially for those once-in-a-lifetime "before you kick the bucket" experiences.

The OolaGuru routinely travels around the world knocking line items off his bucket list—from riding a camel in Dubai, to swimming with a baby elephant in Thailand (both in the same week!), to surfing in Panama or simply driving the OolaBus with the windows down and his Oola hat on backwards meeting people and collecting dreams. He's been to over fifty countries and he's run marathons on four continents. But the interesting thing is that he had to learn from the OolaSeeker how to have *simple fun* every day. He recently put a ping-pong table in his backyard and has committed to evening walks with his wife.

The OolaSeeker, on the other hand, has always been the master of finding free fun every day. You'll see him hiking with his kids in the summer, snowshoeing in the mountains in the winter, and pretty much road-tripping whenever he has a chance. What he learned from the OolaGuru is to start knocking off those big "bucket list" items. He recently completed a solo trip through Spain—working at a winery outside Madrid and running with the bulls in Pamplona. He took a couple of his daughters scootering through Croatia, drifting in a Jeep on the beaches of Santorini, and sipping coffees in Turkey.

The key is to plan, schedule, commit, and figure out how to fund these major life experiences you've always dreamed of. Get out the calendar and pencil something in over the next twelve to eighteen months. Spend an afternoon online learning more about your options and discovering the excitement that's in store for you. Research ways to do it cheaper. Focus on getting what you want, and you'll be surprised at the little opportunities that come along to insure you not only get to pursue that activity—but you get to do it in a way that's much more fun than you originally planned.

What's on your bucket list? And how can you enjoy simple fun every day?

CHASING IT

by Jen Davis

When I was just a little girl, running wasn't exercise—running was FUN! I would run through fields of flowers and weeds, chase the boys, play tag, run around the playground—and I would never get tired. No one had to ask me to do it and I wasn't counting calories burned or distance traveled. It didn't require an app or special running gear. I did it simply because it was fun!

Something happened in adulthood. Exercise became work, an obligation; one of a number of things on my overflowing to-do list that rarely happened. And when it did, it wasn't like I remembered. All that ran through my head was, *I'm not fast enough. My legs aren't long enough. This sucks. Am I going to damage my knees? I don't have a running coach. I'm out of breath. How come I have to stop and take a break. HILLS!*

I would see my neighbors, impeccably outfitted in the latest workout fashion. Whether they were running alone or pushing a stroller, they seemed to run effortlessly, as graceful as gazelles with hardly a hair out of place. I would see others on social media posting times, accomplishments, and pictures of their medals. I was looking for encouragement; however, looking around just caused me to compare, feel less than, and further away from the fun I once associated with running. The negative self-talk danced around in my head every time I strapped on my shoes and reluctantly went out the door.

It is said that comparison is the thief of joy; in my case that was *so very true!* It wasn't until I stopped competing and comparing myself to everyone else, and just started running my own race, that I rediscovered the absolute pure joy of running like I had remembered when I was that little girl.

It was then that I realized that I—yes, me—am a real runner just like the rest of them! And what makes me a real runner is that I get out and run. I just started to be me: real, flaws and all.

Don't be like the rest of them, darling, swam in my head. *Just be you!*

I took the competition out of it all. I stopped posting my mile times and distances. I simply grabbed some comfy shoes, bright socks, and random funky running gear and hit any trail without a plan. No destination in mind, just the curiosity of what's over that hill, around that tree, or can I climb that rock to get to the other side? Jumping in puddles, getting dirty, leaping over streams, flying down a mountainside, tripping over my own feet, creating my own trails, jumping off things for an epic adventure are all part of my daily runs.

I have tapped into my childlike sense of wonder. I stopped taking myself, and life, so seriously. I find fun in every day and in every mile. I realize I have one life to live, and I am only here for a short time, I might as well make it FUN! The zest for life is strong within me . . . my daily runs now feel as if I am on one huge, epic, never-ending adventure and all I ever want to do is explore and learn. It's no longer, *I have to run,* but *I get to run!*

FUN is out there. I found mine on a quiet trail with my feet moving underneath me. For others, it might be something else. Whatever it is, that thing that puts a smile on your face and makes you lose track of time—chase that.

⊚ ⊚ ⊚ ⊚

None of us truly knows how many days we have left on this amazing planet, so take time to enjoy life every day . . . and quit waiting for "someday." Yes, that even means on the crazy-busy, kids-screaming, rush-hour-traffic kinds of days—especially those days! Make time for fun. The only thing better than having little doses of fun every day is turning fun into your full-time gig.

I BOUGHT A GOAT

by Jennifer Webster

was speeding down I-44 in what seemed to be the getaway car. I was so nervous I almost felt as if I had stolen her, even though I bought her fair and square. I had feelings of excitement mixed with disbelief: "What the hell did I just do? Am I losing my mind?"

If my name was Thelma, I would've named her Louise.

I looked in the rearview mirror to make sure I wasn't dreaming. I wasn't. A goat was in the back seat. Floppy ears and with what seemed to be a puzzled look on her face. I think she was having a similar experience: "Why the hell did I get in this car with a city slicker?" They don't make car seats for goats. Her chance of survivability was fifty-fifty, so I understood her concern.

My husband and I didn't grow up on a farm. I've actually never been on a farm. In fact, I knew *nothing* about farming or raising goats. But this goat in the back of my Jeep Grand Cherokee was where our journey of becoming organic farmers began.

I have been a workaholic since birth. I literally had to schedule fun on a color-coded, heavily labeled, perfectly organized calendar. I got my first job at sixteen. I was a cashier at Walmart, and I got my first paycheck and some praise to go with it, then I was off and running. I was the girl who missed out on the parties and fun so that I could cover the weekend shifts. The more I praised the more I worked.

Soon, I was juggling forty hours a week and cruising through high school by taking college credit classes. I was driven, smart, and a 100 percent workaholic by the time I graduated. If my schedule wasn't crammed and people weren't noticing, I wasn't happy. I thought fun was for lazy people—and I wasn't lazy.

Before I knew it, I was married, dragging babies all over, and trying to balance it all. I was the "career woman" that society talks about. The word that best defined me at this point in my life was the word "too." I had too much on my plate, with too much guilt, and I was too exhausted to even think straight. My life was a daily cycle of trying to do everything for everyone and not finding satisfaction in anything. I felt empty and I felt lost. I felt depressed for the first time in my life.

What does a crazy-busy career woman do when she is about to lose her mind? She buys a goat.

It all started with a documentary I had watched with my husband a couple months earlier. This film opened my eyes to what is happening to food production and got me thinking about the quality of what we put in our kids' mouths. My husband and I joked about raising our own food for our family. What started as a joke turned into a passion for healthier living for my family. Some women get hooked on *Keeping Up with the Kardashians* or who's getting the rose. For me, I was hooked on YouTube videos and blogs on farming and raising my own food. My family is the most important thing to me. I realized that I was missing out on the best parts of their lives and feeding them from whatever fast-food joint we passed on the way home from work. I was done.

And I bought a goat for my husband for Christmas.

Today, 7 years later, we are the proud owners of 10 dairy cows, 4 pigs, 100 chickens, 16 geese, 5 ducks, 12 dairy goats, and 26 rabbits ... wait, make that 32 ... *whoops*, now it's 48 ... that thing they say about rabbits is real. You get the point. Remember the movie *We Bought a*

Zoo? Well, I bought a goat and that turned into full-time farming and what feels like a zoo. Eventually, my husband quit his job, and this is now what we do—and we couldn't be happier.

With gratitude, I reflect upon the last seven years. I feel free of my workaholic ways. My husband and I are closer than ever as we work together toward a common dream. The family has bonded over hard work, fresh air, and dirty hands. We now realize that fun isn't always fancy vacations and theme parks. Fun can be found right in our own backyard . . . in an early sunrise on the porch, from a fresh cup of coffee on a cool fall morning, in a soft chair after a hard day of work . . . or rolling down I-44 with a goat in the back seat, chasing your dreams.

Clearly, Jennifer has mastered the art of fun (and farming). But how many women never get to experience a life-changing episode like that because they simply don't see the value in fun? Even Type-A personalities need to unplug and take time off. Here are some tips for having Oola-quality fun.

DISCOVER WHAT YOU *WANT* TO DO FOR FUN. Don't think, *Someday I'll have fun.* Make a list today of what you like to do . . . a list of what you would do if you had all the time and money in the world and no responsibilities of any kind.

If you're out of practice, make the discovery process part of your fun. Grab some lifestyle magazines that look interesting, jump on Pinterest, and spend an afternoon breezing through photos. Start adding ideas and pictures to your "bucket list" journal—or keep a running list on your smartphone to remind you to plan fun new activities.

Some people love to share with others as part of having fun. We challenge you to merge what you love to do in a way that positively impacts others. If you love quilting, why not create some quilts and donate them to a local raffle? If you're a golfer, why not join Big Brothers Big Sisters of America and take a kid golfing? There are countless ways to share your fun with others and make the world a better place, too—even if it's only one interaction at a time. Of course, if it feels like work or just another deadline you have to squeeze into your schedule, don't do it. Oola means balance. Don't let fun time become just another item on your to-do list and be a source of stress.

DON'T USE FUN TO AVOID TASKS YOU HAVE TO DO. One cautionary note about having fun is to always be sure it's part of a balanced life where other responsibilities are being handled in due course. Don't use shopping, workouts, craft time, and other fun stuff to avoid important or unpleasant tasks you have to do.

Confronting your dad, tackling that project at work, sitting down with a debt counselor—you can't put these challenges behind you if you're binge-watching season five of *NCIS* or hanging out at the mall.

You're better than that. Your future is waiting for you to clean up, confront, and complete before you move on.

DETACH COMPLETELY. When you *do* have authentic fun, be sure to detach completely. Don't feel guilty thinking, *There are forty-nine other things I should be doing right now.* With others pulling at your time, remember, you *deserve* this time. You've earned it. It's good for you. And ironically, it's good for those around you, too. Enjoy it.

OOLABLOCKERS

"The path to realizing our dreams is never smooth."

— Susan L. Taylor | @iamsusanltaylor
Former editor-in-chief of Essence magazine and
founder of National CARES Mentoring Movement

n addition to the 7 F's of Oola, there are habits, beliefs, and attitudes that will either hold you back or propel you forward. We call these OolaBlockers and OolaAccelerators. And while your blockers and accelerators may be different from ours, you'll likely recognize a bit of yourself in the responses, traits, and self-talk that we'll discuss in Sections Three and Four of this book.

Blockers, which start in a couple of pages, are the junk that keeps you from showing up fully, thinking of yourself as worthy, or asking for what you need in order to be happy. Not only have we experienced these Blockers *ourselves* over the years, but we see them time and again in the lives of Oola event attendees and those we meet on the OolaBus. Blockers like *guilt, self-sabotage,* and *anger* can keep you from going for what you want—even holding you back *subconsciously.* They're the negative head game that will keep you from living the life you deserve.

In this next chapter, we'll start with the first Blocker: *Fear.* By removing fear and other Blockers from your life, you can move forward with a clean slate—focused solely on the positive new thoughts and actions you want to bring into your life.

FEAR

"I think fearless is having fears
but jumping anyway."

— Taylor Swift | @taylorswift13
At age 26, the youngest woman ever included in
Forbes' Most Powerful Women list, ranking #6

n 1932, during the height of the Great Depression, President Franklin Roosevelt knew he needed to calm a worried nation. After three years of economic hardship, many Americans had lost their jobs. Many more had lost their homes. And most people had lost hope that life could *ever* get any better.

Fear gripped the nation. This is exactly why Roosevelt delivered his now-famous reality check:

"The only thing we have to fear," he said, "is fear itself."

While you probably weren't alive to hear that speech in 1932, it's safe to say you've probably lived through your *own* private hardships a time or two. Maybe you reached the point where *everything* looked grim. Maybe you've been in situations where you made yourself crazy with apprehension—only to find out the actual circumstances weren't that bad. Perhaps you pre-supposed something disastrous—then realized there was actually nothing to be afraid of.

Most of the time, the paralyzing effects of fear are simply unjustified.

Whether it's going on your first job interview, starting your own business, breaking off your engagement, or moving across the country for the first time—these are all things that happen every day. And other people survive them.

As long as your gut instinct isn't telling you there's real danger ahead, our advice is to stay the course, focus on the bigger picture, get all the information or practice you need—then take action in spite of your fears.

WHERE DOES **FEAR** EXIST FOR YOU?

There are only two innate fears that all human beings are born with: the fear of falling and the fear of loud noises.

Every other fear is learned. *And what can be learned can be unlearned.*

If you don't like communicating bad news to your boss, for instance . . . if you're afraid to be in a romantic relationship . . . if you've got a fear of public speaking or flying or heights or enclosed spaces—realize that these feelings have grown over time or stem from a specific incident. You can take steps to remove these fears—especially if they're keeping you from accomplishing something you want to do.

Have you thought through the individual goals *you* need to tackle on your way to the OolaLife? Once you've written them down, you can start to check in with yourself and identify where fear exists for you. For instance, if you want to lose thirty pounds, maybe you're thinking, *I don't want to hire a personal trainer. I'm embarrassed to be the only fat person at the gym. I don't want anyone to weigh me.*

Well, wouldn't the benefits of feeling sexier, fitting into those goal jeans, and being super healthy outnumber the brief moments of embarrassment or awkwardness?

If you're up for a job promotion but the new gig requires public speaking, are you telling yourself, *I'll be a complete disaster in front of an audience?*

And if a past romantic encounter has left you uneasy about meeting someone new, that, too, can be overcome with better boundaries, more caution, and maybe starting things slowly by going out on fun group dates with friends.

In almost every instance, what you're fearing or telling yourself in your head is *exactly* what you need to push through in order to get your life to a better place.

ARE YOU **STUCK** IN ANALYSIS PARALYSIS? OR ARE YOU **IGNORING** REAL DANGER?

Focusing on everything that can go wrong is how people get stuck in "analysis paralysis"—always analyzing their options and never moving forward on their goals.

Unjustified fear paralyzes people. We see it all the time. Someone is presented with a true opportunity. They analyze it to death, thinking of every reason why it won't work. This fear keeps them from taking action and keeps them from growing. Fear blocks their path to Oola.

At the other extreme are people who ignore their fears completely and throw themselves headlong into dangerous situations. Our "gut instinct" is there for a reason—to keep us safe. If you feel creepy every time you think about something you're afraid of, chances are that's your mind and body warning you. Check your facts. Ask questions. Reassess your options. Check out the people involved more thoroughly. Then decide if it's just fear or truly a bad decision.

Find a sweet spot in the middle and take action where and when it makes sense.

◎ ◎ ◎ ◎

THE COURAGE TO LEAVE

by Kristin

On June 25, 2016, at 1:18 PM, I took off my wedding ring and laid it on the front bumper of the OolaBus right below the orange OolaFamily sticker that I had written on thirty minutes earlier. The sticker boldly expressed the dream I knew I needed for my OolaLife: "Release toxic relationships."

I had walked all around the bus, looking for just the right place for my sticker. I found the spot at the front of the bus just above the license plate. I hadn't planned to take off my ring. It wasn't premeditated or preplanned for a photo opp. My mind was calm and clear, my hands steady, my heart resolute. In that moment, I acknowledged a truth I had been hiding from myself for a long time: my marriage was over. It had been over for many years, but like a doctor desperately doing CPR well past the resuscitation time limit, I somehow wouldn't allow myself to give up.

I stood there awhile in the warm sun, looking at the dream I had for my life. I prayed for God to give me the courage to follow through with what I knew I needed to do: don't ever put that ring back on.

Looking at the ring on the bumper, I felt free. A peace came over me. I felt strong in the moment and hopeful for my future. All of these emotions were an outward sign of an internal knowing that had been a part of me for many years. I took a picture of the ring and the sticker, because I wanted to remember the power of the moment.

Soon after leaving the OolaBus, I started to argue with myself; to talk myself out of it for the thousandth time. It sounds strange to say that I honestly didn't think I could leave. I felt as if I was in a complex relational cage, unable to leave.

I'm a classic full-blown, people-pleasing, gold star addict and my highest joy was to earn smiles and words of approval.

He was charming, sophisticated, and single-minded in his pursuit. We had a whirlwind long-distance courtship and were quickly engaged. We were married nine months later, and I carried that co-dependent, people-pleasing pattern into our marriage.

The troubles started right away.

We experienced some good times, especially the miraculous birth of two healthy children; this, after I had been told at age fourteen that I would never be able to have children. We also went through hardships: financial difficulties that culminated in food stamps, foreclosure, and bankruptcy; deep emotional distress and addictions; serious illnesses and the deaths of close family members. I tried to compensate by being the perfect wife and mother: drying the cloth diapers on the line to save on the electricity bill molding myself however I could to make him happy—even looking the other way when he had too many drinks, flirted with other women, or endangered us all by driving drunk.

I didn't live up to his physical standards of beauty and fitness after our kids were born, and he turned from my body with disgust. I felt undesirable and unlovable. I ignored the constant stream of criticism and contempt, which baffled my family and friends. They begged me to leave him, and my parents stepped out of our lives several times because they couldn't handle being around us and witnessed how he treated me. I was deeply lonely. This isolated me further, leaving me connected only to him. I went deeper into the cage.

There was a point when I was so miserable that I fantasized he would die in a car accident. I actually prayed for it to happen. I desperately wanted to be free of him and I couldn't think of another way. I was trapped by my own conditioning to think that I could actively make a decision to save myself. And I knew he would never leave me or willingly accept a divorce, so I saw death as the only way out. At the time, I was still seeing myself as a victim to my past choices, looking for the key to change my future.

I came up with all kinds of excuses, but the truth was . . . it was fear. Fear that I would be seen as the "bad one" rather than the "good one." Fear that I failed my marriage. Fear of the effect of divorce on my children. Fear of not having enough money to do it on my own. Fear of being alone forever because no man would possibly want me. Fear of making another wrong choice in a new relationship. And my deepest fear was that I believed I could not maintain my faith and would be judged by others.

Let's go back to that ring on the OolaBus that sunny day in June. This is where I first realized that the risks of staying in the current situation far outweighed the risks of leaving. I realized that I actually felt nothing for him. In the simple gesture of putting a Sharpie to a sticker, and that sticker on the OolaBus, I found the courage to tell him and our counselor that I wanted a divorce. I acknowledged that, rather than the death of a marriage, I simply called out something that died a long time ago but was never properly grieved.

It feels like the birth of a new life. I don't feel angry or bitter anymore. I feel oddly peaceful. In a way, it feels holy and precious and beautiful.

Author Brené Brown says, "Often the result of daring greatly is not a victory march, but rather a sense of quiet peace mixed with a little battle fatigue." So today I offer up this vulnerability prayer: *God, give me the courage to show up and be seen.* Courage to do the one thing I thought I would never do, so that I can live a life I never thought I could. Courage to leave what I know for what I don't know. Courage to leave behind financial provision and live-in parenting help. Courage to rock my career and provide for myself and my kids financially. Courage to tell my kids I am choosing to end it, even though he doesn't want to. Courage to someday sit with someone new and share my story and hear his. Courage to believe that I am made for the extraordinary and was made on purpose for a purpose. Courage to be a voice of hope for others.

So here I go . . .

. . . Opening the door to the cage and finding it was never locked in the first place. I have had the key all along.

◎ ◎ ◎ ◎

There is an underlying theme in Oola that we mention many times in our books, on stage, and on social media: *You are designed by God for greatness and a purpose.*

Many times that greatness and purpose live right on the other side of fear. Sometimes you will have to find the courage to push through fear and other times you can be pulled through fear by love, passion, and faith.

THE COURAGE TO STAY

by Dorean Leader

This is my love story . . .

As I sat across from my husband of fourteen years, fighting back the waves of nausea as he confessed his infidelity to me, I became intensely aware that, no matter what, from this moment on, my life would never be the same. I would never be the same.

It was the single most shattering moment in my life. I remember a bizarre burning sensation permeating my whole body and, in truth, I wasn't sure I was going to maintain consciousness. I sat there as he "came clean," looking intently at him as he lowered his tear-filled eyes in abject shame. At that moment I became equally aware that, no matter what, from this moment on *his* life would never be the same; *he* would never be the same. I was witnessing the breaking of a man as my own heart was breaking.

I am just as human as the next woman and the blast of horrific and devastating emotions wracked my entire being. There was anger like I had never felt before, shame to the point of wanting to disappear, and a deep sense of worthlessness. And trumping it all was the deepest fear I had ever known.

Over the following days and weeks, I would bounce back and forth between wanting to stay and work it out to being overcome with anger and desperately wanting out of the marriage. More accurately,

I wanted out of the pain. I finally understood how someone could actually die of a broken heart.

There was one sleepless night I actually thought I would simply die as I clutched my pillow for some comfort. With each tear, I was hoping to empty myself of all the hurt and disappointment. The tears that night eventually stopped, but the hurt and disappointment remained.

I woke the next morning realizing I had no choice but to make a choice. I had grounds to leave my marriage, but all through that night I knew I still loved this man. How can I still love the one who broke me? Am I just being weak? Or am I simply afraid that I can't survive on my own?

I always told myself there would be no doubt what I would do if my husband ever cheated on me—I would be out of there faster than you could blink—no questions asked. That's until it happened to me. The truth is, no one really knows what they would do until they're knee deep in it.

Finally, one evening I went to the beach and sat alone on the sand. I found myself lost in the stillness and soul-drenching peace of the setting sun. With the sound of the waves distracting me from my rampaging thoughts, and the mist of the ocean encouraging my whole being to take in every drop of relief being offered me, I surrendered. Right then and there I surrendered to the notion that I did not, and would not, die from a broken heart. I was still breathing and I was still managing my life, my children, my job, and my home . . . I had survived!

I don't actually think I have the words to completely describe what changed in me but something definitely shifted. I realized that for my sake I needed to make a decision. Would I leave the marriage and "shake the dust from my feet" as I walked away, or would I go against every fiber of my being, fight the fear, stay strong, and actually choose to stay?

This would be the single most courageous decision of my life. I had to overcome all the fear and, believe me, there was more than I could have ever imagined. Clearly trust was gone, life as we knew it was gone, the illusion of wedded bliss was gone, but the broken pieces of our love remained . . . and where there is love, there is hope. I had made the decision to not define my marriage by one mistake, no matter how damaging it was but rather by how I—how we—responded to that mistake.

I chose to have the courage to stay.

This was terrifying work and there were many moments I questioned my sanity in choosing to stay. I remember telling my mother, as I lay with my head in her lap, crying out to her, "This is either going to be the craziest thing I'll ever do or the most courageous!"

I had some truly wretched days as I worked at healing, as did my husband. It broke him to see what he had done to me, to us, to our family, but he was determined to endure whatever it took to mend what he broke. One of the first things I told him was that he couldn't make any promises. I didn't want to hear words, I needed to see action. His first action was marriage counseling. I cannot stress how important it was, not only for the immediate disaster we were trying to survive, but also for all the baggage that led up to this tragedy. We discovered there was a whole lot of garbage that needed to be taken out and it was time to really clean house. We worked together on our assignments. This was so unlike him. His effort began to repair the trust I thought was forever broken.

Every day, especially the tough ones, I had to make the active choice to continue in my marriage when many days leaving felt like it would be so much easier. Even today, seventeen years later, a random song, conversation, or movie will bring back all the emotions of this devastating chapter in my life. However, I let faith fuel my choice to move forward because I can't trust my emotions. The days I let my emotions rule, all hell breaks loose and only serves to set us back . . . to set me back.

I now look at my husband and am overcome with love and gratitude that we stuck it out! We did the work, we let go of the fear and worry that would have robbed us of something we weren't even sure would happen. We had hope and we grew stronger, not only as a couple but as individuals. Our marriage is better now—not in spite of the infidelity but, in truth, because of it. Everything we were was destroyed, but that destruction cleared a space to build something far greater, much deeper, and more lasting.

I chose hope over fear. Faith and love were in there—we just needed to dig them out and we did. And because we did we have a deep and meaningful marriage; we came out with so much more than what we went in with.

Thirty-two years and counting, and our love story continues . . .

◎ ◎ ◎ ◎

Fear comes at us constantly in one form or another. Sometimes it's the cumulative effect of lots of little fears over time that hold you back. Other times you'll be faced with a huge life challenge (or opportunity) that will require you to conquer fear in order to move forward.

So what can you do when confronted with fear that is holding you back from living fully?

IDENTIFY WHERE YOUR FEARS EXIST AND HOW THEY LIMIT YOU. Where are you feeling fearful? And how are these fears limiting your life? If public speaking terrifies you, for example, but you know you need to speak to groups in order to grow your business, will your business grow if you give in to the fear? On the flip side, what would your life look like a year from now if you summoned up the courage and became a sensational speaker—charming audiences and growing your business rapidly?

Only when you *identify* your fears—then picture what's waiting for you just outside your comfort zone—can you fully grasp the limits your fears have put on your own future.

MAKE PLANS TO FIX YOUR FEARS. Decide what your action steps will be for overcoming your fears, then start to "future pace" yourself with images of what your life will look like once you're on the other side.

You probably know what you have to do. But are there ways you don't know about for overcoming fears? Could you interview people about what to expect? Is there information you don't have yet? Can you check things out online? Often times, just informing yourself better will calm your fears. But usually there's no substitute for making a decision, jumping in, and just getting real-life experience.

TAKE ACTION TO OVERCOME YOUR FEARS. You're not the only one ever to feel fear. Most moms dread taking their kids to daycare for the first time. Lots of singers *never* get over the fear of performing on stage. And most business owners stress over making payroll in the early stages of their business. But you can only overcome your fears by getting into action.

Where do you face fear and what's the action step you need to take—that "twenty seconds of courage" you need to commit to in order to push through fear?

GUILT

"There is a hidden blessing in the most
traumatic things we go through in our lives.
My brain always goes to, 'Where is the hidden blessing?
What is my gift?'"

—Sara Blakely
Billionaire businesswoman and
founder of Spanx

W e've all made bad choices in the past. We've all said and done things we regret. But when those actions hurt ourselves and other people, guilt often follows.

Guilt over something you did is stealthy. It occupies valuable real estate in your mind. For some people, it becomes part of their "story"—making an appearance when meeting a new friend or surfacing when tackling a new goal in life. Guilt can become your favorite excuse or a recurring explanation. It can even affect your health.

But worst of all, it can keep you from showing up fully. *They'll find out,* you might be thinking. *They'll hate me once they know.*

That's the damage to your OolaLife and your future that guilt can do.

What's sometimes worse is feeling guilt for something *that was never your fault.* If you were sexually abused as a child, if your parents got divorced when you were a teenager, or if you've been physically or emotionally abused by your spouse—this is not your fault. But even though you may know that intellectually, the emotional impact of guilt is still there.

SELF-TALK IS THE **REAL** CULPRIT

If you've been carrying heavy guilt for some time, it may be stopping you from having the life you want. The burden often convinces us that somehow we don't deserve to live a fulfilling life—that maybe we've ruined our chance. This isn't true, of course. But the self-talk often hinders our progress just as we're embarking on an exciting new goal or just on the brink of a major new breakthrough.

THE **GUILT** TRIP

Different from guilt over something you did (or failed to do) is guilt imposed on you by other people's assumptions and opinions.

You never call, your mom says. *You never bring the grandkids.*

A guilt trip is when another person tries to make you feel guilty for acting, thinking, or feeling a certain way (or failing to act)—usually in order to force you to do something.

> *Sweetie, we'd already planned on having you* here *for Thanksgiving.*
> *Honey, my shirts are still at the dry cleaners.*
> *Mom, all the other kids' parents are letting them sleep over!*

What's the underlying message here? *Stop doing what's important to you, and do what I want instead.*

When faced with this type of guilt, recognize that the person delivering it is usually acting on their emotions. They're unfulfilled, fearful, or unacknowledged in some way, and instead of having a mature conversation about that, they're manipulating *you* to meet their needs instead. Don't fall for this tactic. Respond with grace and composure.

Even worse are the subtle guilt trips and I-told-you-so's when something really bad happens:

> *Daddy and I didn't have anyone to explain the documents to us . . .*
> *Why didn't you tell me about their reviews online?*
> *You never answer your cell phone.*

Unless you want the whole world blaming you and dictating your actions, emotions, and thoughts, the only way to respond to guilt trips is with grace and self-control. While explaining why the other person is wrong *probably* won't get you very far, letting them know that you understand their point of view—but have your own opinion, too—will give you the ammunition you need when you tell them you won't be following their advice or agreeing with their version of things.

SAND CASTLES

by Luisa Hogan

H ave you ever built a snowman? I haven't. Florida girl here. But I've built a sand castle before. It's the same idea. You start with something really small and keep adding to it. You give it life, one grain of sand at a time, until you have created something amazing. I grew up on the beaches of my hometown . . . swimming, floating, laughing, resting, and building sand castles. My brothers and I would use those little plastic molds to build our walls, dig a trench around the castle, and let the waves fill it with water. Castle walls and moats protected what was in the middle. When I was a little girl, I would dream of being a princess in one of these castles. That I was so incredibly valuable I needed stone walls, soldiers, and moats of water to keep me and my innocence safe. And there would be this one guy, a prince, who would have the courage to fight past armies, to cross that moat and scale those walls for me.

I can't remember the last time I built a sand castle.

I was fourteen years old and I was at a party with friends. There was beer. And music. And this one guy. He used to work at the store right across from the ice cream shop I worked at. I would watch him when I wasn't busy; he would buy his fountain drink from me. I thought he was cute. He brought me a beer and asked if I wanted to go talk with him in another room. I said sure and nervously sipped the beer. I thought it was odd that we went into a bedroom to talk, but it was a house party and there were people scattered in every room of the house. We sat down on the bed, and as I started to talk he leaned over and kissed me. I stopped talking. Then somehow I was laying on the bed, my shirt was up over my chest, and I felt a heaviness on top of me; a rough jabbing feeling between my legs. I think that was what woke me up. It was dark in that room. I tried to push the weight off of me, but I couldn't lift my arms or kick my legs. I managed to say, *"No!"* I said it a few times. But then his mouth was on mine again and I stopped talking. My eyelids were so heavy. I remember the feeling of wanting to close them so badly. So I did. And it all went dark.

I opened my eyes when my friend came into the room.

"Luisa, I've been looking for you! What are you doing in here?"

The light was on, my clothes were on, and I was alone on the bed.

"I don't know," I said, "but I really need to use the bathroom. Come with me."

We went into the bathroom and I felt the pain. Immense pain. Confusion. There was a little blood. I didn't tell her that part.

She asked me, "Did you guys just have sex?"

I wasn't sure actually. I had plans to remain a virgin until my wedding night. To gift that part of myself to my prince. The one who would scale any wall, fight any army for me. So I poured a little water on my sand castle and told her, "No way, we were just kissing and I guess I fell asleep."

We walked out of the bathroom and heard a commotion in that same bedroom. I poked my head into the room and there was a crowd of kids, staring at the bed, some laughing, some curious. I knew what they were looking at, they were looking at my innocence, right there on that bed. The blood I tried to hide from my best friend just moments before was there for everyone to see. I saw a couple of my guy friends lift their heads and look into my eyes, looking for me to answer, to explain what they were seeing.

Once again, I lied.

I told them I had started my period and I was sorry for the mess I made, but don't worry, I would clean it all up. A little later, my friends and I all drove home in silence. They knew. They had seen it in my eyes. But they didn't hear me say it. I had kicked my most magical sandcastle right back into the sea.

That's the worst part for me. The guilt all these years later of silencing my own voice. Pretending my dreams didn't matter which led to pain and heartache in every relationship I have had since that moment. And guilt over those friends of mine who didn't want to see it, but needed to hear me say it. They needed a chance to fight for me . . . to fight for something good. I didn't let them and for that I ask forgiveness.

I am asking for forgiveness from the innocent little girl building sand castles on the shore, dreaming of her one true prince.

I'm sorry I let your dreams be silenced.

I'm sorry I tore down those walls and let so many weak and passionless people into your life. All you ever wanted was to live happily in that castle until the day your prince arrived. Little girl, you deserve someone to fight for you, to prove that you are worth great acts of courage.

I will fight for you. I will protect you.

But we need to be courageous. Let's speak the words that others can see in our eyes. We can do this together—we can build something amazing again. We can show all the little girls of the world that, no matter how many times the waves try to wash our dreams away, we will build them back up. Because our dreams are not about that prince. They are not even about that moat or the castle walls. They're about that princess we are fighting for. She's worth it.

◎ ◎ ◎ ◎

Guilt over something that was not your fault can be the most harmful because often we believe, deep down, that somehow we caused it, could have prevented it—or even *deserve it*. Not true.

Facing what happened, putting things in their proper perspective, and accepting that you were blameless is the first step to healing.

In cases where you feel guilt about something you do have control over, getting to a place where you accept circumstances as they are, making amends where needed—or just granting yourself some grace and moving on—is the true path to overcoming guilt as an OolaBlocker.

THE MOTHER ON
THE PHONE AT THE PARK

by Meghan Yancy

remember reading some stupid blog when I first started my new role as a work-at-home mom. It was titled something along the lines of "Dear mother on your phone at the park . . . " Some mumbo jumbo that basically made me feel like the worst mom ever.

I was that mom.

While my children were playing at the park, I was off to the side, catching up with tasks on my phone, emailing, and working.

My kids are my "why." They are my everything, and why I choose to be home with them, and why I work hard to build a business. I want to be the one raising them. I want to provide a better life for them than I had. These little people are my passion and my legacy.

Replying to emails and sending video messages while sitting on the toilet. Little fingers poking underneath the crack between the door and floor. Tiny fists pounding and little voices chanting "MOM, MOM, MOM!"

This is my glorious, crazy, chaotic life.

But it is not without conflict, and the conflict is not with my five kids, or my husband—it's with me. I choose to work from home to have more time with the kids. But in order to do so, I need to work hard on my business to make enough money to be able to stay at home and contribute to the family. This often results with me being "with my kids," but not "*with* my kids." And in straight talk, I feel guilty.

It kills me when, on an important call and out of the corner of my eye, I see one of my kids appearing bored playing alone . . . or worse yet, staring blankly at a screen. Or I feel pulled when I feel my phone buzzing with notifications, most likely related to work, as I'm trying to spend quality time with the family.

I see supermoms all over on social media. Homeschooling, cooking organic meals, kids perfectly put together, effortlessly growing their business . . . all with a husband in full support by her side. Deep down, I know this isn't reality, but it does add to the pile of guilt that I'm building.

There are so many days where I feel like a complete failure of a mom. I mean, I freakin' rocked at checking things off my ever-so-long "to-do" list and built my business like a beast, BUT . . . I feel that I totally sucked at being a mom.

Other days, I put everything else aside to focus on the "mom thing." They are some of the sweetest and most special moments, and where memories are made. However, the next morning I suffer from an overwhelming to-do list and an overflowing inbox.

So, this is where the balance comes in. Finding the balance and seeking the growth in all my roles in life as wife, mom, and entrepreneur.

I'm not going to lie. I've led some pretty questionable business calls. Sometimes, you've just got to roll with it. I've had conference calls while in the bathtub and video calls while nursing the baby.

I remember a moment when I was trying to balance it all. My baby was crying and I was trying to get him down for a nap. The teapot was screaming as the steam seeped through the spout. Kids were playing and yelling in the other room. My mind was racing with all the business-related tasks I had to achieve that day. And my sweet six-year-old daughter walked up to me with a blanket in hand and tapped me on the shoulder, "Mommy, can you snuggle with me?"

Irritated and overwhelmed, I responded more harshly than I should have with the whole "I'm too busy" routine. As those words escaped my lips, I instantly regretted it and felt guilt sink into the pit of my stomach. I was too busy to snuggle with my little girl. Really? The mommy guilt flooded me. My very core was ripped to shreds as I knew the mistake I made.

After I finished my call, laid the baby down for a nap, I went to my daughter, crouched down to her level and told her how sorry I was for not snuggling with her. I told her that whenever she wants to snuggle, give me the "snuggle sign" and I will drop anything and everything to make it happen. Of course, her childlike heart forgave me in that instant and we hugged like nothing had happened. Her warm embrace melted away the guilt and her unconditional love captured the parts of my heart that had been wrecked by the conflict of working and being a mom.

Yes, I understand that importance of cherishing our everyday moments. But yes, I also have in me a pull to build an amazing business. And I have become perfectly comfortable pursuing both imperfectly.

I'm learning to work while in the midst of all these beautiful mom moments and have come to believe that kids will not suffer from it. Hopefully, they see my hard work, my devotion, my loyalty, and my passion and it will serve as an example to them. It is a life lesson learned in action.

I know this is my one life to live and I am going to make the most of it. I'm going to be the best mom I can be and tenaciously chase my dreams and crush my business goals. I work through the guilt trips that I put myself on by finding the balance every day.

Some days, that means not taking that call or stepping away from the computer to do Legos with my son—and I frickin' *hate* Legos. And some days, that means I am the mother on the phone at the park. To all supermoms, raise your glass and say cheers to the missed naps, the snot-covered shirts, drool on your iPhone, and taking calls on the toilet. I don't judge you, I respect and support you . . . because I get you. I am you.

◎ ◎ ◎ ◎

It's imperative to release guilt from your life. Whether it's guilt about something you did or something someone else did to you— whether you were the driver or passenger on a guilt trip—follow these three ways to lessen the impact of guilt in your life.

FORGIVENESS IS THE KEY. The first person to forgive is yourself. Forgive the harsh words, the stupid choices, and the part you played in what happened. Ease your mind about the decision that you made. If you need to make amends and haven't, release yourself from *that* guilt and—if possible and safe to do so—commit to making things right. Have compassion for yourself. You've carried this burden for a long time.

Next, forgive others who played a part. *Everyone* does the best they can with the skill set and knowledge they have at that moment. No one is perfect. Everyone makes mistakes. Remember that forgiving them does not in any way condone what they have done or the pain they have caused. It simply releases its hold on you.

And finally, free yourself of the regret you have for the way your life was changed. It's a new day. And you now have the chance to quit looking back. Choose a new direction and thrive.

CHOOSE GRATITUDE OVER GUILT. Is it possible to find beauty in the mess? What if the mistakes you made in your past taught you lessons that are setting you up for greatness in your future? What if the strength you gained when something bad happened is preparing you for challenges you will need to overcome in order to do amazing things in this world?

What if all the events in your life, both good and bad, are all part of your journey, leading you to something really cool and impossible to foresee. Be grateful for the lessons learned, the strength gained, and stay faithful that it all plays into a greater purpose for your life.

LEARN. If, like us, you've made mistakes resulting in guilt, then— once you've done the work of letting go and moving forward—don't make the same mistake again.

Yelling at your kids, cheating, overspending, getting into relation- ships too quickly, making financial decisions that put your family at risk . . . everyone does things in life that cause regret and lead to guilt. Making the mistake makes you human. Repeating the mistake makes it a problem.

ANGER

"I've learned that people will forget
what you said, people will forget what you did,
but people will never forget how
you made them feel."

—Maya Angelou
American poet, civil rights activist, and author

F rustration is a normal response to life's crazier moments. But unfortunately, that five to ten minutes of uncontrolled fury—or persistent and violent anger—has a far greater cost when it comes to your relationships, your life, and your future.

For one thing, anger has a ripple effect. It affects not just you, but those around you, too. Take your kids, for example. An angry outburst will silence them, of course—but in the worst possible way. When you remain calm in the face of stressful circumstances, you become their safe harbor in any crisis—whereas erupting in anger makes you unsafe, untrustworthy, and someone to be avoided when the going gets tough. Not only do you relinquish your role as their confidante and mentor just when it matters most, your anger changes the game from "let's learn and grow and excel" to "let's not make her mad."

And what about the other long-term effects of your anger?

Studies say just five minutes of anger impairs *your* immune system for as long as six hours—so imagine what harboring anger for a lifetime will do. And if you're habitually vocal with your anger, you should know that half of all children who witness persistent anger in their home will suffer chronic anxiety, hyperactivity, low self-esteem, and depression. Yikes.

WHAT'S **TRIGGERING** YOUR ANGER?

If you begin to see a pattern of one thing that repeatedly sets you off, our advice is to quickly create a plan to process that trigger or remove it from your life.

For instance, it's common to feel frustration and anger start to well up when sitting in traffic—especially if you're running late for work or picking up the kids. If this is a trigger that "sets you off," strive to leave fifteen minutes early or seek alternative routes. Remove the trigger that makes you angry.

Similarly, if you know the house will explode with energy once the kids get home from school at 3:00, prepare yourself. Get your important work done early, make those must-do phone calls before 2:30, and find an extra fifteen minutes of downtime to relax before they walk through the door.

For most women, even more triggers can be found outside the home. Being under-appreciated at work, getting projects dumped on you late in the day, a random social media post, being qualified but overlooked for a promotion, even a lack of direction from supervisors that keeps you from doing your best job can be a trigger—*if you let it*.

But nowhere does anger get triggered more forcefully than in our romantic relationships—with the man we say we "love" often getting the brunt of our outbursts. He might be triggering some unfilled need from long ago and not even know it—until *you do the work* of identifying these triggers for yourself first.

SIXTY SECONDS YOU CAN **NEVER** TAKE BACK

Lashing out in anger is not only uncool, it can be dangerous—because what you do in the next sixty seconds could be the sixty seconds that changes your whole life if you hit someone, get behind the wheel, or harm yourself in any way. This not only blocks your Oola, it can totally change the course of your life.

You can't take back angry words or actions. *And you can never get that time back either.*

◎ ◎ ◎ ◎

IN THE AIR AROUND ME

by Leslie Hart[’]

Handsome and strong, Josh came into my life at just the right time. I was a struggling twenty-three-year-old single mom raising my son Mason who was just fifteen months old. Although Mason could always win me over with his chubby round face, deep blue eyes, and adorable smile, I was feeling overwhelmed trying to keep things together.

It had been a few months since Mason's father last saw him. The man who created this child with me now rejected both of us. We were truly on our own.

Though I had a full-time job at a local warehouse, I waitressed on the weekends just to make ends meet. It was there that I first laid eyes on Josh. I think it was his cute smile and dark hair that first got my attention. But what I soon fell in love with was his shy and reserved demeanor. His quiet nature spoke of strength. Mason and I needed some strength in our lives.

At first it was a glance, then eye contact. Soon, there were rushed but witty hallway conversations—then ultimately, a first date. Before I knew it, Josh met Mason and just seemed to become part of our little crew. Playing hide-and-seek with Mason around the house and helping me tuck him in at night, Josh gave me glimpses of what it

---

[’] Pseudonym used to protect contributing writer.

would be like to have a little help and someone to share my life with. It was a hint of what it would be like for Mason to have a father figure in his life again. It felt good. I remember snuggling with Mason on our "big man chair"—Josh laying on the sofa next to us—thinking, *Everything is going to be all right.*

Our lives had come together so beautifully, but they would soon unravel—and the result has been a lifetime of pain.

One night as I headed out to work the graveyard shift, I saw that Josh and Mason shared the big man chair like they had so many times before. But this night felt different.

Mason was screaming. While Josh tried to settle him down, big tears kept rolling down his cheeks. His eyes pleaded with me. *Don't leave,* they seemed to say. His little hands kept reaching for me. This was new for Mason. He usually didn't mind me leaving. In fact, he was pretty comfortable with just about everyone we knew. And it wasn't the first time I'd left him with Josh either. Still, Josh assured me that everything would be fine.

"Mason is just a momma's boy," he reminded me.

I understood that. For months, it had been just Mason and me, so of course he wanted his mother around the clock. Still, something was in the air that night. My heart sunk to leave for work. As I walked outside, the old metal door slammed behind me—separating my home life from my work life. With each step toward my car the crying faded. I told myself that Mason must have stopped crying, but in my heart I knew it was the distance and the door that made me unable to hear him. I went to work.

When I got back that night, everything was silent. Mason was asleep in his bed. Josh was asleep in mine, smelling of beer. *Monday Night Football,* I thought, though I didn't approve of him drinking when it was just he and Mason.

The next morning, Mason seemed listless. He had vomited overnight onto his pillow and didn't want to eat much. Since my nephew had just had the flu, I assumed Mason had picked up a tummy bug at my parents' house over the weekend. Josh and I tried fluids off and on throughout the day with little success. By nightfall, I had to go to work. Josh agreed to stay with Mason but I still worried greatly. My son just lay there on the beanbag chair as I left for work again—not a fuss, not a peep from him. As he watched me walk away, it broke my heart to have to leave. I worked another late night, making a phone call home to check on Mason, and even calling the clinic for advice.

"Keep trying to give him fluids," the nurse had said, "and if he keeps vomiting and isn't taking anything in twenty-four hours, bring him in to keep him from getting dehydrated."

Eventually, exhausted from my graveyard shift, I arrived home and strained to open the heavy metal door. Though it was 2:30 in the morning, oddly, Josh was still awake. The smell of fresh-baked pizza was in the air and our favorite game, Monopoly, was laid out on the coffee table inviting me to play. Although the pizza and board game was a great gesture, the conversation felt forced and I felt in my gut that something was wrong. Josh tried to make conversation but was jittery—just not his usual self. When the clock struck 4:00 AM, I realized it was time for bed. Like always, I checked on Mason first. He was sound asleep.

The next morning, the doorbell rang. It was my landlord with some papers to sign. I was so tired that I'd lost all sense of time. I signed the papers and quickly went back to bed. Most mornings, Mason was my alarm clock, so I knew I didn't have much more time before he would come running into my bedroom, smiling and full of energy, excited to take on the day. This was always the highlight of my morning.

But as I awoke on my own, stretched, and glanced at the clock, I saw it was noon. Mason had not woken me up. I instantly felt panic rush over me. I ran to his room. That's when I saw him; he was motionless and not breathing. I was frantic and called Josh's mom—a close friend of mine.

All I could manage was, "He's gone. Mason is gone."

"Take him to the hospital immediately and I will meet you there," she urged.

I grabbed Mason in my arms; Josh and I ran to the car. The only thing that mattered was getting my son to the emergency room. Though it was only a few blocks away, the drive felt like eternity.

When we arrived, I rushed Mason's lifeless body inside and placed him on the bed in one of the sterile rooms. That was when I saw him clearly for the first time. He was black and blue under his chin, and there were bruises on the side of his head and ears. The nurses quickly moved Josh and me to a small room nearby and closed the door. We sat for what seemed like hours, waiting, wondering how this had happened. *What did we do wrong?* I thought. *What did I do wrong?*

When the doctor came in, he confirmed my worst fears, "Mason is dead."

He looked disgusted and asked, "What happened to this child?"

I was frozen. I was hoping he was going to give me a medical explanation for what had happened to my son.

Josh didn't say a single word. What did I miss? How could this happen? Did he fall and hit his head? Did he climb up onto the table and fall? I kept going over the possible scenarios in my head, repeatedly trying to make sense of the chaos in front of me.

For the next two days, things were quiet; not much happened. A few people stopped by to express their sympathy for my loss. But we still lacked a complete picture of what really happened. We still didn't know why my child died. As Josh and I were preparing for his funeral, he and I headed to the apartment to get Mason's little clothes and some pictures of him. We were met by two unmarked police cars, then separated and taken in for questioning.

Josh confessed what he had done.

Angry over Mason's crying, he had violently shaken him. My beautiful son—who was the love of my life—had died from injuries caused by shaken baby syndrome. In less than two minutes, the damage inflicted, the coroner said, was equivalent to Mason falling from a five-story building. He had severe hemorrhaging to his brain and a detached retina.

All this happened on a night I entrusted my precious baby to a man that I was dating. It was the night my son cried for me not to leave. Josh couldn't handle the crying and, in a moment of frustration, it got the better of him; he acted senselessly. In that moment of lack of self-control, lives were changed, flipped upside down, and a precious, beautiful child became an angel with wings.

Twelve years have passed and Josh is in prison hundreds of miles away, but the damage his anger caused is still with me—and the pain of that loss still lingers. Though time has healed me somewhat, there are still days when it takes all I have to get out of bed. Other days, I'm sustained by the hope of a new life that grace and forgiveness has provided.

I've worked hard to rebuild my trust for others, to find my faith in God and believe that this is all part of His master plan. But in all days, the anger is still there, floating in the air around me.

Anger leaves a wake. If, like us, you read Leslie's story and felt anger, you felt the wake. This story demonstrates that anger has the power to affect people even when they're not directly connected to the event. And now, even twelve years later, the negative effect of that anger spans time.

What if anger doesn't stem from a single act, but rather is a trigger you must deal with repeatedly and over time?

UNDER THE SURFACE

by Dusty Hardy

We'd dated for five and a half years and been married for almost sixteen years. Our time together was equal to half of my life. After a few previous separations and reconciliations, and many smaller, less formal fall-outs, I wanted to believe that we still had a chance. I so adamantly wanted this to be true that I refused to consider anything else. Why would I?

That's essentially what we told our three kids months before he moved out: we were creating some space between us to explore why we were so unhappy and argued all the time. It was our attempt to avoid divorce, he said. We wanted to stay married and be happy.

I believed him when he assured the kids that everything was going to be okay. We had never been dishonest with each other and we were both committed to raising three honest, truth-seeking, curious, and emotionally intelligent beings—ideally, by example.

On New Year's Day, I opened an email from my husband letting me know that this time he wouldn't be coming back. By *email* . . . really?

I read it over and over for a week, letting the words sink in. It was well written and included a review of how stifled we both felt in our relationship, how fundamentally different we are in our approach to everything from fitness to running our business and more. He assured me there was no blame. That it was just who we are. He explained that he wished we'd figured out how to be the best versions of ourselves while together, alas, we hadn't been able to. He described an amicable divorce, one without judges and attorneys and ugly fights. One where we could rise above the status quo, say we'd given it our best shot, but realized when it was time to try something else. One where we remained friends.

I told myself then and repeat it now: *I am so grateful that he had the guts to call it out for what it was, otherwise we might still be unhappy and unhealthy together.*

I didn't feel grateful then but thought if I repeated it enough it might come true.

Keeping this news mostly to myself for over a month, I joined a couple of girlfriends for dinner. There had been plenty of time for the pain of rejection, the guilt of how I'd contributed to this mess for so long, and the worry about what was next to settle in. They were already well into a bottle of wine when I arrived. Before I ordered my meal, just as the cabernet touched my lips . . . the tears flowed full force. I apologized over and over that I should have warned them about my situation before showing up and publicly losing it. My marriage was over. I was scared. There was no way I could possibly survive this emotionally, financially—and my poor kids. Oh, and he wants to be friends? Really? I recently told him I wanted him to just disappear; kind of like dying but without actually dying. I told him that I didn't want to be his friend and that I didn't like him.

I was so hurt and so afraid, but it was about this time that I realized my deep hurt and all-encompassing fear had really turned into an exhausting anger. I'd never experienced anything like it before. Like a pot ready to boil, my anger lay just under the surface and took over anytime my phone would buzz with a text from him. I was already angry before I answered his calls, but a simple text would take it over the edge. I'd been mad before. I'd been angry, too, but it always seemed to just kind of disappear after a day or two; it was *never* like this.

I tried everything. I adopted the "no contact" strategy of inter-acting with him (thanks to the many "a woman scorned" blogs I was constantly reading) thinking that fewer dealings with him would likewise limit the chances for anger. I tried to distract myself with travel, girls' nights out, and work. I listened to hypnotherapy ses-sions on YouTube that focused on letting go of past relationships, releasing anger and resentment, and clearing negativity. I surrounded myself with family and friends, who, while I exhausted them with my journey, offered encouraging words and never-ending promises that everything would be all right. I flip-flopped between feeling sorry for myself, sorry for my soon-to-be-ex-husband and my kids, and finding moments of clarity that promised to get me through this, but they were all underlined with the anger.

Wrestling with the anger as the holidays approached was honestly the most difficult thing I have ever done. It was compounded by new information and new arguments regarding the terms of our pending divorce—things that created additional hardship, both emotionally and financially. I looked at my Oola goals, read through my workbook from OolaPalooza, and pulled out another goal sticker. I noticed the goal that should have been in the workbook was not there. So, I wrote down a new goal . . . to forgive my husband.

I sent a very vulnerable, honest, and *not angry* email to my hus-band. I admitted that anger had prompted or entered almost every interaction I'd had with him over the last year. Most importantly, I forgave him.

I forgave him for being selfish and I acknowledged I had done the same. I thanked him for some things and explained that while his thanks or appreciation had always been important to me in the past, from this day forward I would be fulfilled instead by simply knowing that I forgave. That I am committed to letting go of anger, fear, and hurt.

He didn't respond to the email; he didn't need to. It was enough to write it and take a deep breath. My goal was complete. I feel lighter and am confident that, no matter how painful or scary this transition continues to be, I'm stronger, more compassionate, and more loving having experienced it. I do suspect the anger will surface again, but I am now equipped with the experience and wisdom to recognize it and make choices about it that will serve me and those around me.

◎   ◎   ◎   ◎

Anger has no place in the exciting and positive path you're on. Whether it's angry outbursts or harboring resentment and feelings of victimhood from the past, anger eats away at your soul and robs you of the bliss and joy you deserve.

So what can you do to process your anger and remove the triggers from your life?

STOP BEING A VICTIM AND PUT ANGER INTO PERSPEC-TIVE. If anger was directed toward you in the past—or if you're experiencing it right now—work to reframe it into something less threatening by asking, *Could this situation be pushing me in a better direction?*

If your spouse cheated on you, did your eventual divorce lead to a completely new life? Did your alcoholic father actually make you more independent? Did the arguments over household chores lead you to hire some help so you actually have quality time with your kids? Only *you* can put a positive spin on the triggers in your life and on any past anger you endured.

DECIDE HOW TO APPROPRIATELY VENT YOUR ANGER.
Don't let your anger build up like steam in a teakettle until it explodes. Speak your mind, confront others' anger with calm responses, ask for more mature behavior—and, most importantly, have these crucial conversations as soon as possible so resentment doesn't build.

CLEAR THE ANGER THROUGH POSITIVE NEW HABITS.
Meditation, exercise, healthy eating, laughter, exploring new hobbies—anything that puts you in a positive frame of mind will help you clear the inclination toward anger and clear the remnants of anger that was directed toward you in the past.

SELF-SABOTAGE

"We ask ourselves, 'Who am I to be
brilliant, gorgeous, talented, fabulous?'
Actually, who are you not to be? You are a child of God.
Your playing small does not serve the world."

—Marianne Williamson | @marwilliamson
Author and international lecturer on
spiritual, personal, and political issues

Y ou deserve an extraordinary life. Regardless of what you've done—or have failed to do—you have an incredible future within you.

By now, you've been working hard to identify where you need to grow in the 7 F's. You may have begun to think about your Oola goals and started on your OolaPath (which we'll walk you through at the end of this book). You're planning and growing and taking big steps. Soon, your stress will begin to ease. You'll become more balanced. You'll finally feel on track to achieve your dreams.

But just as you're on the verge of the perfect OolaLife, did you know that you actually run the risk of losing all progress?

Negative self-talk—hidden in your subconscious mind—will begin to say, *You don't deserve this. You're not good enough. You're not smart enough.* Even worse, this furtive form of self-sabotage can actually cause you to *take actions* that will undo all the progress you've made.

If you've ever worked hard to lose thirty pounds, only to gain all the weight back . . . if you've ever met the perfect guy, only to over-think and blow it up for no reason . . . if you've ever been presented with a lifetime opportunity for your career, but failed to move forward with it, *that* was your subconscious mind controlling your actions.

Why does it do that?

Over your lifetime, your subconscious mind—which runs your body's systems, takes in information, and helps you make decisions—becomes programmed to act in your best interests. It protects you from harm. So every time you try to achieve—but fail miserably—your subconscious mind reacts to that painful disappointment by saying, *Okay, so we're never doing* that *again.* It stores the information so it can "protect you" the next time you take similar action.

Now that you're about to start down a positive path, your sub-conscious mind will likely tell you to stop. Persevere past these messages, and it might wreak more havoc. Start to rack up actual achievements, and it will probably make you do things to unravel all you've accomplished.

YOUR SELF-TALK IS **LYING** TO YOU

Regardless of what your subconscious mind says, you are smart, successful, beautiful, and accomplished. You're capable, lovable, talented, and interesting. Like the thousands of women we meet at Oola events, your life has so much potential.

So where do these negative "I'm-not-good-enough" thoughts come from? From the crap that people have told you that you've started to believe.

Maybe your father barely acknowledged you and rarely applauded your achievements. Maybe your mom repeatedly told you how irresponsible you were. Maybe a teacher or a coach embarrassed you for giving the wrong answer in class or making a mistake in competition. And you probably grew up with neighbor kids who laughed, gossiped, and made fun of you from time to time.

Later, when you started your career, maybe you didn't get recognition for your ideas or were told your input didn't matter. If you started a business, perhaps your family told you it wouldn't work—maybe even begging you to get a "stable" job instead of admiring your talent, honoring your judgment, and encouraging you in your dream.

Bit by bit, these hits to your self-worth programmed your subconscious to keep your life unexceptional, safe, and ordinary.

YOU ARE **WORTHY**

Stop telling yourself a story. Stop believing the hurtful comments and belittling remarks. You deserve to live the fulfilling life of your dreams. You can handle whatever the world throws at you. You are worthy of all you want and more.

You're also worthy of being loved for who you are. And being loved starts with how you talk to *yourself*. It starts with how *self-loving* you are.

So change your self-talk to words of praise, encouragement, and acknowledgment. Love yourself as much as you love your children or your spouse. Give the world a great example of how to love you *by loving yourself well*—not in a narcissistic way—but by standing up for your needs, celebrating your own achievements, and staying focused on your dreams.

BREAKING UP WITH ED

by Alyse Hall

S ticks and stones may break my bones, but words will never hurt me. Yeah . . . right!

"You look fat in those jeans," Ed said. Part of me wanted to die whenever Ed spoke to me. It seemed like he was always there to tear me down and pull me away from anything great in my life. I would tell myself his opinion didn't matter, that I wouldn't let it get to me, but it always did.

I knew he wasn't good for me, and I wanted him out of my life, but I couldn't get away from him. I just wanted to be normal, young and free, enjoying time with my friends and family. Pursuing my dreams and creating memories. But no matter what I was doing, Ed was there to tell me NO.

Every cell of my being was strong enough to not get into a relationship with Ed. I was raised in a loving and strong family that taught me that I was destined for greatness. My parents were fully supportive of my dreams, even when they were different from theirs.

But as a teenager, I let him in. At first it was just an occasional conversation. Over time, he insidiously claimed more and more space in my life while simultaneously forcing out self-worth and self-love. Before I knew it, he controlled my life.

Our relationship started at the very time I began being bullied from girls in my class. Simply, I wasn't like them. I was shorter, stocky, and my Italian skin was darker than theirs. And that was different enough for them to single me out and start making me the target for their jokes and taunting.

"I am strong and I can get through this," I told myself repeatedly. I didn't want to tell my parents about it, but Ed was there. And although I knew he wasn't good for me, he provided an odd comfort in a progressively out-of-control situation.

Finally, I broke and told my parents everything. Exhausted and crying, I said, "Please help me! I can't handle the bullying any longer and I am starting to believe what these girls are saying. I feel that I am losing the battle between who I am and who they are saying I am!"

My parents were destroyed to hear that their daughter was struggling in these ways. They told me that everything would be okay and that they would transfer me to a different school at the end of the quarter. I felt relief in this. I saw an end in sight. I faked a smile and found the courage to face these bullies every day, knowing that soon I would be able to leave them in my past.

I also found the strength to break up with Ed.

My new school was my refuge, a fresh start. I thought that this was where I could finally be me and pursue my passions again without the onslaught of evil words. I had barely got into a rhythm of this new school and meeting new friends when my past crept into my present. The bullies from my old school started reaching out to me on social media. And worse yet, they started reaching out to my new friends on social media, telling them that I was a bitch and a bad person. I couldn't start over again. I couldn't move to another new school. I couldn't deal with this again. *I am strong,* I thought to myself, *but I am not this strong.* I started to feel weak and, before I knew it, Ed was back in my life.

He told me that maybe if I just lost a little weight, I would not get bullied anymore. Maybe if I just cut my food intake down to 500 calories a day and worked out at least two hours a day, burning 1,000 calories or more, I would get skinny and they would like me. Then I would fit in.

So, I listened!

No matter how much I tried to love myself for who I was, I would listen to Ed.

Soon, yet again, Ed controlled every decision in my life. I would get anxiety when my family was planning a family get-together, because I knew there would be food there. There would be pasta and bread . . . my favorites. "Look at yourself. You are already fat, and if you go to that family party there will be food and you will eat it and get fatter." Ed said.

Before I knew what happened in my life, I was ninety-five pounds.

I would look in the mirror and see my ribs sticking out from under my bra. I would think, *Oh, my God, what have I done to myself? God, please help me. Please save me from this.* But as soon as I would get an honest glimpse of my frail body, Ed would tell me that I was still fat and that I could do better and that's why people hated me. "You are pathetic, suck your stomach in," Ed would tell me.

I missed out on family vacations because of Ed. I missed out on fun with friends because of Ed. And I missed out on any chance at a real relationship . . . because of Ed.

At age twenty-two, with the encouragement of my family, I broke up with Ed for the last time.

It was during my seven months of therapy for exercise bulimia that I realized how destructive Ed had been in my life. I became aware that my relationship with ED (Eating Disorder) started shortly after the bullying started and intensified throughout my teenage years. Although it didn't kill me physically, it killed my spirit as a young woman and robbed me from so much. In therapy, I was asked to write out everything bad that Ed would tell me . . . and the list was long. When asked to write out everything that I loved about myself, I just sat there; my mind and the sheet of paper in front of me were blank. My eyes welled up with tears as I realized that although Ed didn't kill me physically, he killed my confidence, self-worth, power, and dreams. I chose to end it here. I looked at the blank page and started with, "I love my smile."

It has now been six years since I broke up with Ed—the scariest thing I've ever done. And although he is like a bad ex-boyfriend lurking in the depths of my mind, I have overcome this part of my life. I have triumphantly found deep love for myself as a woman and now as a wife, expectant mother, successful doctor, and friend. Every day, I hear women say what they don't like about themselves . . . Their hair. Their body. Their arms. Their legs. Their smile. Their nose. The list goes on and on . . .

When I hear this, I know that even though they may not have an eating disorder, they do have an Ed in their lives. And although we all are different, we all share an inner strength and deserve the life of our dreams. If we are going to be free to love others and chase our dreams, we need to love ourselves . . . and we *all* need to break up with our Ed.

◎ ◎ ◎ ◎

Words are powerful; they can build you up or break you down. Choose your words carefully—not only the words you use with others, but also the words you use with yourself.

But how do you overcome a lifetime of negative self-talk and toxicity around you? How do you find strength and a voice when it feels as if no one is listening? Missy did it, one step at a time . . . literally.

INKED

by Missy Wollman

I t was Saturday. The air was stale and the lights where dim; exactly how you would picture a place like this. I was lying on my back. The faux brown leather table was uncomfortable. It was trying its best to support me as I squirmed in a mix of anxiety and pain. I'm not sure what was more unnerving, the buzzing sound of the gun or the pain of the needle stabbing ink into my wrist. I wasn't looking for art, I was looking for a statement. A statement not to others, but to me. A permanent reminder of where I came from and where I'm going. I specifically wanted it on my wrist, written upside down, so that I could read it daily as a reminder of the badass within.

It simply read: *She believed she could, so she did. #LiveOola*

I had just finished a kid's run with my son on the Thursday before, a 5K on Friday, and a 10K that morning. As I crossed the finish line, my son asked for a double high five. Not just a high five, but a double . . . and that's a big deal. Little did he know, or anyone, how big of a deal it was.

My mind drifted back to when I was thirteen years old and sitting around the dining room table at my grandma's house. Looking in from the outside, our family seemed normal, or as normal as could be for a small-town family get-together. My mom and grandmother had finished preparing the food and were bringing it to the table.

My father, a man of few words, was humble and very hardworking; he was out pouring concrete, missing another dinner. My brother was doing what brothers do; talking smart and irritating me. Suddenly, Pat walked in. My throat tightened and my body went numb. I strained to pull air into my lungs, but I couldn't. I needed to get air. I needed to go outside, so I ran for the door and my mom followed closely behind. Terrified, she asked, "What is wrong?"

All I could say was, "We need to leave . . . now!"

My brother stayed in the house and I convinced my mom to drive away in the car. I didn't care where, just away. After ten years of pain and secrets, I finally had the courage to tell her the truth. With my head down and my voice weak, I finally said, "It's Pat."

Pat was my grandmother's boyfriend and he started sexually abusing me when I was three years old. He said that it was "our little secret" and I wasn't supposed to tell anyone. I was three, so I didn't.

I held onto this secret for all these years—and all the shame and guilt that came along with it. I ate to feed the pain. A piece of me felt that if I gained weight, maybe I would no longer appeal to him and he wouldn't touch me anymore.

The weight came on but he didn't stop. I lost myself over those ten years. I lost my innocence. I lost the idea of what love was. I felt weak, used, and worthless. I hated myself.

The short ride home felt like forever. My mom took me in the house and sat me on the couch. She sat in disbelief as she tried to process what was said. It was too much for her. She went straight into denial and the room went silent.

When my dad got home, my mom took him by the arm and pulled him into the adjoining room. Moments later, my dad emerged crying; I'd never seen that before. He walked over to me and held me safely in his arms in a way only he could. Even at thirteen, I could read the mix of deep sorrow and intense rage in his eyes. He loved me, he was my rock, he was my protector, and he felt that he had failed his little girl. He just kept saying over and over, "My baby girl, my baby girl, you didn't do anything wrong and I love you."

I wish this moment could've been the turning point in my story. I wish this is where everything in my life changed for the better.

But it didn't.

The abuse stopped, but the pain, the weight gain, and self-hate didn't. Time didn't heal. Time only made it worse. I had zero confidence and I was sabotaging my entire life. I couldn't shake it. I carried this with me from the time I was a toddler, through high school, and even into my marriage.

Throughout the years, I was desperately searching for that one spark or magical moment where I felt powerful and I could love myself again. It was after hearing the OolaGuys speak at a live event, and reflecting on all the searching, reading, counseling, and support throughout my life that I realized that if I truly want change, it starts with me. I started putting one foot in front of the other and I just kept going, and going . . . and going. Think Forest Gump, but a Midwest girl version.

What started as a couple steps on a random day has led to a complete transformation. Just as every unwelcomed touch took away a piece of me, each step seemed to bring it back. I've lost over 100 pounds in the last year and I am still going. In those pounds shed on country roads, treadmills, and dance classes, I also shed twenty-six years of shame, guilt, anger, and self-hate.

Today, I believe in me. I have learned to become my own number one cheerleader. I feel beautiful and sexy. Instead of not feeling worthy of love from my amazing husband, I now enjoy looking my best. My kids have been changed, too. They're confident, active, and living a healthy lifestyle. I now know the difference between good relationships and bad, and make no room in my life for the bad ones.

It seems that as my confidence continues to grow—and the love for who I am as a woman grows—so do all the other key areas of my life.

I realize that everyone has challenges. They can break you or they can change you. I'm changed and I'm back. I believed I could—and I did. And if you don't believe me, I'll show you my tattoo.

Melissa's story is just one example of the journey to healthy self-love: treating herself well so she can be available to the life that's awaiting her. What about you? Is anything holding *you* back from living your OolaLife? Or do you need to overcome self-sabotage and begin pursuing the extraordinary future that's within you. Let's take a look below.

IDENTIFY THE SOURCE OF YOUR SELF-SABOTAGE. When you look in the mirror, who do you see? Do you see a capable, confident, captivating woman? Do you see someone who has goals in life with plans to achieve them? If not, what's the story you're telling yourself?

If negative, self-sabotaging thoughts exist, why do you think they're there? Where do they come from?

Only when you identify the source of your self-sabotage and negative self-talk can you begin to eliminate its impact from your life.

TAKE STEPS TO BOOST YOUR SELF-WORTH. When your parents, your spouse, or your friends use belittling words with you, it's like death by a thousand cuts. It's anchoring the idea of inadequacy inside your head. To counteract this hit to your self-worth, first ask for more supportive and encouraging dialog. Ask for helpful remarks instead of hurtful criticism. Stand up for yourself.

Then, replace what you get from other people with a lot of atta-girl's and high fives *from yourself* whenever you accomplish even the smallest achievements. Celebrate yourself daily—in the mirror, if you have to—with a big smile, words of praise, and a few words of encouragement for tomorrow. It doesn't matter whether you ate healthy that day or met a sales challenge at work, or finally finished a project at home, you deserve to be applauded—even if it's only self-praise. When others see you treating yourself well and happier than you've ever been, they'll show up in a whole new way for you. That kind of confidence is irresistible.

DON'T SETTLE FOR ORDINARY WHEN EXTRAORDINARY IS WITHIN YOU. You were designed by God for greatness. You are here for a specific purpose. Remember that where you are now is not where you're destined to stay. Tell yourself daily, *This is just where I am. It's not who I am.*

Then, anchor that affirmation by writing it on a card, wearing the Oola affirmation band or adding it to your smartphone so you can repeat it every day to yourself. I AM . . . designed by God for greatness.

CHAPTER 14

LAZINESS

"I hate housework.
You make the beds, you wash the dishes
and six months later you have to
start all over again."

— Joan Rivers
Comedian, actress, writer, producer,
and television host

f there's one thing that impresses us about women, it's how good they are at juggling the fifty-seven things they have to think about in a day. Not only does this make you a natural multitasker, it makes you a born prioritizer, too.

So why do some priorities rise to the top of your list while more important ones get pushed down to oblivion?

Values.

Everyone has two or three very high-value systems they focus on. For example, if you naturally think about and spend energy on your family and your field (career), those are your two highest value systems. If you find it difficult completing tasks related to finance and fitness, these are likely your two lowest value systems.

Luckily for the world, everybody's high and low value systems are different. It's why some women feel called to be home with the kids, while others feel an inner pull to crush it in the workplace. This uniqueness and authenticity keeps the world from being a boring place.

However, values are still the major drivers of our actions.

While you might never slack off where it matters most, you can get really lazy when it comes to lower valued activities. Are we right? You don't procrastinate with things you value, but you do procrastinate with the stuff you don't care about.

This is basic human nature, of course, but living Oola means you have to pay attention to it all. You have to find a way to overcome laziness so that a failure in a low-value area of your life (for example, poor finances or a loss of health), doesn't affect your high-value areas like Family and Field, along with the rest of the 7 F's.

NO ONE CAN DO **YOUR** PUSH-UPS FOR YOU

Lots of Oola Women delegate the parts of their life they're not good at or that they don't care about. You don't have to be awesome at everything.

Most business owners, for example, delegate accounting, marketing, social media, and more—so the owner can focus on building the business. Sometimes, stay-at-home moms hire a housecleaner so they can focus on homeschooling or childcare.

What low-value priorities can you delegate, outsource, or assign to someone else?

Of course, there are some things you just can't delegate: family relationships, time with your spouse, your own fitness, faith-based activities, time with friends, and time spent developing your career. Decide which parts of your life you *can* hand off . . . and those you can't. Unfortunately, you can't pay someone else to do your push-ups for you.

IT STARTED WITH A CHRISTMAS CARD

by DeAnn Barth

Martha Stewart was my role model when I first started having kids and was thrown into this world of being a "stay-at-home mom." Like Martha, my house was always spotless. My children left the house with their pacifiers always matching their outfits, and I didn't walk out the door until my hair was perfect and I had a smile on my face. I didn't take a single nap when I was on maternity leave. Ladies, may I repeat that again . . . not a single nap. Super mom!

On the outside, you would've been impressed. You would have said, "Wow! That lady has it together." The reality was, I didn't. As I left Martha for constantly scrolling Pinterest to find my next super-mom idea, I lost my grip on reality. I would yell at my kids if they messed up the perfectly folded laundry, and I would give my husband the evil eye if I saw his dirty clothes in a pile on the floor—actually I would just "cut him off" for a couple of weeks.

By kid number five, I couldn't keep up anymore and I was feeling depressed. The Pinterest-perfect life had gotten the best of me and I decided to prioritize; actually, I made a conscious decision to become lazy.

It started with our Christmas card. I was running out of time. I didn't have the kids' outfits picked out or a photographer booked—no theme, and I had no idea about the perfect location. So, I did what I thought was best: I got lazy. I posted a picture of last year's Christmas card on Facebook and said, "Here you go everybody: Merry Christmas, here we are from last year. We basically look the same. Feel free to print this bad boy and hang it on your fridge." I was waiting for backlash from friends and family, but the reaction was quite the opposite and it opened the possibilities of *what if.*

What if lazy wasn't all that bad. What if I cashed in the Pinterest perfect life for a life of lazy?

The next thing that fell victim to my lazy ways were leftovers and food storage. I opened the fridge to start making dinner, and way in the back I found a long-lost Tupperware container from last week. I think it was spaghetti and meatballs, but I was afraid to look. I walked over to the sink and I started to crack the patented tight seal when I remembered my Christmas card. I immediately walked over to the garbage, thought about it for a minute, hesitated, and then threw it in the trash can. Liberating. This has now become status quo. The funny thing is that this past Christmas, I got all new Tupperware; I give it six months, tops.

Laziness continued. I accidentally spilled a bag of chips in the pantry. I looked at the vacuum, smiled, and called over the dogs. Problem solved.

Folding clothes straight from the dryer, I discovered I had three unpaired socks. Rather than search for their mates, I threw them away. More lazy.

The dishwasher just finished running, but I have one dirty dish in the sink. I dropped it in and reran the entire load. Blasphemy!

At times, I would fall back to my old ways of perfection but it didn't last long. On the first day of school in the fall, all five kids left the house with perfectly pressed clothes and their style was on point. Their lunches were magazine-worthy. Think whole wheat tortilla with cream cheese, spinach, and turkey cut into cute little pinwheels, accompanied by perfectly cored and pared apples with sun butter and raisin sprinkles—not *peanut* butter, *sun* butter. By week three, they were lucky to get Ziploc bags of dry cereal thrown at them as they headed out the door . . . fifteen minutes late.

Being lazy in some areas of life has given me the time to make my marriage and life better and more enjoyable. It's okay if my pantry is unorganized and I leave dirty dishes in the sink overnight. The world isn't going to end if I go to dinner and a movie with my husband instead of making sure the laundry is finished. I'm happy to sacrifice the perfect meal for the kids for a quality conversation.

However, I also learned that I must keep my laziness in check. It's easy being lazy. I am totally fine never spending another minute on things that don't matter, but I always need to be watchful that prioritizing doesn't turn into an excuse to avoid the hard work necessary to reach my potential and be a good example for my five kids.

To my mentors, Martha and Pinterest, I bid you a fond farewell. I've outgrown you. I'm off to take a nap to prepare for the shit storm that is about to walk through the door at 3:30 PM.

No one likes to be called or categorized as lazy, but if we're honest, we all have our moments. Whether it's procrastination or straight up avoidance, we all have things in our life that if we dig in and overcome, will add value and more balance to our life.

Sometimes we make a conscious choice that "this changes today." Other times, life will deliver circumstances that offer very few options *other than* to dig in.

TOGETHER

by DelRae Messer

grew up watching sunrises and sunsets. I didn't have insomnia or an infatuation with the sun. I had parents who believed in hard work; waking up early and going to bed late. It was a characteristic that was handed down from their parents to them, and they instilled it in me. I understood their point of view. We were a family of six growing up on a farm in the Midwest. If you weren't working, you weren't surviving.

I carried this work ethic throughout high school and into college; excelling at sports and always getting good grades. I held onto a very simple philosophy: follow your heart and work like crazy. If you do that, all things will work out.

My junior year of college, I unexpectedly got pregnant and shortly thereafter found out that I would be raising my baby as a single mom in a co-parenting situation. I was scared but wildly excited at the same time. My options were to quit school and move back to my parents'—or continue and go at this alone. I knew this would be a challenge, and I oddly loved a good challenge. This would certainly be more difficult and also more important than anything I'd done in my life up until this point, but I was up for it. So I put my head down and I forged on.

When my daughter was born, I kicked my hustle into high gear. In addition to the diaper changes, nighttime baths, regular feedings, cuddle time, and checkups at the pediatrician's office, I was working part time and going to college full time. I was absolutely exhausted, and when she cried at night, it took all I had just to get out of bed. But this was my life; busy became my normal.

My daughter and I were inseparable. We became a team. Wherever I went, she was right by my side. We graduated college together. We got our doctorate together. We opened a clinic together and sometimes, we even saw patients . . . together! We worked out five to six days a week together and cooked healthy meals together. We frantically hustled through life, together.

A couple years after getting my doctorate and launching myself into the real world, I found out I was pregnant with my second daughter. I started to feel the stress of my reality mount. I started feeling the crushing weight of student loan payments and the cost of raising two girls alone and on one income. The financial stress was tearing me apart. I felt that the only answer was to work harder. I continued to revert to my childhood ways of working like crazy. I went from working hard, to working harder. I went from being busy, to being busier. I thought that this was the way to our salvation.

Before I knew what happened, I found myself working eighty hours a week and becoming what I never thought I would be: an overwhelmed shell of a mom. I was completely unfulfilled and slipping further and further away from my purpose—my "why." I was unhappy and my relationships suffered.

Soon, my girls and I found ourselves at the bottom . . . together.

I was emotionally, physically, and financially exhausted.

How could this have happened to me? I put in the work. I put in the time. I can't even think about how many times I wanted to just lay on the couch and be lazy, just to take a break from life, but I never did and this is what I got? Life felt unfair. I wanted to give up. What was I missing?

Instead of giving up, I had one more ounce of hustle in me, and so I stepped outside of my life to look at it objectively and see what I was missing. As I examined my life down to the details, I found my answer: I was lazy!

I wasn't lazy showing up. I wasn't lazy with my workouts. I wasn't lazy with taking care of my patients. I wasn't lazy being a mom. I was lazy with my time.

While I "frantically" went through life, I was spinning my wheels and going nowhere. I was taking the work ethic that my parents had instilled in me and scattering it everywhere without a plan or a purpose. Could being less lazy with my time and planning my day and my life really be the answer? Could it really be that simple?

I was on the verge of losing everything, so it was worth a shot. I started with organizing every room in my house to at least clear the clutter around me. I wanted to see clearly again. I learned how to efficiently delegate and time-block. I started to organize my day, my week, my quarter, and my year. I had a planner and it was color coordinated and filled out perfectly . . . and I followed it. Every day, I put my time and energy on the important things in my life and removed all the "time sucks" from my life. The hustle was always there, but I was being lazy in planning where to focus it.

I felt empowered by the momentum and the growth in my business so I decided to take everything to the next level and reclaim my life with my daughters. I hired an assistant and delegated everything that was not income producing: cleaning the house, doing the laundry, running errands, planning events, and even getting groceries.

My whole life, I had thought I was a hard worker and there was no way that I was lazy. What I realized was that I was lazy about the most precious gift of all . . . my time.

Today, with a teenager and a toddler, the financial stress has lifted, and I run my day effortlessly and rarely with stress or anxiety. I am blessed that I am finding the time to do life again with my daughters . . . TOGETHER.

◎　◎　◎　◎

If you, too, need to overcome laziness and procrastination, recognize that your dream life is waiting for you just on the other side of that procrastination. So what's the proven formula for getting past it and into action?

READ YOUR GOALS DAILY TO STAY CONNECTED TO YOUR LARGER PURPOSE. Where are you being lazy? What priorities are being pushed down on your list? If your goals are not being met because you keep putting off those tasks that will get you there, re-read your goals every day to stay inspired and proactive.

BE TACTICAL BY BREAKING DOWN LARGER GOALS INTO SMALL STEPS. Sometimes laziness stems from sheer overwhelm. You don't even try to tackle your goals because the amount of work you need to do feels virtually impossible.

We get that.

But why not break down your big goals into baby steps that are doable and that provide frequent wins for you? If you want to buy your first home, for example, but don't have the down payment, start by saving just the first $1,000. Next, get pre-qualified for a mortgage. Then research lower-qualifying homes or special programs for first-time buyers. Investigate how you can make or save more money.

Small steps will keep you motivated, focused, and proactive—instead of lazy, overwhelmed, and idle. And the positive traction and momentum will get you *believing in you* again.

DO THE WORST FIRST. Do what you don't like before moving on to the fun stuff. If you show up for work appointments on time but can't get to the gym—if you go to the gym but can't balance your budget—recognize that we're all disciplined in some areas but lazy in others.

Tackling the unpleasant tasks first in your day will free your mind to pursue enjoyable tasks with passion. Trying to move forward with other deadlines, projects, and incompletes hanging over your head, on the other hand, is downright miserable. Do the worst first.

ENVY

"The spirit of envy can destroy;
it can never build."

— Margaret Thatcher
First female Prime Minister of
the United Kingdom

T he world is an infinite place. There's more than enough to go around. But lots of women go through life feeling bad about themselves because someone else has more . . . or they're better . . . or their life is just *different.*

Of course, it's normal to compare your life to others' and say, *I'd like to own a house like hers. I wish I'd gotten the promotion she did. I'd love to take a trip like that.*

This perfectly normal emotion—jealousy—comes from comparing yourself, then wanting what other people have. Jealousy is normal as long as it passes through you. But when jealousy sticks around and grows into envy—that's when it becomes an OolaBlocker. So what's the difference between the two? With envy, not only do you want what someone else has, *you don't want them to have it . . .* and that is dark. Envy will not get you what you desire, in fact, it will *keep* you from what you desire.

REMEMBER, YOU'RE RUNNING YOUR **OWN** RACE

President Theodore Roosevelt once said, "Comparison is the thief of joy." He knew that constantly judging yourself against some impossible standard of living or random level of success can actually rob you of the joy you get from the awesome aspects of your own life.

Besides, most people haven't researched what it would be like to maintain that house, do that job, or travel to that exotic locale. It's possible you wouldn't even like those things once you acquired them. Your job instead is to decide what's right for *you,* authentic to you—then pursue it with all your heart.

WHERE ARE YOU **ALREADY** CRUSHING IT?

As you assess your current life and make goals for your future, you might discover you're *already* crushing it in four to six of the F's of Oola. Perhaps you live in the countryside in a historic farmhouse with your loving husband and three terrific kids. Maybe you get to pursue your favorite hobbies or volunteer while the kids are at school and still have plenty of time to garden or decorate a picture-perfect house.

Well, many women would love to trade places with you. And many more are wondering how you do it.

All too often, we allow society to define what an "ideal lifestyle" is. We watch celebrities on TV and think they've got it goin' on. We read lifestyle magazines and feel bad about our own circumstances.

Your life is unique. So is your path. Don't fall into the comparison trap.

◎ ◎ ◎ ◎

SHE'S PERFECT
by Danielle McDurfee

I walked into the bathroom and there she was . . . fake smile, fake hair and fake personality! And the most annoying—her fake positive attitude. *Look at her!* I said to myself as I washed my hands and gave her a halfhearted grin. It was the best I could muster up in the current situation. She was that popular, cute girl who dated the popular athlete—and I wasn't.

Everyone in school and the community loved Vanessa: girls, guys, adults, kids, teachers, coaches and even *my* parents. Oh, Vanessa this and Vanessa that. But whatever. I could tell just by looking at her that she wasn't what others made her out to be. I knew it was just a matter of time before others would see what I saw. There is no way she can keep faking being this nice and this pretty forever. She will screw up eventually and when she does, I'm going to be there to witness her fall from glory.

She looked back at me, smiled to reveal her perfect teeth, and said, "Hey Danielle, how are you doing?"

I rolled my eyes slightly and said, "Fine. How about you?"

Not that I cared, but I knew it was the polite thing to say. Of course, her response was, "Great!" And then she proceeded to tell me about school, her life, and of course her boyfriend . . . ugh! She actually tried to carry on a conversation with me. What a bitch. But damn, she's good at faking it. I must admit that I almost fell for it myself, but no way, I am not that gullible. I'm not that stupid.

We finally graduated high school and all went our separate ways. The sun seemed a bit brighter not having to walk in Vanessa's shadow. Actually, I got a tan for the first time that summer. That fall, I entered college and loved it. Made great friends. Went to cool parties. Dated a very handsome guy . . . or should I say, I dated a bunch of very handsome guys. But the best thing was, I found my career path and was off and running. Although I was miles away from Vanessa, rumors of her life seemed to always float my way at the most inopportune times.

She joined the military . . . I guess she wants people to think she is some GI Jane or something.

She deployed to Iraq to serve our country . . . of course she did, why wouldn't she? She's perfect!

She returned a hero, got a degree, and got engaged to that popular, good-looking athlete guy . . . still hate her!

Three years passed and I heard less and less of Vanessa as I continued building my career and enjoying parties, friends, and guys. Travelling was my newfound passion. So when a dear friend asked me to leave the snow and cold for Spring Break on a beach in Pensacola, I didn't even ask questions . . . sign me up! After working hard, I was anticipating this trip for weeks. I couldn't wait to put on my bikini and soak up some much-deserved rays while sipping mai tai's in Florida with my girlfriends.

The day arrived and I got the text, "Babe. 5 minutes out."

My girlfriend was on her way to pick me up for the ride to the airport. Flip-flops, sunglasses, and three bikinis was all I needed, but for some reason my bag was overweight. I forced a smile through the strain on my face as I dragged my suitcase down the steps of my condo in my high heels and out to the street. The car pulled up and out jumped Vanessa. WTF! Who invited her? Blinded by her smile and her personality, I was instantly back in high school. She grabbed my bag and effortlessly threw it into the trunk. I guess I didn't need that sunscreen in my bag since I'd be in her shadow the whole trip.

On the twenty-minute drive to the airport I had a running internal dialogue of conflicting emotions: *This is my vacation and I'm going to enjoy it no matter what. I bet she looks amazing in a bikini. But I look good, too, don't I? Maybe I can just avoid her. It won't be that bad, Danielle, just be positive. This is gonna suck.*

I fell asleep on the four-hour flight or maybe I passed out from the stress, but either way, I was soon in Florida and on *my* vacation. I avoided conversation with her the whole way in the taxi; she talked a lot but I wore my headphones. Problem solved. We got to our vacation home and I proudly thought that I had this whole "avoiding her" thing figured out. Until she uttered those four words that changed my life forever: "I'll room with Danielle." Just kill me now!

It has been ten years since rooming with Vanessa in Florida. And in those ten years, Vanessa and I have travelled to many beaches, gone to some of the best concerts, shared all our secrets, and enjoyed our greatest moments in life. We've been bridesmaids in each other's weddings and supported each other mentally and physically through pregnancy and the birth of our babies. Vanessa is even the godmother to my firstborn daughter.

What I realized in those seven days was that there was nothing fake about Vanessa. She is exactly who others told me she was. She is sweet, kind, funny, beautiful, and now my best friend. When people meet her and ask me if she is truly that nice, I laugh and say, "Yeah, it's kind of annoying but she is."

◎ ◎ ◎ ◎

It's easy to be in competition with someone we know well. This is where comparison will bring out the worst in us—and possibly cause us to lose a great friend. Unhealthy competition can keep you stuck in envy.

But envy also comes from prejudging someone we don't know, then *assuming* their life is great. You compare yourself to "the competition" and end up feeling less than. But think about it: could there be aspects of her life that are difficult, hurtful, or depressing? Or do you have more in common than is apparent at first glance? What if you put aside your jealousy and envy and get to know that other woman as a person? You can never know fully what's in someone's heart—good or bad—when you compare, judge, and assume.

THE OTHER WOMAN

by Shannon Rheault

remember the first time I spoke with her, how jealous and angry I was! She was the "other" woman—my ex's new wife—*and* she was spending time with *my* children!

I remember the utter turmoil and the uncomfortable feeling of complete helplessness knowing that a woman, other than me, would influence my babies' lives and I had *no* control over it! I wanted to throw things, I wanted to hate her, I wanted to be the only "mom" in my children's lives—yet there she was. I'll never forget the day when I told my own mother that "she" had baked cookies with my daughter, and my mom literally said, "You best be careful!" I was scared. I was a single mom, working nonstop to provide for my children, keep the bills paid, and do my best to keep my sanity. *I did not want this, nor did I choose this.* I wanted more than anything for my children to dislike her as much as I did, but they didn't.

She was kind, she was thoughtful, she was considerate, and she was understanding. She was a lot like me and it wasn't long before I had to acknowledge it. She made life easier for my babies who were reeling from their parents' break up. Though she'd had no part in that, she helped them adjust to the change *they didn't ask for* and *they did not choose.*

In reality, she made my life easier.

I remember letting go of the hurt and forgiving the past. That was a big moment for me. I realized that we weren't here because of one person's actions but because of life choices that we all had made. Life had thrown us some curve balls, there was no need to lay blame. I could hold on to resentment and let it destroy me and destroy my kids, or I could let go.

Letting go is what saved me from a life of resentment and fear that would have destroyed all of us.

And when I let go, I cannot describe what happened—what's been happening—in our family! Our Christmases are amazing, we share meals, we celebrate birthdays, and "the other woman" and I even do girls' nights with my daughter! We've been able to stick to family traditions for more than twenty years. If you stop to consider our history and connections, you'd likely think we're an odd group. Our families and friends thought we were weird; they just didn't get it. But as the years went by and they have come to understand, they have all embraced it. I've since remarried and have two younger children who—along with my ex's stepson—see us all as one family. They love each other and don't even consider that there's no blood relationship between them.

What is more special than anything is how this woman has proven that she deserves my children's love and my respect. When I have faced some of the most difficult times in my life she was there for me, over and over again. When I was travelling for weeks at a time for work and the kids needed a mom, she was there. When I lost my job and didn't have enough money to pay for Christmas gifts for the kids, she secretly provided them for me and never once asked for recognition. When her mom passed away, it was a very difficult time for her. I remember coming to the family gathering after the funeral and her dad coming to hug me. He told me that we were such special women that we were able to push aside resentment, anger, and fear and embrace a special relationship—that we were an example to other blended families out there, to other women out there.

Not a lot of people refer to "the other woman" as a "gift" *unless* it's dripping with sarcasm—but I can. The woman I initially viewed as my biggest threat has become one of my greatest gifts.

You, too, will be happier, less stressed, and more authentic if you focus on what you already have in your life—instead of being envious of what others have. In fact, envy *keeps you* from discovering and getting what you truly want. To overcome envy for good, these tips will help you focus on your own path.

AVOID COMPARING WHO YOU ARE AND WHAT YOU HAVE. We've been taught as a culture that we're all pursuing the same thing: money, a high standard of living, the perfect man, a slim and toned body. But the reality is that you have unique gifts and abilities and dreams and desires, so comparing yourself to some fixed standard isn't even fair. While one woman might have material aspirations, another might have creative aspirations. We're all just different.

Unfortunately, when we allow society to define what a great life is, we take the focus off of our own needs and desires and already-awesome life—not realizing that what you *already have* is very attractive to someone else. It's all a matter of perspective.

Instead, why not define "the good life" on your own. Once you do—and start pursuing it—you really have no need to be jealous or envious of anybody.

GET INSPIRED BY OTHERS' ACCOMPLISHMENTS. Rather than being envious of what others are doing, use it as inspiration for what's possible. If someone has the marriage you want, the business you want, or the kind of financial statement you want to have, why not try to learn from her—or even recruit her as a mentor? She can inspire you and lead you to see those goals and dreams happening in your own life.

This is especially true if you're already solid in six of the Oola categories. If there's one category in which you're struggling, reach out by saying, *Hey, this is my challenge. I'm looking to learn from you.*

SEEK COLLABORATION IN ACHIEVING YOUR OWN GOALS. Small thinkers focus on competition, while big thinkers focus on collaboration. If you can combine forces with others—instead of being envious of what they're doing—you can make great things happen in the world. And your efforts might just have a ripple effect that benefits millions of people.

So rather than always compartmentalizing your life with thoughts like, *I have to have the perfect life* and *I have to do everything myself,* why not draw other people in so greater things can happen?

FOCUS

"It is our choices that show what we truly are,
far more than our abilities."

— J.K. Rowling | @jk_rowling
Billionaire author of the
Harry Potter book series

t's often said, "You get what you focus on." And whether it's saving for your first house, improving your marriage, reaching a new goal in your business or anything else you want to accomplish, spending the necessary time and pulling in the necessary resources is the *only* way to accomplish it.

Unfortunately, most people's focus is either scattered or misdirected.

This is even truer for women who have the multiple commitments of job, household, and family—not to mention the goals you've made in getting to Oola.

So what can you do?

BECOME A LASER BEAM, NOT A FLASHLIGHT

Today's world offers infinite opportunities to waste time. Hanging out on social media, watching TV, spending unnecessary time on the phone—these are time bandits that will rob you of your future. Also disrupting your day are those "urgent" things that come up, like finding last-minute supplies for your child's homework project or planning an impromptu birthday party at work—squirrels you simply don't need to be chasing.

These things will keep you from focusing on your larger goals and a balanced life. So how about considering *instead* what your life would look like if you unplugged more, volunteered less, and simply said "no."

Instead of overscheduling and working on a broad array of tasks, you could focus your time and energy—like a laser-beam—on just those things that will get you closer to your goal.

AVOID THE OOLA A-BOMB

Misdirected focus is also where addictions live: shopping, alcohol, drugs (including prescription medication), gambling, pornography, social media—these aren't just OolaBlockers, they're Oola destroyers. It's like dropping an atomic bomb on your OolaLife.

It's rare to find a family not touched in some way by addiction—an environment where there is no energy toward goals. In fact, all available energy is spent feeding the addiction and doing damage control as things unravel.

Help exists if addiction is holding you back from your OolaLife. Call it out, deal with it. You are stronger than you realize. You deserve it, your dreams are worth it, and your loved ones are likely praying for it every single day.

WE ALL HAVE THE **SAME** AMOUNT OF MINUTES

Our advice instead is to focus on what you *need* to do versus what you *want* to do. Author and life-hack expert Tim Ferriss suggests going cold turkey—something he calls the "low information diet." No news, no Internet, no TV for one week to one month—just focusing like a laser beam on something you really want to accomplish.

You would wake up every morning knowing exactly what to work on or who to call. In fact, you'd probably have a checklist of specific to-do items that would get you closer than ever to your goal.

◎ ◎ ◎ ◎

UNPLUGGED

by Amber Cooke

When I became pregnant with my son, I joined an online forum for expectant mothers. I was a new mom who was feeling overwhelmed and had so many questions. When the pregnancy insomnia would strike, I would just sit and browse through the thousands of posts by other mothers-to-be. I loved it!

Around the same time, I started to understand how to navigate Instagram and Pinterest. It felt good to unplug and scroll. Kind of like watching TV, but better!

I discovered thousands upon thousands of bloggers out there. There was a blog that covered virtually any topic I could dream up: motherhood, homeschooling, fitness, nutrition, self-help, relationships, homesteading, interior design, and I even found a blog on how to find jeans that fit a pregnant woman.

Social media opened an entire new world for me.

Now, I didn't even need to leave my house to find a community of other women who were in the exact same boat as me. All I had to do was sit and scroll, or stand and scroll, or even lie down and scroll.

Their faces became familiar and soon so did their homes, their lives, and their experiences. I spent hours checked out of my own life while seeing what was new in theirs. They were having beautiful, drug-free births and exclusively breastfeeding their babies . . . while they simultaneously scrapbooked and painted the baby's room perfectly. They spent hours each week pureeing organic vegetables for their toddlers, and the toddlers actually ate them! *Gasp!* Their kitchens were pristine and white and they always had fresh flowers in the center of their always clutter-free tables. Their hair was perfect and their six-pack abs returned six weeks after delivery. Their husbands were always smiling and supportive.

I became absorbed and I would think to myself, *how is all of this even possible when I have absolutely no idea what am I doing here? I am so not up to par with these women.*

Some of this obsession eased as my child became mobile. I was much too busy (or tired) to care. Or so I thought. Because it never really went away. It only transformed.

I soon discovered so many other areas of my life where I was falling short; I just had to scroll. I did not have a big enough house; nor did I own it, for that matter. I did not start exercising right after my baby was born, or six months after that either. I didn't do enough activities with my baby. I didn't have beautifully presented organic meals ready for my family each evening. And, of course, I certainly was not pleasing my husband as well as I could in all areas of our relationship.

I couldn't shut it off. I just kept scrolling and clicking. It was even affecting my sleep. There is even a name for it. Ironically, I discovered the term on a blog, it's called *Pinsomnia:* the inability to get enough sleep because you keep clicking "See More Pins." With my husband sound asleep next to me, I would manipulatively tell myself, *Go ahead, just click it one more time, then you, too, can go to sleep.*

It was during one of those sleepless nights that I finally realized this was not good for me. Not only was social media stealing valuable time from me and my family, it was leaving me feeling "less than" as a mother, wife, and woman. Instead of it being a resource to help me be better, it actually made me feel worse.

My focus was no longer on my own dreams for a happy life; it was on everyone else's. My focus shifted from a healthy pregnancy and birth to what everyone else's pregnancy looked like. It shifted from how I wanted to raise my child to how they were raising theirs. It shifted from what I wanted to eat and look like to what they physically looked like and ate. My focus even shifted from what my husband and I wanted for our lives to what *they* had and *they* wanted. The worst part is that my dreams were beginning to be replaced by their dreams. I wasn't just losing time, I was losing "me."

I now understand that much of what we see on social media and blogs is either fake or polished to impress and attract readers and followers.

I know that I *am* good enough! I am worthy of my *own* dreams—not theirs!

I now research blogs related to my dreams. I now use social media to learn about things we want to do, recipes that I want to cook, activities we want to do with the kids, and information that supports us and our goals. Not only have I taken back valuable time for me and my family by unplugging more, I've learned how to use social media to put me on the path to fulfilling my future hopes and dreams rather than enticing me to follow someone else's.

What started out as something fun and meant to add value in Amber's life quickly turned into something that was stealing her joy and valuable time. Time is the only commodity that is finite, which makes our minutes so valuable. Be careful that you're not making decisions today that can steal years from your future. You can't get that time back.

CAPTURING A MIRACLE

by Brittany Jacobson

My iPhone was capturing a miracle. I was trying not to shake as I was watching the little screen, but soon found my eyes drift to the man in front of me. My dad was wearing his San Francisco 49ers jersey. He was sitting on a stool with an acoustic guitar in his hands and his frail and shaky fingers played a song by memory from my childhood. I cried as I reflected on the events of my life.

I had a very normal, simple, suburban upbringing in Northern California. We lived in a nondescript tan condo with a dark brown terracotta roof on the corner of John Drive and John Street. Mom and Dad had bonded over their mutual love of music and their three daughters. My school was within walking distance and I had friends on every corner. Our house was filled with the sounds of my dad playing his acoustic guitar every evening and the giggles of us young girls dancing to the music in our nightgowns and curlers. After the music and the dancing, we would get tucked in and say prayers . . . and I would secretly wish upon a star that our San Francisco 49ers would always win. My dad and I loved the 49ers. We watched the games together, went to games together, and got our jerseys signed together. It was our thing.

In fact, one of my fondest childhood memories with my dad was when I was eleven. I popped out of bed without an alarm. I was *so* excited. Today was *the day* . . . the day that my dad and I had been waiting on for years. Most girls my age would only be this excited if they were going to Disneyland for the first time or on a shopping spree, but I wasn't like most girls.

I contained my enthusiasm, so I wouldn't wake my younger sister who was fast asleep in the bunk below me. I then looked toward the crib on the other side of our tiny bedroom to make sure my excitement didn't wake my youngest sister. I could see her closed eyes through her curly blonde hair; she, too, was fast asleep. I wanted to take a superhero leap from the top bunk, but I resisted and slowly and quietly climbed down the ladder. If my sisters woke up, I wouldn't get the alone time with my dad that we loved so much. I tiptoed over to my dresser and slowly pulled open the top drawer. It was perfectly folded as if on display. I pulled it out and slipped it over my head. I felt strong wearing the red and white. I glanced down with pride at the large number 8 on the front of my Steve Young autographed 49ers jersey. Today is Super Bowl XXIX and *our* 49ers are in the big game.

I slowly opened the door to my bedroom and turned myself sideways, leaving just enough room for me to sneak out and minimal light to sneak in. I was so excited to help my dad prepare our traditional Texas sheet cake and crab dip for our Super Bowl party. The smile on my dad's face showed a mix of excitement and nervousness. Mine was just excitement.

I'm glad we won the game that night, but to me this time with my dad meant way more than a win, even a Super Bowl win.

After that game, through middle school and high school, while still focused on the players, stats, and games, I was becoming more focused on academics and competitive swimming. I would wake up most mornings at 3:30 AM to get to swim practice and I took extra classes because I thought high school was silly and I wanted to graduate early. After graduation, I went to college to study public relations and communications. I'd never been away from home, and I felt empowered by the knowledge that I was the first in our little family to receive a college degree.

College was filled with friends, studying, boys and parties. It was exactly what I thought it was going to be and I loved it. On Labor Day weekend, I went to a nightclub with my friends. The music was thumping and the drinks were flowing. I'd never been to a bar before. We walked to the counter, the bartender looked at me and said, "What can I get you?" I froze. My friend stepped up and said, "Bacardi and Coke." Great choice. It tasted sweet and I loved the way it made me feel. That was the first time I had ever drunk alcohol in my life.

It didn't take long, and by my senior year, I had snorted my first line of cocaine.

Ten years later, I found myself sitting on a strange bed with a shoelace tied tightly around my upper arm. My vein was engorged and a needle was resting gently on my skin. Some random guy I met earlier that evening, looked into my eyes and said, "If you do this, one of three things are going to happen to you. You will either end up in jail, be in rehab, or you'll be dead. Are you sure you want to do this?" I reflected back at my previous ten years of alcohol and drug use that led to this moment and I said, "Give it to me." Heroin became my God that day.

It wasn't long after that moment that I found myself sitting alone in the grass next to a river by my parent's place. In my right hand, I had a syringe loaded with more than enough heroin to end it all. I wanted to cry, but I felt nothing. I slowly pushed the needle into my arm, emptied the syringe, and lay back. I had lost all control of my life over the last ten years, but I still had control over ending my life. I felt comfort in that. I closed my eyes, my breath slowed, and I slipped into unconsciousness. As I lay there unable to move and waiting to die, I heard a very soft voice repeating, "Take a breath, breathe again, breathe again, breathe again."

The next thing I remember was waking up in a hospital bed with my parents—who I emotionally left years ago—standing beside me. My mom held my hand and I felt love, real love, for the first time in years. On December 23, 2012, I chose sobriety.

Exactly two years into my sobriety, a CT scan revealed that my dad had a rare brain tumor the size of a grapefruit reaching down his neck and squeezing his carotid artery. The doctors informed us that the only option was surgery to remove the tumor, but that no one had ever survived this type of operation. While he was in surgery, I was conflicted between feelings of gratitude and guilt. I felt so guilty that my focus shifted from my family, my dreams, and my goals to drugs. I was so angry that I had lost ten years with my dad. But, at the same time, I felt so grateful that I got sober and that I was there to reconnect with him over the last two years. And I was grateful that I could be there for him when he came out of surgery. The doctors seemed surprised and shocked when they said that the surgery went well, and they got the entire tumor.

"Although your dad may lose coordination in his hands, lose mental capacity, and never play music again," they said, "he is going to make it."

It was seven months later when my iPhone captured the miracle. While walking with my dad to a 49ers game, he saw a guitar shop. He stopped and walked in. Wearing his finest Niner's red, he grabbed an acoustic guitar off the shelf and began to play. I couldn't believe what I was seeing. He hadn't played like this since his surgery and we thought he may never play again. Although in recovery he couldn't remember my mom's name, the day before, or who was president, he began playing a song from memory, just like when I was a little girl.

The scars from the needles in my arms have faded, but they are still there. I am okay with that. I don't focus on them, but I do notice them from time to time. And when I do, they remind me of the ten years I lost and the great pain I endured. I don't look at them for long, I simply notice them and go back there for a moment so I never go back there again . . . and just like that, I keep moving forward.

◎ ◎ ◎ ◎

What dream could *you* accomplish by overcoming your scattered focus? Is misdirected focus pulling you further away from your dreams? How about addictions? Are you losing valuable time?

How can you carve out time to focus on your goals, yet still give your family and career the attention they deserve? We've got a three-part formula. Let's take a look:

KEEP YOUR EYE ON THE LIGHTHOUSE. You've got a bright, shining goal in the distance. You just need to stay the course to get there.

But over the last twenty-four hours, how many minutes did you spend moving toward your "lighthouse" goal? If you're busy running your kids all over, then serving on a committee you could care less about, then finally dropping into bed exhausted at the end of the day, ask yourself: *How could I do a better job of focusing on the most important dreams of my heart?*

One trick is to write down three or more "high priority" tasks on a 3x5 notecard every night before you go to bed—tasks that you want to accomplish in the next twenty-four hours (as you'll learn more about in Chapter 26). Day by day, little by little, you'd move closer to your lighthouse goal. In fact, in just one year, you could take over 1,000 steps toward the life of your dreams.

AVOID THE SQUIRREL SYNDROME AND THE TIME BANDITS OF LIFE. To eliminate the stuff that wastes time in your day, first you have to identify them. Unfortunately, some time-wasters aren't as obvious as you think. For instance, did you run to the grocery store after work because you forgot to put bread on your list? Did your sister call for the third time this week to complain about her husband? Did you really spend three hours on Pinterest looking at travel photos of Peru?

These are precious hours you're *not* spending on your goals.

Visualize instead what your life will look like a year from now if you avoided these interruptions and devoted the time instead to the necessary tasks that will help you get your OolaLife.

BE CHOOSY ABOUT YOUR COMMITMENTS. Okay, we get it. It's flattering to be asked to chair the school fundraiser, plan the family barbecue, or spearhead the lunch-and-learn program at work. But could your time be used more effectively if you committed to less—and then only to those things that will move you forward in the direction of your dreams?

There is great power in the word "no." And usually, you don't need to back up that response with an explanation. If you *do* feel you need one, why not admit you've spent a lot of time over the years committing to building other people's dreams, but that now you're focused on your own?

SECTION FOUR

SECTION FOUR

OOLAACCELERATORS

"I am constantly amazed by Tina Fey.
And I am Tina Fey."

— Tina Fey
Actress

OolaAccelerators, the next seven chapters, are where the real fun begins. You'll learn new daily practices and proven success behaviors like gratitude, discipline, integrity, and wisdom that will help bring your life into balance—and lead to stunning personal growth—faster than almost any other way. You'll not only get tips to help you incorporate these daily practices into your life, you'll also discover new insights from women who relied on these Accelerators at different points along their journey.

What do they say worked for them as they learned lessons and created new behaviors on their way to the OolaLife? You'll find out in this section.

GRATITUDE

"I don't have to chase extraordinary moments
to find happiness — it's right in front of
me if I'm paying attention and
practicing gratitude."

— Brené Brown | @brenebrown
Author of Daring Greatly and Rising Strong

Another reason we think Oola Women are amazing is that, more often than not, you're the "first responders" to life's ups and downs. While us guys want to "rub some dirt on it," you bandage the scrapes, kiss the boo-boo's, calm the fears, counsel the reckless, and become the fixer.

You go into instant action mode whenever a loved one is in trouble. And while it may not be on your schedule, it's in your DNA. You don't overthink it. You just do it.

You deal with the chaos.

But have you ever thought about putting a positive spin on these chaotic moments? Have you ever said, "Yeah, reality bites, but I can still be grateful about other things in my life that are working. I can still be positive even in the face of pandemonium." Gratitude not only helps us stay balanced during life's crazier moments, it actually brings about the support, opportunity, and abundance that keeps us balanced.

Having a grateful heart—and staying in a state of grateful anticipation—is very Oola.

GRATITUDE HEALED MY BROKEN HEART

by Jacque Book

"You're not going anywhere, young lady," warned the mild-mannered doctor at my local urgent-care clinic. Though I'd suffered from rheumatoid arthritis for years, I thought the chest pains I'd been experiencing all night were just another flare-up.

Weren't they?

Little did I know at the time that I'd just suffered a rare but increasingly seen condition called *Takotsubo cardiomyopathy*: broken heart syndrome.

Of course, the previous few weeks had been stressful to say the least. With more than one family crisis, tons of last-minute orders of my custom jewelry to finish, and the normal stress of the holidays, my blood pressure was up and it had gotten harder and harder to catch my breath. I was constantly worried about everything. There seemed to be no relief in sight. So it was little wonder that I was suddenly gripped by an attack that's brought on solely by severe stress and whose sufferers are 90 percent women.

It wasn't a heart attack exactly. Instead, the overwhelming stress hormones in my body shocked my heart and caused half of it to stop beating.

As the first of the emergency responders began to arrive and crowd into the little urgent-care exam room to hook me up to monitors and begin their cardiac protocol, my husband Sam was jostled farther and farther away from me—a look of worry, love, and sadness on his face. Later, in the emergency room, I watched my heart on the ultrasound monitor. I could see that the upper half of my heart was eerily still while the bottom portion pumped madly to compensate for the lack of blood pressure to my arteries.

It's not what I thought would happen to me now, I reflected.

After several hours of tests and a pantheon of medical terms that would have made a brain surgeon panic, my new cardiologist returned to give me his prognosis: I'd live a normal life by taking beta blockers every day, but a portion of my heart muscle was likely damaged permanently.

In profound shock, but ever proactive, I considered what I could do. Then I remembered a chance visitor I'd had six months earlier at my jewelry design studio—an energy healer who told me I was more powerful than I knew.

"You can manifest everything you want—well-being, success, money, family tranquility," she had said, "if you just visualize it being so."

She admired the artistry, love—and, yes, the gratitude—that I brought to my jewelry designs, calling my studio a "happy place" . . . a peaceful, beautiful environment created by my gratitude.

While the conversation had struck me as odd at the time, it now got me thinking, *If gratitude and visualization could help me create beautiful jewelry, could it also help heal my damaged heart?*

Slowly, I began to think of things to be grateful for.

I thanked the nurses who drifted in and out of my room, calling them by name, to their surprise. I appreciated the visitors who kept up a steady stream of conversation in the background—even though

I was tired and just wanted to rest. I slept on and off over the next two days and, upon awakening, spent the first few moments in grateful reflection about those things I could appreciate in my world: the trees outside, the machines in my hospital room, even the elderly patient next door who seemed to wake up grumpy and stay that way.

Several times a day, I also visualized a healing golden light entering my body and restoring my broken heart and my broken spirit.

I immediately noticed how much more positive I was about my future. The stress that had nearly brought me to death's door didn't seem so important anymore. I vowed to no longer be a victim, to talk openly about things, listen to my gut, speak my truths, and be authentic in all ways. I even reassessed who I spent my time with and how I lived my life.

We're not guaranteed tomorrows, I thought to myself, *so I resolve to live life to the fullest today.*

When I finally went home, I continued my visualization practice in the one place I knew I'd remember to do it every day: the shower.

Every morning, as I stepped under the steaming cascade of water, I'd close my eyes, breathe deeply, and envision healing light from above entering the top of my head and flowing downward—clearing any pain, removing any harm, and healing what needed to be healed . . . leaving only that which was for my best and highest good. Eventually, I added a second ritual: to breathe in light from the universe and take in love from my guardian angels, filling myself so much that I could no longer contain it all—then radiating that light back out to the world to heal others in need.

After six months of this practice, my cardiologist called me back for my first echocardiogram since being hospitalized. As we viewed the ultrasound images together, it was clear that one area of my heart still hadn't recovered. It was frozen.

"Even if that part never heals," he said, "you'll still have a full life."

But I could tell he was convinced it would never work well again. What more could I do?

And then it hit me. *Be grateful.*

I vowed to continue my "gratitude practice" and find the good in everything I did. Every morning, I'd spend my first ten minutes finding several things to appreciate. I even challenged myself never to list the same thing twice. If I started my day with gratitude, it gave me the proper perspective to go through my day gracefully. If life hurled something at me, I'd see myself as a stately tree, bending and swaying—instead of breaking—whenever adversity appeared.

"I'm grounded," I'd say, knowing I could handle anything.

Over the next few months, I found myself happier and more positive than I'd ever been in my life. I was especially grateful for my husband of twenty-four years who had supported me through the dark times and loved me more with each passing day. Not only that, but my energy was boundless. Where before I'd need several naps a week, now I'd work a ten-hour day, go to dinner and a concert, then still have energy when we returned home at eleven o'clock.

I gave up all my "stories" and let go of my cynical opinions—instead going through life as an observer without judging anyone. I started a new job and met exciting, fascinating people. Life was never dull.

Then, one year later, I returned to my cardiologist's office for my annual echocardiogram. To my surprise, my doctor walked in with a smile on his face.

My heart was healed! Every part of it was working perfectly.

"A year ago, I didn't think it was possible for the damage to heal. In fact, I've never seen this type of recovery before," he said. "But I compared today's test results with your test last year, and I couldn't believe my eyes. I've looked at it from ten different angles and your heart is completely healed."

So what has my "gratitude practice" taught me? It taught me that happiness is not something you find or that other people give you. Instead, it's something you choose on your own. And making small changes like being grateful? That creates a shift in your outlook. You can wake up every day and live your life, or wake up every day and let life happen to you. Whether you drive the bus or ride the bus, it's always your choice. I chose gratitude, and it healed my broken heart.

Jacque learned that being in a state of gratitude is something you practice over time. It's a habit. But how will you know when you've achieved true mastery? How will you know that you can be grateful no matter what shows up?

Here's how: when something bad—and totally unexpected—hits you and you think, *There's no way* anyone *could be grateful about this.*

Or could you?

ONE PHONE CALL FROM MY KNEES

by Denette Jacob

As the wind turned crisp and the colors in the landscape began to change, I could feel the outside air trying to find refuge inside the comfort of our aging farmhouse. Late summer is always a magical time on our farm, and I remember one of those days with complete clarity.

Our family was huddled around the table enjoying our traditional Sunday "pizza night"—a time full of smiles, pepperoni, and one-liners. As I watched this simple family moment, I leaned over to my husband and said, "How can our life get any better than this? We are truly blessed."

We have four healthy children, I thought. *We're financially stable. And we're finally pursuing our dream of restoring this old farmhouse into a family home—something we've talked about since we got married twenty years ago.*

As with many dinner tables in late summer, the conversation turned to football. When you're from a very small town in the middle-of-nowhere America, the Friday-night lights of high school football pit surrounding communities against one another—but pull local families together.

It's not just a game, it's a way of life. And this was my son Jared's year to shine.

The coach and the community reminisced about his impressive rookie season the previous year, and anticipated seeing him run more yards and score more touchdowns in the upcoming season. Jared bought into all the hype because, well, he is Jared. He was confident, tall, strong, and full of energy. Not only did he have the words to inspire his teammates, he had the skills to back up those words.

But four days after that family pizza night—four days after I'd declared to my husband that our life was perfect—I got the call.

We're all just one phone call from our knees, I thought, as I hung up the phone. This was the call that did it.

As the doctor explained, "Your son's tests came back, and that back pain he's been experiencing is due to a rare form of bone cancer."

That phone call changed our family forever.

Suddenly, Jared wasn't on a football field fighting for extra yardage—he was in a sterile hospital room fighting for his life. Football pads and cleats were traded for tubes, needles, and a room full of intimidating machines.

Through it all, Jared possessed an amazing spirit. He did everything in his power to make sure that those of us around him kept a smile on our faces and a skip in our steps. To give you a glimpse into Jared's heart, when a curious four-year-old at a public pool asked him about the scars on his hip, Jared replied, "shark attack," then grinned as the kid's expression changed from freaked to impressed.

Jared's resilience and determination was inspiring. Even though he was told he'd never walk normally without some form of assistance, the year after his surgery Jared went on to win the dance-off contest at a high school dance.

Cancer may be in him, but he would not let it define him, I thought.

But after two years of countless rounds of chemotherapy, extensive surgeries, and multiple alternative therapies, Jared's body was exhausted, even though his smile endured.

On the afternoon of December 8, 2010, as we stared at the same sterile and confining walls of Jared's hospital room, my body felt the fatigue of emotions that had been running through it for months. I always did my very best to stay strong for Jared and shed my tears in private, but this particular day was different.

I couldn't contain the overload of emotions. Nothing could hold them back.

In a random moment, I cried uncontrollably. I moved to the bathroom to hide my outburst. And as I looked in the mirror—I can still remember the smell of bleach—Jared asked his dad, "Why is she crying?"

"Mom, come out here," he said.

Tapping the bed with his hand, he invited me, with his irresistible smile, to sit beside him. As he wrapped his frail arm around me and drew my head to his shoulder, he asked me to not to cry and promised that—no matter what happened—he would be okay. Unable to speak, I simply nodded.

"You're the best parents ever," he told his dad. He was so grateful for all we were doing for him. It was a moment of genuine gratitude—and a moment of peace—that will forever fill my soul.

As the day wore on, Jared's condition worsened.

I remember the feeling of comfort as we held hands, my rosary intertwined in Jared's weakening grip. His dad held his other hand and we prayed—asking for an enormous miracle to flow into the hospital room and call Jared to sit up with a huge smile on his face—hoping he would jump out of bed and get on with the life he always dreamed about.

Why shouldn't this happen? I thought.

Throughout his life, Jared had always figured out a way to be on top of his game, a way to win no matter the obstacle or the opponent.

Then it happened.

Jared took one more earthly breath—then pure stillness and peace came over him. It felt as though his dad and I were walking hand-in-hand with him, through the gates of heaven, until he sensed God's love and let go.

As he had just told us, Jared was okay. He was pain-free, full of happiness and living in the arms of Jesus.

His dad and I are blessed to have been there when he received the highest trophy given to mankind: eternal love, peace, and gratitude.

In the days that followed, as I tried to comprehend what had happened, I would find myself sitting on the floor of Jared's room, going through his things in an attempt to feel closer to him. It was in one of these moments that I discovered Jared's greatest gift to us: a handwritten letter. On the second page, about halfway down, Jared wrote:

I'm grateful that God chose me for cancer and not my mom or dad. I'm grateful that God chose me for cancer and not my sister or brothers. I'm grateful that God chose me for cancer and not my cousins, aunts, or uncles. I'm grateful that God chose me for cancer and not my friends.

The last sentence read:

I am grateful that God chose me for cancer so I could teach others how to be strong—JJ Strong.

Now, as I look back at my life as a mother, I'm filled with blessings and grace. I can honestly say that my body and my spirit are filled with happiness, my smile is now genuine, and my heart is content. If, in order to spare me the deep heartache and pain, God had given me the choice of either not being Jared's mom or of having Jared for just nineteen short years, my answer would never change.

I chose Jared, and I'm forever grateful that God chose me to be his mother. I would live through all of it again for the memories created, the lessons learned, and the chance to truly know the meaning of pure gratitude.

◎ ◎ ◎ ◎

This poignant story from the OolaSeeker's sister Denette confirms what we've learned about the power of gratitude in women's lives. As we travel around in the OolaBus—meeting people and hearing about their goals and dreams—we're reminded that people who are living Oola "get it" about gratitude.

They're high on life, wearing sincere smiles, having found gratitude in all things.

They constantly remind us that being grateful for what you already have helps you feel more abundant—while worrying about what you don't have keeps you in a mind set of disappointment and lack.

Focusing on what's good, what's plentiful, or what's improving in your world helps keep you in a state to receive even more of what's good, plentiful, and improving. It's like you're saying, *This is all cool. What else is out there for me today?* It keeps you in a state of anticipation.

To get your mind right, focus on what's going right. Living Oola doesn't necessarily require money, time, connections, education, or special circumstances.

- If you've got a loving family who "gets you," be grateful.
- If you've got friends and mentors who inspire you to follow your dreams, that's even more Oola.
- Waking up every morning in a place that's serene, inviting, or energizing—with birds singing outside or the excitement of the city calling to you—hey, lots of people only dream about that.
- Then there are your unique talents, or your kids who remind you to play full-out and love unconditionally.

⊚ And don't forget you've got opportunities to start a business, move to a different city, start a charity, go back to school—or anything else you want to do.

These are all things to be grateful for. Of course, one thing that most of us can be grateful for is our health and vitality—enabling us to enjoy activities that we simply couldn't enjoy if we were unwell, depressed, or mentally depleted.

So how can you live more fully by inviting more gratitude into your life? Here are three things you can do today:

PRACTICE GRATITUDE EVERY DAY. While some days are meant to be celebrated, others simply have to be endured. But in all days—regardless of what happens—be grateful in all things.

To help you stay in a state of gratitude, we recommend that you start writing in a Gratitude Journal. It's not something other people will read—it's just for you. We've been keeping ours for years.

Every evening, as you end your day, jot down those things you're grateful for—whether it's something you have now or something new that showed up for you that day. It may even be something that felt bad in the moment but that's wrapped in a lesson and may be leading to your OolaLife.

While your "gratitude list" may include the same stuff for a while, in time, this will change as new things enter your life and your dreams come true—only to be replaced with new dreams and goals for the future.

EMBRACE THESE TWO LAWS. In life, you don't get what you want, you get what you expect—not in an entitled way, but in a "this is happening" sort of way. Your expectations actually become a powerful force that attracts the opportunities, resources, and people necessary for you to achieve your goals and add new elements to your OolaLife.

There's even a universal law that says if you set goals and *ask* for things in a state of grateful anticipation—then believe they'll show up—you'll actually *receive* what you ask for. It's called the Law of Attraction and gratitude boosts the law's effect.

However, the Law of Attraction is not a genie in a bottle that you simply rub in order to get what you want in life. You can't just dream about what you want, then expect it to appear. Along with practicing the Law of Attraction, you also have to practice our other favorite law: the Law of Action.

Every day, wake up with a clear vision of the life of your dreams, and then take small action steps that will get you there. When you take conscious action toward achieving your goals, you're sending a powerful signal that you actually expect that life to show up. The Law of Attraction works, but only when you follow the Law of Action, too.

MAINTAIN A STATE OF GRATEFUL ANTICIPATION. Once you get into the practice of being grateful, you'll discover that opportunities to be grateful exist every day. But here's the key: these opportunities *will only be found* if you proactively seek out things to be grateful for.

What kinds of things are we talking about?

Watch for big things, like a phone call that up-levels your career, or randomly discovering your dream house before it goes on the market. Look for little things, like finding a parking space near the entrance, or getting a refund check in the mail. You'll soon see that opportunities are hidden in every encounter, and that "unexpected" new relationships, happy coincidences, little conveniences and other forms of good *routinely show up* to make your life easier or more enjoyable—all of which you can be grateful for the moment they happen.

When you meet each new day with the expectation that something amazing is going to happen for you, it keeps you in a state of grateful anticipation—dreaming of what you *will have,* while also feeling gratitude in the present for what you *do have.*

LOVE

"Eat like you love yourself.
Move like you love yourself.
Speak like you love yourself.
Act like you love yourself."

— Tara Stiles | @tarastiles
Supermodel and creator of Strala yoga

When the rock group Queen sang about this "Crazy Little Thing Called Love," they didn't know how right they were. Love is complicated, whether it's romantic love, familial love, self-love—or even those intense feelings of affection you get when you say you "love" a good book or the latest handbag from Prada.

But what complicates love for women *especially* is this internal compass that says you're supposed to love everyone. Those nurturing maternal instincts of yours—which are awesome—want to make sure everyone's happy, cared for and valued. It's your natural inclination to get attached to others in a loving way.

But, beyond your own kids and spouse, is that really possible? Or even healthy? And what about getting lots of that love for yourself?

GIVE AND RECEIVE: **COMMITTING** TO A LIFE OF AUTHENTIC LOVE

What we've found with the women we've met through Oola is that love can be a tremendous accelerator in one's life and an incredible force for good in the world at large—both when you're loving others and especially when you *yourself* are receiving love. But the love you give has to be authentic and pure. It has to be applied in a smart way. And it's a learned skill that takes practice.

Of course, the best way to get better at love is to start loving *yourself* more—giving others a clear example of how to love you, then receiving that love without complaint.

The truth is, people *want to love you*. Let them.

◎ ◎ ◎ ◎

SOMETIMES LOVE CHOOSES YOU

by Andrea Hanson

I believe love first chooses you, then it's our choice to continue to love. To work for love and to fight for it. To grow together, not apart. To focus on what is going right, not what is going wrong.

Our love story began—though we didn't know it—seven years before we met. I was a junior in high school while Chad was enrolled in the University of Minnesota engineering program.

On a cold fall day, Chad was driving down a quiet country road in southern Minnesota just miles from his parents' home—a road he had driven a thousand times before. This night, however, was different. It was late and he was tired. He'd been up late the previous night studying for final exams. Overcome by fatigue, he found himself off the road, into a ditch, and upside down in his car.

Chad's life had changed in the blink of an eye.

He woke up in the hospital with countless challenges and an unknown future ahead. Chad was paralyzed from the chest down—fighting for his life, on a ventilator, and learning to adapt to his new reality. After four and a half long months of surgeries and rehab, he was strong enough to come off the ventilator, drive his own power wheelchair, and leave the hospital to live with family.

Life was now very different for Chad. Once fiercely independent, he now needed to rely on others to help him with the everyday tasks

229

he once took for granted. Though this was difficult, he never lost his drive to live a normal life. Depression and self-pity never swallowed him up. Instead, he focused on the beauty and kindness in those around him. He would see others with challenges and be grateful for what he had.

Graduating from college, he landed a job with the Minnesota Department of Transportation at a salary that allowed him to build his own home. Personal Care Assistants (PCA's) were now a part of Chad's "new normal." They would come each morning and evening to help him get in and out of his wheelchair, brush his teeth, and stretch his body to prevent his muscles growing tight from lack of use.

While Chad was in a groove with his engineering career and life in his own home, I was turning twenty-two and hunting for jobs with a college diploma in my hand. I wanted to teach and assumed the dream job in education would follow. Instead, I had landed only a part-time position teaching high school math. Living in an old house that seemed to require repairs as routinely as mortgage payments, money was tight. I quickly found myself looking for extra work to make ends meet.

My mom's friend mentioned that a young man was looking for part-time help just few blocks away. I walked up to his house—young, nervous, and with no idea what to expect. As the door swung open, I saw a good-looking guy with ice-blue eyes quickly smile at me and introduce himself. Chad assured me I could learn the ropes in no time. He had an easy way of conversation that made me feel relaxed and at home. Captured by his smile, dry sense of humor, and beautiful eyes, I forgot he was in a wheelchair moments after meeting him.

In those first few weeks learning to be Chad's PCA, I was awkward, unsure, and shy. The agency that had processed my application told me never to share personal information or build a relationship with a client. As Chad asked questions about my life, I often turned them around and asked him instead. My heart was saying yes, but my head said, *Be cautious; this is complicated.*

Still, his positive attitude was magnetic. It was a light that slowly drew me to him. As the weeks passed, I couldn't help but begin seeing Chad differently. He ticked the way I ticked. We both loved learning, jokes that required thinking, deep conversation—and he was the first guy I'd ever met who actually thought I was funny. God was beginning to write our love story, and I began asking for more shifts from the agency.

One afternoon and a few months into knowing Chad, while helping him organize his office at the Minnesota Department of Transportation, he shyly asked, "Are you hungry?"

I thought, *Is he asking me out to dinner?*

The man I worked for *was* asking me out—and my heart was thumping in my chest.

"Yes!" I answered.

As we sat down at the table in a crowded steakhouse, I remember asking what he needed help with—not wanting to embarrass him in front of the other customers who were inevitably staring at the two of us. I knew how to help him get out of his wheelchair at night, but now I was navigating through new waters, learning how to "do life" with Chad. At dinner that night, while cutting up his pork chop so he could use his own fork attached to his wrist splint, I began imagining what life with Chad might feel like. And I couldn't get enough.

Within a short while, I knew I needed to open my heart to what was possible. I needed to break down any preconceived ideas I had of what love looked like. During each of my three-hour shifts, we connected, not physically but intimately, progressively, and on an intellectual level. I had butterflies in my stomach, unending smiles, and an anxious feeling—wanting to see him more and more. I knew Chad was experiencing something similar as he would find random things for me to do around his house to keep me there as long as possible.

Finally, I worked up the guts to say, "So what are we? Friends? Or something more?"

He put it back on me: "I don't know. What do you think?"

Time seemed to stop as we shared stories, found common interests, and enjoyed new experiences. Without looking for it, we were falling in love. Two short weeks later, he asked me to be his girlfriend.

Because in my heart I fell in love with Chad—not simply a man who couldn't walk—I found it alarming to begin receiving stares and probing questions from others. It brought concerns that I had never considered before. I get it, we have our challenges, but Chad is a catch—a real gentleman, kind, handsome, smart, and in my eyes, he could have his pick of any girl. But his wheelchair poses a roadblock for many.

After much prayer and with immense vulnerability, I mustered up the courage to ask him, "Are you dating me because you're afraid no one else will come along? Are you worried that your wheelchair means you should grab the first girl who shows interest?"

I needed to know: was he choosing me *for me* or because he thought this was the best he would get? My question didn't offend him; instead, he was grateful I had opened such a real part of my heart to him.

"Andrea, I'd choose you every day for the rest of my life," he said, "regardless of our capabilities. I'm blessed that you chose me."

Over the next nine months we grew closer. Each date brought a new adventure. Often, we would find a hiking trail and take the unpaved path as far as we could with his chair before it got too treacherous. We both strived to live life to its fullest. Then, one beautiful fall day, traveling about a mile into the woods, we found a small clearing of trees. Sitting on his lap, with us overlooking the beautiful

St. Croix River, he pulled a ring from his wrist splint and asked me to be his wife.

Today, almost ten years into our marriage and blessed with our daughter Mari, we are both grateful that God used Chad's tragedy to bring us together. Chad and I both believe that our love has been strengthened through the challenges. The more we've let this attitude drive our lives, the more God has showered His love and goodness on us.

I'm thankful that I didn't listen to others when they questioned if I should commit to the challenges of Chad's life. "Challenge" is a relative term—to me, helping Chad with daily living is just part of a regular life, not obstacles to overcome. I get to be his hands and feet while he brings stability, love, and joy to me daily.

I've learned that all marriages require hard work. But while many couples live their struggles privately, our "challenges" are merely more visible to others. As Chad teaches me constantly, life is well lived when you remember that you have 100 percent control over how you view the world. Love is powerful, and attitude is everything.

◎ ◎ ◎ ◎

What does love look like in your life? Does it come with conditions like, *I will love you if. . ?*

Pure love comes without conditions and pure love moves you toward your OolaLife. But is it possible to sustain authentic and pure love? Is it possible to love well for a lifetime?

DANDELIONS

by Barb Braun

"Barb, are your kids taking over your kitchen?" a neighbor asked. I looked around thinking that there must be something crazy happening behind me. It wouldn't surprise me if one of my daughters tried to make a dessert to impress a boy only to leave the kitchen a complete disaster. Could it be another animal that my son David—you know him as the OolaSeeker—is attempting to raise in the sink? I've seen it before. A litter of mice, a turtle, various birds, and even baby skunks. But to my surprise, I turned to see nothing that looked out of place. As a matter of fact, I think the kitchen looked immaculate. I loved my kitchen. The bright orange countertops; spotless. The stainless-steel sink; shiny. The intense patterned laminate floor; buffed. Obviously, it was the early eighties when my neighbor was asking her question, but nevertheless, my kitchen was where we spent much of our time, and I took pride in its functionality and design.

Our kitchen was truly the heart of our home. In this little room, in this little house, on this little farm in the middle of North Dakota is not only where we gathered two to three times every day to eat as a family, it's where we shared our lives with each other. I can recall so many memories of just sitting back and watching all the kids interact, laugh, fight, make up, pray, and tell stories of their day. In the moment, it seemed as though time stood still and these days would last forever. They don't. And although these moments faded into memories, some things have stayed the same even to this day.

The one constant is that Tony, my husband, has picked me flowers. His "flower" of choice is a dandelion. He has done this almost every day during the summer months for fifty-two years. He proudly presents this little yellow flower to me with these precise words, "These are for my beautiful girlfriend, aren't you glad you met me?" I sometimes act as though I'm not impressed, but secretly I am, and in all honesty, he secretly knows that I'm impressed. He walks away with a confident smirk on his face and I quickly walk over to the sink like a flirtatious teenager, fill up a little glass jar half full of water, place the dandelion in the jar and set it on the window sill on display for all to see. It was this dandelion that my neighbor saw that day. And why wouldn't she question it? These are the weeds that everyone is trying to battle and kill in the spring and all throughout the summer, and I look as if I'm protecting this one flower—or should I say weed?—with my life.

"Kids these days!" was my most common response when my flower was noticed by one neighbor or another. But, deep down, I knew then and I know today that this isn't a simple weed in a jar. It is an expression of Tony's love for me. His ongoing pursuit of me.

This dandelion and all the dandelions since have always represented us. The yellow flower symbolizes the sun and the hope each sunrise provides. The globe resembles the moon and reminds us to end each day in gratitude. And the dispersing seeds floating in the wind represents the stars as a reminder to always dream big, regardless of our age.

No matter how many times you step on a dandelion or mow it down, it comes back stronger. Just as the dandelion opens every morning to welcome the sun and closes every night, we have committed the last fifty-two years to always going to sleep with prayer, not anger, and waking together to start our day.

I realize Tony will not be around forever. Neither will I. He assures me there are dandelions in Heaven. I hope so, because whenever I see one I know I am loved.

The OolaSeeker's mom, Barb, knows what it means to love the simple things in life. What about you? How can you practice love more authentically and accelerate the journey to Oola? Here are three suggestions:

LOVE YOURSELF. You have unique qualities that are different from everyone else. Recognizing the differences in who you are—and loving yourself for these differences—not only makes the world a better place, it's what makes you genuine, authentic and real.

It makes you imperfectly perfect.

Putting yourself down over inconsequential things, on the other hand—like that funny freckle on your cheek or the fact that you left college to raise a family—creates negative self-talk and robs you of an appreciation of the very things that make you unique. Why not appreciate instead that you're one-of-a-kind and can build an incredible life being 95 percent of perfect?

Remember, too, that you have to love *yourself* before you can expect others to do so. *The world is taking its cue from you.* Give it the best example of how to love you—by loving yourself first.

UNCONDITIONALLY LOVE OTHERS. While toxic people need to be approached only after you've "suited up" in full hazmat gear, those who remain in your life deserve to be loved unconditionally for who they are—imperfections and all. Without conditions.

If you've ever found yourself thinking, *I'll love my husband if he takes out the trash . . . I'll love you if you go to the college I choose . . . I love you even more when you bring me gifts,* realize that *that* kind of thinking is passive-aggressive, *conditional* love. It's love that depends on others doing what *you* want. You've put a price on it. These conditions set you up to be disappointed by everyone. When you're never happy and no one can ever do enough for you, that makes you a pretty miserable person to be around.

Instead, why not begin expressing words of empowerment, compassion, and appreciation? Express *that* kind of love to people you care about and watch them show up in ways you've never seen before.

LOVE WELL. Some women are "enablers" and don't even know it. They encourage or allow self-destructive behavior in others—like ignoring a teenager who's partying too much or overlooking the red flags of a husband who works late every night.

Other women are "helicopter moms"—hovering and controlling their kids' every move, protecting them from every disappointment, and doing even the smallest tasks for them, just when kids should be learning new skills and maturing year by year.

Although it comes from a nurturing place and a good heart, that's not loving well.

While your protective instinct is strong, sometimes you just have to let people stand on their own, lose their way . . . fail. It's the only way they can learn to work through disappointment, overcome pain, and gain the confidence they need to be a smarter, stronger, wiser person.

DISCIPLINE

"It's hard when you feel down and you think,

'Why is the world doing this to me?'

But you have to pick yourself up again.

That's what makes you a better athlete."

— Jessica Ennis-Hill | @j_ennis

Olympic gold medalist, founder of Vitality Move events,

and Dame Commander of the Order of the British Empire

Rarely will you find a woman who's succeeded in creating the life of her dreams who doesn't *also* have a strong work ethic. Oola is not for the faint of heart or the undisciplined.

But what is discipline, really? It's doing *what must be done*—even if you don't want to at that moment. It's battling through the daily grind, putting in the extra hours, using sheer force of will.

But it's also doing things consistently—like practicing the piano sixty minutes a day. Writing one more chapter of your book every week. Or saving something every month for early retirement.

YOU ALREADY HAVE ALL THE
DISCIPLINE YOU NEED

If you think about it, there are already habits you follow, tasks that get done, and stuff you consistently spend time on. Unfortunately, they're often counterproductive to the goals you want to reach. Take social media, for example. If you've ever clicked over to check out a friend's post on Facebook, then found yourself down a rabbit hole still following links an hour later, that's sixty minutes you didn't spend on accomplishing your dream life.

If you spend $5 every day on a coffee on the way to the office, then another $12 eating lunch—that's $340 a month that you could have invested in for your future.

Sound familiar? You already have habits—maybe just some wrong ones.

So what if you spent the same amount of time, energy, and focus on *new* disciplines that would get you closer to your goals? You could still have coffee every day (we're not crazy), but make it at home six days a week and limit that venti, blended caramel macchiato quad-shot (topped with whipped cream) to just once a week. You could still check out Facebook for a few minutes, then spend the remainder of the hour exercising to get fit, or meditating to lower your stress level.

Do *that* for twenty-one days and look at the new you that emerges.

COURSE-CORRECT WHEN NECESSARY

Of course, there will be challenges to keeping up with your disciplines. The clutter of life just happens. Your job is to be persistent, course-correct if necessary—but always stay focused on your bigger goals.

Other times, you'll need to instantly tap into the power of discipline to push through an obstacle . . . or simply survive.

NAKED AND AFRAID

by Debbie Harris

I t was the morning of my thirtieth birthday, and I had never felt more lonely and lost. As usual, I celebrated my birthday alone. Well, not entirely alone; as a result of rotating work schedules that kept my husband and me apart, the evening of my birthday was spent with my three kids.

As I gazed around the room, looking from the outside in, it appeared as if I had it all—the career, the car, the house, the family, the typical suburban life. Yet I felt diminished. In my pursuit of the ideal life, I had neglected my own passions. And by failing to take care of myself, I began a downward spiral of self-loathing. I developed a negative body image, which constantly challenged my self-worth. I wasn't happy.

I had spent my twenties climbing the ladder; my work as an elder-care professional was my life and I had let it define my being. However, in my pursuit of professional success, I felt as though I had lost myself. After what seemed like a lifetime's effort of taking care of others, I felt I was losing my own life in the process. I knew I had to start living a life that actually felt good; a life I could sustain and that I knew to exist in my heart; a life that I was proud to say was mine and where I could be the truest version of "me."

Reflecting on my life, I reviewed the vibrant dreams and aspirations that laid dormant for over a decade and watched as they returned in full color. The first goal I set was to run a marathon. I knew nothing about marathons—not even the distance. I realized there was nothing stopping me from running but me. Like a rocket waiting to launch, I felt as though my fuse had been lit and I was on a mission: to live and to find my true self.

Over the course of the next year and a half, running became my obsession. Running was the one thing that gave me clarity and allowed me to fully be myself. I started small, running a half-mile without stopping. I became disciplined, increasing my distance rapidly. In a three-month period, I ran six half marathons, four marathons, and one triathlon. The miles I had put under my feet . . . the endless hours of nothing but myself versus my mind . . . the voices telling me to stop—the 1,500 miles changed and energized me, giving me the strength and an appetite for more.

Having once looked in the mirror disgusted by a reflection that seemed to show my own self-doubt, unachieved dreams, self-hate, and negative self-talk, I began to see something new, something strong, something powerful, something that helped me fall in love with me again. My inner voice had shifted from doubt to one that encouraged me, pushed me—a voice that made me be better. I had become my own biggest fan, and nothing felt impossible.

In the midst of my own transformation, I was flipping through the TV channels late at night and came across the show *Naked and Afraid*. At first glance I was horrified.

A man and woman surviving naked in the wild for twenty-one days? I thought to myself. *Ridiculous.*

Yet here were complete strangers stranded in a dangerous and desolate location without food or water . . . and they were completely naked. Their only prize was their pride and sense of accomplishment.

I was captivated.

In fact, I said to myself, *If this thirty-one-year-old mother of three from Wisconsin can find the discipline to do this, I could go on to do anything!*

I applied and was accepted.

My preparation for the show involved more than just learning how to start fires. I began to experience my life more deeply and with more passion than before. I took time to closely observe my children—the magic they held, the captivating blue of their eyes. I paid more attention to my body. I would lay in bed at night just thinking, soaking in the familiar warmth and comfort. Everything I ate I appreciated more, knowing that I would soon be hungry. I savored every bite. I took nothing for granted.

Before I knew it, I was on a plane heading to Guyana in South America. I committed to staying fully present; I didn't want to miss out on a single moment of this experience. I knew nothing about what was to come but I did know these two things: I was going on the adventure of a lifetime, no matter how insane it sounded to others; and I was determined to accomplish my goal to finish all twenty-one days in the jungle, surviving naked with nothing but one item and a random naked stranger.

During my twenty-one days in the jungles of Guyana, I endured the harshest environmental conditions I have ever experienced. Physical pain, extreme lack of food and clean water, endless nights without sleep, and exposure to every environmental challenge a jungle climate can offer became par for the course.

Through it all, I felt more alive and grateful for my life than ever before. In fact, I created a daily discipline of gratitude—being grateful for available water, that the fires hadn't gone out, and that the palm leaves that made up our A-frame shelter had kept the rain off of me in the night. I would meditate and practice affirmations. One of my favorite quotes kept echoing in my head: *She believed she could, so she did.*

The habit of discipline paid off in constantly working to improve our living situation. We regularly hunted for food, finding grubs in the nuts of the kukrit palm. We cooked fish, snake, even small reptiles. Every morning I awoke expecting to feel closer to death, but in reality I never felt more alive.

After twenty-one days, I emerged from the jungle—having discovered a discipline I never knew I had, and experiencing renewed gratitude for life. On the flight home, waiting to hold my babies in my arms again, everything I thought of seemed foreign: a bed, a chair, a fork, a glass to put water in, people, lights, running water, the list goes on. Three weeks of the daily grind doesn't seem long and typically flies by pretty quickly, but three weeks living primitively in the jungle seemed endless.

As I returned to my former life, I began to create new disciplines around the gratitude that had kept me going in Guyana. I realized that community and giving back, random acts of kindness, volunteering—these are the things that I've become more conscious of and grateful for.

You always hear about a "near-death experience"—one that awakens the soul of a person to live their life with greater passion and to pursue their dreams. My twenty-one days in Guyana was a "near-life experience," challenging me to live life to the fullest and giving me an awareness about myself and about possibility that I never had before.

Hopefully, you don't have to find yourself naked in a South American jungle with a complete stranger like Debbie did in order to discover the discipline within you. The discipline you need to change your life is already there.

You are more disciplined than you realize. For instance, if you don't think you have it in you to pick up a second (or third) job to get out of your current financial mess, you do. Let's use an extreme example to prove the point. What if the only way to save your child from a life-threatening disease was to earn the money to pay for treatment? Would you find the discipline within you to make that happen? You would.

Discipline in the short term is one thing, but there will be moments in your life when you'll want to develop enduring discipline to achieve a long-term goal.

FREEDOM

by Lindsey Elmore

When I left Alabama for pharmacy school in San Francisco, it was the farthest I had ever lived from home. I was terrified and I cried the whole flight. I was a complete wreck when I landed and a friend of my mom's picked me up at the airport. She had to pull over twice between Oakland and Napa to let me throw up on the side of the road. I had never been so scared to do anything. For two more days, I cried. I listened to David Bowie songs on endless repeat and was sure my life was over. Finally, I stopped and stared at the city skyline and said, *This is my dream, and I can't believe it's here. I will do this.*

I managed to go to the first day of orientation and reality hit me. I was about to take out loans, *big loans,* to pay for this education at the number one pharmacy school in the U.S. Earlier that summer, I'd been on the phone with the loan company. When I told the loan officer I needed $56,000, she replied, *$15,000?*

"No, $56,000," I said. And that was just for the first year's tuition and living expenses. Every year after that, I'd need to borrow more.

I was a blessed kid. My grandmother and grandfather lost every penny to their name in the 1960s when they opened a service station, but through discipline and hard work, they saved every bit of money they got from then on. They taught me these same lessons, but I also benefited from their resolve: I never worried about clothes or food or shelter as a child. In undergraduate school, I had a full academic scholarship, and my grandmother paid for rent, books, and more. I had it made; all I had to do was put gas in my car and food on the table. Suffice to say that I didn't understand or truly appreciate the value of money.

As I sat in orientation, I heard the dreaded news, "If you take the loans and don't finish the degree, you are still responsible to pay back all of the money you borrow." I was in the audience making lists of pharmacy schools closer to home, trying to see if they took transfer credits; I honestly did not know if I would finish the journey to a doctorate in pharmacy in San Francisco.

Then came the moment. I knew as soon as I cashed that first student loan check that my fate was sealed. I stood there with the check in my hand. *Oh, crap,* I thought. *This is real. I just accepted $56,000 from the almighty U.S. Government and State of California, and they expect to be paid back.*

I cashed the check. I was "all in" and failure was *not* an option.

Four years later, I graduated at the top of my class, with two years as class president under my belt, a couple of national honors, a diploma—and a going-away prize of $157,000 in debt.

For two years, I effectively ignored it, hoping somehow it would magically go away. I paid some minimum payments here and there, but during my time in residency (which is like purgatory after pharmacy school), I chose forbearance on most payments. This means I basically told the loan lenders that I didn't have the funds to pay the loans and would get back to them later. They said sure, just know that you are still accruing interest. I ignored the interest. The number was so big already that I couldn't fully grasp it, so what's a little extra interest on the top?

When I finally finished residency, I got my first real job and was making more money than I ever had before. People told me, "This is your big chance to pay off the loans. You've never had any money. Continue to pretend that you don't. Pretend you're still living on a residency salary, and put everything else toward loans and retirement savings."

I did that. I wrestled my way down to $120,000, and the grave reality of how interest compounds and builds and makes debts never disappear sunk in. I aggressively pursued the debts with the highest interest rates and still didn't seem to be making any progress.

Then I got even more serious. I tightened up my budget, forgot about retirement, and committed 10 percent of my income toward extra monthly payments for loans.

My family noticed my increasing discipline toward paying off my loans (which thrilled them because I was never disciplined with money). Then my grandmother—my dear, wonderful, giving-beyond-every-form-of-giving grandmother—came to me with a deal: she said she had an inheritance she'd been saving for me, but that I could have it now if I put all the funds toward repaying my student loans. This generous gift got me down to almost exactly what I had taken out in my first year of pharmacy school—about $56,000.

It was then I started running. I got a bit (okay, a lot) obsessive-compulsive about checking my loan app, and each loan I paid off was a personal victory. Every extra dollar I had went to loans.

In August 2014, our company brought in the OolaGuys for an event. They talked about goalsetting, personal accountability, and the importance of being awesome in 7 key areas of life. On December 17, 2014, at that event, I stood on stage and vowed to pay off the final $32,000 in student loans I had remaining by December 31, 2015. At this point, I had a strategy, a method, and the drive to be rid of this monkey on my back forever. I didn't know if I could—I only knew that I had to.

And I did. I called my grandmother with the news and we cried. She had been worried for years I would never pay off my loans, and there were times that I had the same misgivings. After graduating with $157,000 in debt, I ultimately paid $220,000 for my education to be a pharmacist. It took so much discipline to not drive through that coffee line, to not go out to eat at that new restaurant, to not stop at the mall, and to not take that trip with my friends. But, there is no better feeling than freeing myself from debt, and I have never carried debt since.

I admit I had help along the way: my grandmother and the fact that my degree gives me good income. Even so, paying off debt still took discipline. It was a choice between another pair of shoes, one extra glass of wine at dinner, a new gadget, or more money paid toward my debt.

I can't tell you how much I have grown through this: from the scared girl who landed in San Francisco to the powerful, debt-free woman I am today. I not only received my doctorate in pharmacy, I got a bonus "adulting" degree in finance and discipline. Being free from debt is unlike any other freedom. With financial stress behind me, I can focus on the horizon and the bigger dreams that are in front of me.

◎ ◎ ◎ ◎

Could you, too, be disciplined enough to achieve the OolaLife of your dreams? Patience and persistence are the keys. But you've gotta take that first step. Here are some tips to get you going.

SIMPLY START. Life happens. We get that. But some women find that after the clutter of life is over for the day, they've done *nothing* to move their life closer to their dreams or goals. Don't let this be you.

Every day create a task list of three or more things that you will do to move closer to one or more of your goals.

If you've wanted to start an investment account and begin saving for your future, spend thirty minutes reading online reviews of the top five companies—then choose one of them and open an account at their website. Want to travel internationally? Spend twenty minutes applying for a passport online, then call three local places that can take your passport photo. And if one of your goals is to eat healthier, spend ten minutes going through your cabinets and refrigerator, tossing all the junk food that's just too tempting.

One, two, three. Done. In just sixty minutes on a random weekday—when life is busy and chaotic and overwhelming—you've just moved forward on three of your goals. Simply start, and see how much you can accomplish.

CHALLENGE YOURSELF FOR TWENTY-ONE DAYS. Experts say it takes twenty-one days to establish any new habit. By practicing a desirable new behavior every day for three weeks, your brain actually becomes "reprogrammed" to automatically take those steps that will get you to your goal.

Well, imagine if you created one new habit every ninety days—like going to the gym three times a week, or saving 12 percent of your weekly paycheck, or writing in your gratitude journal. You would begin to see your goals achieved easier and faster than you thought possible.

To help you create your first new habit, check out the free "Oola 21-Day Challenge for Women" at our website: *www.OolaLife.com/women*. You'll get daily reminders, tips, and inspiration to keep you on track for a life with less stress and more balance.

BE PERSISTENT. Some goals are so big, they won't be completed tomorrow. Be patient. But also be disciplined enough to continue doing those things that will get you to your goal.

A balanced life doesn't occur overnight. It occurs over time. It's composed of seasons when you'll have to be out of balance. Sometimes your life will have to get a little sideways. Persist through these seasons. Course-correct, if necessary—but be patient and proactive if you want to achieve the balanced OolaLife of your dreams.

INTEGRITY

"I try to live with the idea that karma
is a very real thing.
So I put out what I want to get back."

—Megan Fox | @meganfox
Actress

D o what's right. Keep your word to yourself and others. Underpromise. Overdeliver. That's the meaning of *integrity* in our modern-day world.

But unfortunately, living in integrity isn't always easy. We rarely face questions that can be answered with a *yes* or *no*. Instead, we're faced with gray areas, fuzzy math, wink-wink morality, and "acceptable" excuses.

So what can you do?

ADHERE TO WHAT IS RIGHT

As you are on your path to your OolaLife—pursuing great goals and big dreams—never lose your moral compass. Be kind, be patient, be persistent and do what is right.

Don't be in such a hurry to reach your dreams that you compromise your values in an attempt to get there faster.

HOW BEING A PERSON OF INTEGRITY WILL **ACCELERATE** YOUR LIFE

Of course, you can justify your bad behavior with a dozen different excuses, but beware of the consequences. Even when justifying and overstepping seem easier, faster, and less stressful—you end up paying the price when remorse and your damaged reputation stay with you long-term.

Being a person of integrity, on the other hand, will actually accelerate the attainment of your goals. When people see you as trustworthy, honest, mature, transparent, and forthright about setbacks, it creates a vibe and momentum around you that's compelling. People *want to be associated* with those who actually do what they say they'll do. Your integrity instills confidence. You become reliable, consistent and bankable.

One other point of integrity is also important: pay your bills on time. There's an old saying: *Pay the laborer his wages before his sweat dries.* Being prompt is just another way of keeping your word to others.

Of course, integrity around money is fading fast from our culture. But as we'll see in the next story, taking charge of one's financial responsibilities is not only virtuous, it's empowering.

IT'S IN MY BLOOD

by Jamaryn Braun

I was sitting on the couch in our living room, staring out the large window. As if framed in a picture, was the pergola that my dad and I built over the summer. Building the pergola was a mix of hard work, which I enjoyed, and messing around with my dad, which I enjoyed even more. I was only twelve at the time, but when my dad asked for help I was eager to volunteer. The project consumed much of my summer but I didn't mind. In fact, I wouldn't have wanted to be anywhere else. With three sisters and a little brother, time spent alone with my dad was special. I had many questions about life and he seemed to always have the right answer. We talked, we laughed, we built, and I learned. It was awesome.

I learned so much from my dad that summer. He was very hard-working, and with the help of my mom, they had built a pretty sweet life for the five of us. It was one filled with love, travel, adventure, traditions, and crazy experiences. As I sat on the couch reflecting on our summer project, my mom and dad walked out of their bedroom toward the couch for our evening prayers. This was how we ended every evening and started our bedtime routine. This night seemed different. They seemed stressed, not smiling. They seemed nervous, not relaxed. They were distant and disconnected.

They walked over to the couch and stood there in silence. They were looking at each other, as if to say "you first." Even at twelve, I knew something was seriously wrong. After an uncomfortable amount of time passed, my dad started talking. He said that he was sorry for what he was going to tell us and that they loved us very much. Then he said it. "Your mom and I are getting a divorce." We started laughing. This had to be a joke. We have the perfect family. When they didn't laugh, we knew that they were serious. My older sister stood up and ran downstairs to her room. The rest of us just sat there stunned . . . crying. Hugging us tightly, my dad assured us that things would be okay.

He was wrong.

Life as I knew it changed in an instant. My dad moved into a tiny apartment a couple days later. Shortly after that, my siblings, mom, and I had to leave the beautiful home Mom and Dad had built together. No more running around in our sport court, cuddled in blankets around the couch watching movies together, or hanging out under the pergola we built watching the sunset behind the mountains. Instead of packing bags for a family trip, we were packing plastic Target bags for the overnight stays at Dad's place. My mom was sad. My dad was sad. My siblings were sad. I was sad, angry, and scared.

As weeks turned into months and months turned into years, things began to improve. We settled into the rhythm of our new family dynamics. Our parents committed to doing holidays together, going to church together, and out to eat as a family most Sundays. My parents always said, "We are family always and forever, no matter what."

As the waters calmed, and we all healed and adjusted to our new normal, one stress remained: money. I didn't know the details but I knew things were tight. I caught portions of conversations and many of them involved debt and the stress of supporting two households. Financial things that were once never even a consideration were now passionately debated. Soccer camps, school clothes, trips . . . it was all stressful. Even a simple coffee run. It seems overnight we went from carefree financial living to tight budgets and depleted college funds. It was as if the stress around money was always in the air. Even when it wasn't spoken, I could still feel it.

I was scared, but at the same time I felt oddly empowered. I realized I was going to be responsible for my own future. This experience taught me that the decisions I make today affect my life in a positive or negative way for years to come. I was seeing this firsthand with my parents. This left a mark and I made a commitment: to always be responsible with money.

I graduated high school and started my bachelor's degree in accounting and finance. Realizing I was responsible for my own college tuition and expenses, I worked hard, picking up work tutoring kids and working retail at the mall. I received academic and soccer scholarships to cover some of the cost of tuition. Life taught me that debt equals stress. I was committed to not borrowing money. Along with working part time I budgeted every penny. Splurges were few and far between. It is amazing how good a latte can taste when you save for it all week . . . I promise you it's better.

It was hard to see friends who had student loans or family help enjoying themselves: traveling, driving nice cars, going out to eat, and buying cool clothes. I love nice clothes and traveling and I wanted to join in the fun. Yet I constantly reflected on what we went through as a family, and I stayed committed to being responsible with money. I worked through the summer and took summer school to stay ahead.

Going into my sophomore year, even with the scholarships and side work, I was going to fall short. I was stressed and faced with an interesting dilemma: student loans, ask my parents for money, or find some other way. I thought about this for a while and knew that I had to figure it out on my own. I was committed.

As I was driving home, I heard a very familiar commercial on the radio but I actually listened to it for the first time. Get paid to donate plasma. *Interesting,* I thought.

I could help people who needed plasma. Awesome! (I remember my cousin Jared needed plasma when he was going through cancer treatments.)

I could study while donating. Bonus.

Most importantly, I could make the money I needed to pay for school on my own. Perfect.

Although my arms had more tracks than a junkie, and my rich friends would never understand . . . it worked. I donated as often as the regulations would allow and continued to donate plasma throughout my undergrad years. I guess if you are going to become a "regular" somewhere, a plasma donation center isn't that bad. My boyfriend and I have started many of our date nights there. While I imagine most people wouldn't call this romantic, I disagree; finding a guy who is responsible with money is sexy.

As I finish up college and get ready to head to Manhattan to take on the world, I am lighter knowing I am not carrying with me the weight of debt, and empowered because I figured out a way to do it on my own.

I still remember the day my dad (the OolaSeeker) dropped me off in front of 30 Rockefeller Center for my interview. I leaned down to give him a hug (I'm *way* taller than him . . . even when I'm not wearing four-inch heels). He had tears in his eyes as he watched me walk into this next chapter of my life. I never did ask him the reason behind his tears, but my guess is it was not because of disappointment because he couldn't pay for my college, but because he was proud of me that I figured it out on my own. Little did he know, it was in my blood.

◎ ◎ ◎ ◎

No matter what you're going through, staying true to your word (to yourself and others) is something you will never regret. It's not always the easy way—but it is 100 percent the right way.

So, what if you fully intend to keep your word but "busy" gets in the way? What if you want to be all things to all people—and help those you care about—but there aren't enough minutes in a day?

SAYING YES

by Sarah Robbins

M y love affair with the word "yes" began when I was a child growing up in Troy, Michigan. I said yes to many opportunities there. I said yes to being on the dance team. I said yes to being a cheerleader. I said yes to being on the track team and I said yes to all my friends whenever they wanted to do anything or needed anything from me. When I look at my childhood, I smiled a lot, had serious energy, and was always up for anything.

When I was sixteen, my parents needed to move from Troy, Michigan, to Shawano, Wisconsin; away from all my friends, my dance team, my track team, and everything I had known up to that point in my life. This was the first time in my life where everything inside me screamed *"No!"*

When I heard the news, I felt empty, but that emptiness soon filled up with worry, fear, and millions of unanswered questions. Where is Shawano, Wisconsin? Will people there like me? Will I fit in? Do they have a track team?

After doing some research, new questions arose. Are there more cows than people? Will I have to trade in my "cool" clothes for overalls? Do I have to like the Packers? Are we going to have to learn to ice fish to survive? I cried in the back of the van all the way to Shawano.

After screaming *"No!"* for the first six months of my life as a

Shawanoan, I started meeting great people, making friends, and becoming more open minded to my new reality. I started saying yes to life once again. I said yes to amazing experiences that created lifelong memories.

Saying yes to everything continued through college and into adulthood. When my boyfriend got down on one knee and proposed, I said, yes! When the opportunity to start my own business two years later at age twenty-five presented itself, I said yes! Author a book? Yes. Start a publishing company? Yes. Travel twenty-six days a month speaking and crushing business? Yes. Sponsoring 164 children in India? Yes.

When those around me would say no out of fear, often finding themselves stuck, I would look risk in the face and say yes to opportunity. At twenty-nine, I was happily married and making over a million dollars a year. Saying yes served me well.

With each yes, however, my obligations began to pile up. I loved all of it: making people happy, growing my business, traveling, and serving others, but my schedule was full—overflowing, actually. I was finding it hard to keep up with all the demands and people that I said yes to. Trying to be all things to all people was overwhelming. I was overcommitted and overscheduled.

It was when I said yes to expanding our family by having a child of our own that this became abundantly clear. I realized, especially with a new baby, that I can't say yes to everything and everybody, even if I want to.

Gabriel was born twelve days overdue—fashionably late, just like his mother. On the way home from the hospital I got a frantic call that I needed to get on a business conference call immediately. I said no. I could hear her head turn and her eyes roll over the phone . . . *screech!* After saying no, I calmly said, "I know you got this, good luck!"

I realized I needed to come up with a tactical approach to saying no. I decided that if I must say no, I would offer a solution. I can't make it to the meeting next week, but you can video me in. I won't be able to speak for your company, but I have a friend and colleague who is an expert on that topic; I'll put you in touch with them. I won't be able to get on the call, but I know the perfect person who can take it from here.

Early on, saying no was terrifying. I was afraid I would disappoint others and that I would miss opportunities. But I anchored every no with the complete understanding that saying no to certain things, would allow me to say yes to the best things in my life.

Since breaking up with the word yes, or at least making yes simply a friend with benefits, I have been home twenty-six days a month, I've made my health and my family a priority, I've kept up with the demands of others without letting people down—and the craziest thing is my businesses have hit record numbers. In the process, I've also empowered many people to do things on their own.

Saying no to certain things has opened the door for me to say yes to the best things . . . being a wife and mother, all while being a businesswoman without being stressed, overscheduled, overcommitted and overwhelmed. I now have a greater ability to manage my time and manage my life. It's about finding a happy balance of yes and no that feeds into my values, my purpose, and the bigger vision for my life.

◎ ◎ ◎ ◎

Not overcommitting and saying "no" when you mean it—even when it's tough to do—is one way you can achieve a reputation for integrity. That's what Sarah learned. And you can, too. Here are three imperatives that will help you maintain integrity.

KEEP YOUR WORD TO OTHERS. KARMA'S A BITCH. Dishonest behavior and promises not kept will come back to haunt you.

Our advice is to always decide in favor of decency. Do the right thing. Overdeliver. Create solutions where everybody wins.

Honoring your word throughout a working relationship—especially in business—will cause more opportunities to open up for you. You'll establish a reputation as someone who's not only great to work with, but who can be trusted with bigger projects and more important duties. Delivering on time, showing up prepared, and paying bills promptly shows not only that you respect other people, but that you see them (and their time and work) as valuable.

KEEP YOUR WORD TO YOURSELF. When you repeatedly lie to yourself, over time you'll quit believing in you.

If you've ever made a New Year's resolution, for example, only to realize on January 15th that nothing's happened yet—that's a broken promise *with yourself* that can chip away at your self-worth. Score enough of these disappointments and your subconscious mind will get the message that moving forward is not important. It's no different from a friend or colleague who repeatedly agrees to meet you at 4:00, but shows up between 4:30 and 5:00 every time. You simply don't believe her anymore.

Start to create *instead* a culture of success in your life where you set small, achievable goals—then accomplish them—as a way to believe yourself again.

Say you commit to going to a gym today . . . simply drive by. Yay! You went to the gym for the first time in forever, and you're not even sore. On Day Two, go inside, take the tour, and sign up as a member. Go home to your spouse and proudly declare, "Two days in a row! Can you see the difference?"

On Day Three, actually turn on the treadmill, then stand back and watch it roll. That wasn't so bad! And on Day Four, get on the treadmill and walk half a mile. Has your fitness level improved this week? No, but your mind set has. You've actually started to believe yourself again.

Use that momentum to progressively challenge yourself and make positive changes in your life.

DON'T OVERSCHEDULE, OVERPROMISE, OR OVERCOMMIT. While you may be well-meaning, your integrity level drops whenever you overschedule and can't honor your commitments.

Of course, women are masters at juggling twenty-seven things at once—we see this in our own households. But there's a downside to being really good at multitasking: it's easy to say, "I can squeeze in one more thing."

Don't do it. Don't overschedule, overpromise, or overcommit. Say no, then delegate and prioritize.

You know what we're talking about.

When you head out for a meeting or take the kids to school, how many times have you "made a quick stop"—*knowing* it will make you late for the school bell or another commitment you're actually supposed to be focused on? Instead, why not try to do *one thing less*? Rather than cramming one more thing onto your to-do list, why not *remove* one thing so you can arrive stress-free, organized, and on time.

This applies to other areas of your life, too. In fact, women will often say "yes" to a new project, when that new commitment will only add stress to an already stressful life. While it's flattering to be asked and wonderful to be acknowledged, your tranquility should come first. The same thing goes for business commitments if you're an entrepreneur. While your heart might be saying, "I can do that!" oftentimes, we see well-meaning women miscalculate the time it takes to meet deadlines or achieve benchmarks. Underpromise and overdeliver instead.

PASSION

"The question isn't who is going to let me;
it's who is going to stop me."

— Ayn Rand | @aynrandinst
Author of Atlas Shrugged, philosopher
and creator of Objectivism

Passion is the trump card. Not only can it overcome virtually any OolaBlocker that comes your way, it's also been the driving force behind every modern convenience and lifestyle benefit we enjoy today. We fly in airplanes, own smartphones, and shop online because—at one time—people were passionate about human flight, mobile technology, and building the Internet.

What are *you* passionate about?

A goal fueled by passion will inspire you to overcome all Blockers and spark your creativity, ingenuity, and determination. Hopefully it's a goal that, once you accomplish it, will uplevel everything you do— from how you live, to who you hang out with, to how much money you make, and more.

TRUST THE PROCESS TO FIND
WHAT YOU **NATURALLY** LOVE TO DO

If you got outside your life and actually focused on *you,* chances are good your true heart's desire would emerge. Unfortunately, passion and purpose are two things that can easily get buried by paying the bills, managing toxic relationships, and plain old everyday stress.

That's why we encourage you to trust the process of this book. Set your goals, work to eliminate the Blockers, embrace the Accelerators, take action, and begin your journey to the OolaLife. As you start to achieve your goals, your purpose and passion will appear.

◎   ◎   ◎   ◎

TAY-TAY, THE INTERN

by Taylor LaGuardia

It was 9:00 PM and pitch black outside. I was just finishing up a six-hour drive down I-93 from Vermont to southern New Hampshire. The freeway was hilly and narrow and the shoulder of the road was not an option. The speed limit was 70 mph, but with a tailwind, we were going 50. The air outside was freezing cold, and with no heater, the air inside matched its fierce bite. My fingers were numb and I hadn't felt my toes inside my shoes for the last three hours.

Climbing another big hill seemed routine, especially in the mountains of the Northeast. Gear down to third, put my foot to the floor, and hope there is enough power in the back of me to match the grade I face in the hill in front of me. But this hill was different. Nearing the top, with the pedal to the floor, the bus stopped, and like an exhausted marathon runner at the finish line, it refused to go forward another inch. The intense cold seemed to lessen as the adrenaline kicked in; I started to feel sweaty and flush. I'm only twenty-two. I am thousands of miles from home in a state I have never been in, and I'm now stranded on the side of the road in a vintage Volkswagen Surf Bus. With no taillights, no headlights, and cars flying by at 70-plus mph, I felt like I was in a death trap.

I contemplated my options. *Do I stand on the side of the road in the rain and cold or stay inside the bus?*

I didn't learn the answer to this question in college. But after forty-five minutes of waiting for a tow truck to arrive, I was done. I called 911. Soon, I found myself in the back of a New Hampshire Highway Patrol car, and I'd never been happier in all my life!

As I sat there waiting for a yet another tow truck to arrive (yes, this wasn't the first, and it wouldn't be the last), I reflected on the choices that led me to this moment. As a little girl, I was passionate about following in my family's footsteps and becoming a doctor. It's all I thought about and all I wanted to do. During my senior year in high school, I took a marketing class to round out my schedule. I got hooked and I felt the tides shift. Should I instead pursue a career in marketing? What are my parents and grandparents going to say when I tell them I want to go in a different direction? But, I felt it in my heart that this is what I wanted to do. I sat my parents down to break the news to them and to my surprise, they were completely supportive.

"Follow your heart" is what they told me, so I enrolled in college to pursue a degree in business and marketing.

I was a junior at the University of St. Thomas in Minnesota, deep into marketing, when I had a slight panic attack. Okay, a *major* panic attack! Is this really what I want to do with my life? Is this my purpose? Is this what I'm designed to do? It was a big decision. After all, this is how I am going to spend the rest of my life.

Suddenly, I knew I wanted more for myself. My deepest desire and greatest passion is for helping people. This was tied to my desire to be a doctor, and my desire to communicate via marketing. I love working with people, guiding them and serving them.

Now, just one year from graduating, I felt like I was starting from square one. No plan, just a passion for helping people. In a panic, I called my dad. After listening intently, he asked a very simple question: "If you could do anything and money was not a consideration, what would you do?"

Calmly, I said, "I would want to do what the OolaGuys do for a living."

"Then contact them and see if you can do an internship," he replied.

That sounded completely crazy, but the more I thought about it, the more excited I became. I had clarity, and thought, *What do I have to lose?*

I reached out. Surprisingly, they got right back to me. And I was even more surprised with their very simple and interesting reply: *Can you drive a stick shift?*

With passion, I exclaimed, "Why, *yes*, as a matter of fact I *can* drive a stick!" (A more honest answer would have been "well, kinda.")

I thought back to a cold Wisconsin morning, just four months after getting my driver's license, when my friend Kelly took me out on the icy country roads and taught me how to drive a manual stick shift in a small blue Pontiac. She told me that I may need to know how to drive a stick one day. I guess this was that day.

Two weeks before my senior year in college was scheduled to start, I pushed the pause button to follow my passion. I agreed to work for free, driving the OolaBus across the country collecting the dreams of America. "Tay-Tay, the Intern" was born.

I immediately contacted my academic advisors to advise them that I would be withdrawing from school one year shy of graduation to drive a 1970 VW Surf Bus across the country. I also wrote letters to the financial committee, my professors, and the dean of the university. By their reactions, I am pretty sure they felt I would be leaving college to sell weed out of the back of the OolaBus, and not hope.

But I immediately jumped out of school and into the driver's seat . . . and I have never felt more alive.

The four months that I spent on the road driving the OolaBus city to city (and donut shop to donut shop when the OolaGuys were along for the ride) were the most amazing four months of my life. The dreams I collected, the people I met, and the countryside I explored, provided me with more knowledge and life experience than I ever could have learned in a classroom.

My assignment was simple: meet people, listen to their stories, let them know that they are awesome and designed for greatness and a purpose, hand them a Sharpie and a sticker, and tell them it would be our honor to carry their dream for their life on our bus. It was my favorite assignment in all my years of college.

Little did I know when I wrote the letter to the dean to leave college, that in helping others find their purpose, I would open my heart to find my own.

After completing my internship, I went back to college and finished my degree. I knew with certainty that completing my degree was the next step in pursing my passion and purpose.

I am now living in Vail, Colorado, and my internship has transitioned into a position at Oola Corporate Training, where we teach Oola in the workplace. On my days off, I hit the open road in my Infinity with automatic transmission, heat and air . . . and even a seatbelt. I'm grateful for the passion that got me here, that got me through that night on the side of the road, and that still guides me today.

We spend so much time in our heads doing what makes sense on paper that our passions are often overlooked. Our mind questions decisions, worries about outcomes, and fears change. But our heart is where passion lives and passion can trump them all.

Whether it's hopping on the OolaBus and working for free, or pursing your dream to become a superhero, follow your heart . . . no matter what.

AMAZONIAN KICKASS WAR GODDESS

by Tiffany Smith

I looked down at the notecard that was just handed to me and clutched it in a superhero death grip. I thought if I held it firmly enough, no one would notice the card shaking. I slowly started to read what was written on it in my mind, mentally rehearsing. The words seemed to float above the paper, but I knew it was my eyes refocusing in disbelief.

"Calm down, Tiff! You were made for this. You've worked your whole life for this," I yelled to my brain.

I wasn't sure if I was nervous or just insanely excited for the next few minutes of my life. Standing on the red carpet in my blue dress and bright yellow heels, I took a deep breath and read into the microphone, "Please welcome:

Robert Downey Jr.—Ironman
Scarlett Johansen—Black Widow
Chris Helmsworth—Thor
Chris Evans—Captain America
Samuel L. Jackson—Nick Fury"

Moments earlier, I was walking down Hollywood Boulevard toward the legendary El Capitan Theater. I was mesmerized by the beauty of the old concrete building dressed with an impressive gold marquee, which was adorned by red, orange, and blue lights. It proudly displayed the words "*Avengers* Premier."

I made my way through the crowds of people, the cheers, and the blinding flashes of cameras before entering the theater. I felt as though I had stepped back in time to the glittering past of 1920's Hollywood. I was caught up in the moment as a fan of Hollywood, the movies, and especially superheroes, but I wasn't there to enjoy a movie. I was there to work.

I'd landed my dream job earlier that year working for Marvel comics. My job that evening was to work the red-carpet premier of the *Avengers* movie; whatever they needed. But at the last minute, the producer said, "Tiffany, I need you to announce the actors and actresses for the show."

He handed me a notecard with names on it, pointed to where I should go, and quickly walked away. As I looked at the notecard he handed me, it wasn't the actors and actresses names that shook me, it was that I was literally getting to introduce my childhood heroes. Soon, I would be calling Ironman and Captain America and they were going to answer my call. I was even going to call for Thor . . . pinch me!

After the premier and literally watching the *Avengers* movie with the entire cast, WOW was my reaction. I went home, lay in bed, and reflected on the moments of my life that led me to this memorable evening. Putting the pieces together, all the moments big and small that led me here, it made sense. It was like holding a handmade tapestry and looking at the unorganized and confusing mess of threads on the reverse, then turning it over and seeing the most beautiful and intricate piece of art on the front. That art was my life. I began to see the beauty in everything that had happened in my life, whereas in the past, it had seemed somewhat random.

The common thread that had pulled my tapestry together was passion.

I was born in Southern California, but grew up in Hershey, Pennsylvania, far from the bright lights of Hollywood. As a young girl, I remember watching Saturday morning cartoons with my dad and sharing in his obsession with comic books, superheroes, and everything Marvel and DC Comics. While most young girls dream of being a princess, and carried away by their prince on a white stallion, I wanted to be an Amazonian Kickass War Goddess who ran with the big boys. My first crushes were Clark Kent and Peter Parker—obviously, I love the nerdy types. My costume of choice wasn't a Cinderella dress, it was Wonder Woman's. Comics were in my blood.

The real question in my mind was, *How do I get from Pennsylvania back to Hollywood and become a superhero?*

The answer seemed easy: graduate high school, jump on a flight, and make it happen. My parents encouraged me to follow my heart but only after getting a college degree. I was fifty-fifty on the college idea, but I took my parents' advice and enrolled at Syracuse University.

Before I knew it, my wardrobe was winter ready and predominantly orange. Majoring in broadcast journalism, I felt out of place with all the students discussing whether they wanted to do news or sports. "Hey Tiff, what's your dream? CNN or ESPN?" they would ask. Um . . . neither! I just needed my degree, and then I was heading to Hollywood to pursue my dreams.

Passion for my dreams pushed me through those four years and I graduated with honors. Without knowing what happened, I was now pretty comfortable in front of a camera and found so much joy in interviewing people. My parents were proud—and they'd been right to press me about college. What I'd thought was a bit unnecessary turned out to be a very valuable step on my journey. College was an integral part of the tapestry I was creating, even if at the time I could only see the messy back side.

After graduation, I followed my heart and moved to Manhattan into an apartment with three friends on the Upper East Side. I got a job as a booking agent's assistant at a modeling agency. This wasn't my dream job, but it paid the bills and it would support me while I pursued my true passion. It wasn't Hollywood, but it was one step closer. My job at the agency was to reach out to models and confirm their appointments. When they showed up, I would help them get settled and get ready for their auditions. After watching audition after audition, I learned what casting directors looked for and quickly realized that I could do what those models were doing . . . I could totally rock an audition.

Now was the time; uncertainty and fear flooded my mind, but passion flowed through my veins. I knew that to work for DC Comics or Marvel—to be a real superhero—I was going to have to move to Los Angeles. My parents and my only sister lived on the East Coast. All my friends lived on the East Coast. But, my dreams were on the West Coast. With crazy passion, no job, and only three months of living expenses saved, I got on a flight to California.

As I stepped off the plane at LAX, I was greeted by the warm Southern California sun and palm trees, but to me, it was like the scene in *Indiana Jones and the Last Crusade*, when Indy was asked to cross the invisible bridge. I took a deep breath and, with faith and passion, I stepped out of the past and into my future.

Just two weeks and multiple auditions later, I got my first job— working for G4TV's *Attack of the Show*. Shortly thereafter, I was hosting Marvel live streams, which led to the memorable evening hanging with some of my favorite superheroes.

Currently, I'm the host of *DC All Access* and am pushing myself even further by focusing on acting. I'm not sure what my future holds, but my tapestry is far from complete. I'm going to continue following my heart and push through all challenges, fear, and doubt with passion. Who knows? Instead of interviewing superheroes, maybe the next stitches in my tapestry will be to *become* the superhero. Move over Superman, it's time the world met the Amazonian Kickass War Goddess.

◎ ◎ ◎ ◎

Are you ready to add a little more passion to everything you do? Are you ready to start living the life *you* want versus traveling a road dictated by others? Take a look below at what we know works to bring more passion to your Oola journey.

REDISCOVER YOUR TRUE PASSION, NOT SOMEONE ELSE'S PLAN FOR YOU. You weren't built by accident. You're built uniquely for a purpose that not only serves the world, but it also inspires and motivates you.

Unfortunately, most women find that their deepest desires have been masked by what *other people want you to do.* You get a business degree because your parents expect it, when you secretly want to pursue a career in the arts. You agree to start a family right away, even though your real passion is to travel the globe. You love being a mom, doing organic gardening, and cooking healthy meals, but that's not considered an "important" career.

If this sounds familiar, you're not alone. On the way to pleasing others, being politically correct, paying the bills, and securing the "future," most women have sadly lost track of their own true desires.

So what's one way out of this predicament? Start removing the clutter and obstacles in your life that are holding you back from following your heart.

When you begin to eliminate fear, the weight of debt, laziness, self-sabotage, and toxic people, your true self will begin to emerge. You'll start to get a glimpse of what's inside of you, and your heartfelt passions will come to light.

TURN YOUR PASSION INTO THE ULTIMATE OOLA CAREER. Of course, passion is the fuel that will help you achieve your goals and change your life *even if you don't have* the knowledge, contacts, funding or opportunities right now.

Unfortunately, many women get so caught up in the clutter of everyday life, they don't see an opportunity for them in an activity they love. They don't realize that social media, e-commerce, and other technology has changed the equation by creating opportunities in blogging, photography, travel, publishing, entrepreneurship, forex trading, spiritual leadership, developing new inventions, and providing unique services.

The OolaGuru's wife lights up when she's creating custom jewelry, even though she has a teaching degree plus many other responsibilities with the kids and at home during the day. And many businesses have grown out of women's passion for chemical-free households, quilting, surfing, scrapbooking, hunting and shooting, hiking, writing fiction, ecotravel—the examples are endless. In fact, today, it's more possible than ever to turn your passion into a full-time career, thriving business, or side gig that pays the bills.

ANTICIPATE ROADBLOCKS AND LET PASSION CARRY YOU THROUGH. Your road to Oola will not always be rainbows and butterflies; you will encounter bumps, potholes, and detours. You finally commit to getting in shape but then you sprain an ankle. You finally build up an emergency fund and then the furnace breaks. After a rough patch with your spouse things are going fairly well, but then an offhand remark turns into a heated argument.

In these moments, you'll want to stop because it is hard to see a way through. Let passion pull you through these challenges. Remember why your health is so vital to your future. Remember why you want to feel the freedom of being debt-free. Remember why it's so important that you are in a loving and committed relationship. Your "why" will give you passion—and your passion will see you through.

HUMILITY

"I want to serve the people."

— Malala Yousafzai | @malala
Pakistani activist and youngest recipient
ever of the Nobel Peace Prize

W orking on you is not only Oola, it's vital. Much the same way a flight attendant instructs you to "put the oxygen mask on yourself first before helping others," working on *yourself first* helps you become a more balanced and capable person—which in turn allows you to better serve others.

But while we've spent most of this book talking about *you*, encouraging you to work on *your* dreams and pursue *your* OolaLife, *life isn't always about you.*

In fact, some of the greatest leaders we know—and many of the most successful women we have met—are also the most humble humans on the planet. They listen more than they speak, they're quick to deflect praise, and they are first to accept the burden of responsibility when things don't go right. It's never about them being put on a pedestal. It's about serving those around them and having a purpose that is tied to something greater than themselves.

By making themselves small, by being humble, they are able to create something really big.

Embracing humility, just as they do, will help *you* achieve the life of your dreams. Being modest and reserved makes any situation less about you and more about the people around you. But don't confuse humility with weakness. Being respectful and kind, putting others first, being transparent, and responsibly owning the mistakes you made will give you a quiet confidence.

Instead of excusing, explaining, or posturing, you can spend your energy (and reputation) on collaborating, connecting, creating, and moving forward.

◎ ◎ ◎ ◎

STARTING OVER

by Kim Stoegbauer

The housing crash in 2008 was humbling for everyone, but especially for our family. My husband and I had been riding the appreciating market since we graduated from college in 1999. We bought our first house in 2000, and for the next several years, we were flying high in the luxury property business. He worked for a large national homebuilder as a sales manager/broker, while I worked as a real estate agent and co-owned two real estate offices.

On the side, we were fixing up and flipping homes left and right. We couldn't buy enough homes or flip them fast enough. Things couldn't have been better. We were young, more successful than we ever thought we would be, and at thirty-one we moved into our dream home—a beautiful, custom home in a neighborhood we coveted for years. We poured our hearts and money into this home, renovating and updating every detail before moving in our growing family.

We were proud of what we created and thought it would never end.

Little did we know, the real estate market would come to screeching halt in 2008. We found ourselves drowning in mortgage payments on multiple homes with quickly decreasing values. We sold off what we could as quickly as possible, while continuing to work our respective real estate jobs, all while balancing family life.

Even back when the market was hot, I had always tried to put

281

others' needs first—my clients', my husband's, my children's—but one incident became the tipping point for me.

One afternoon, I was at home with the kids—my three-year-old son and my one-year-old daughter. I needed to present an offer to a client over the phone, and since decent deals and contracts were now few and far between, I had no choice but to make the call with the kids playing nearby. I decided it would be best to "hide" in the garage, but several minutes into the call, my little ones tried to find me. I could hear them calling for me, so I grabbed the door handle to the garage and held it as tight as I could so they couldn't open it. It scared them and I could hear them hysterically crying and calling for me on the other side of the door. Yet, I took a deep breath, kept my composure and finished the call.

With more bills than money, I needed this deal. My family needed this deal. What was probably a few minutes felt like an hour. When the call ended, I opened the door and fell to my knees, hugging and kissing my babies, begging for forgiveness.

At that honest moment of pure regret, I knew things had to change immediately—even if it meant less money, fewer things, and a smaller house. That was the last time I put work before my children.

I immediately called my business partner and said I was done. I couldn't do it anymore and I didn't care about the consequences or money. It was time to put my family first.

Deep down, I knew we'd be okay. *The only thing that matters,* I thought, *is that we're happy and healthy.*

So with my amazing husband completely behind me, we simplified. We chose having less for being home more. It was scary, but instead of focusing on what we didn't have, we were grateful for what we did have.

This time at home allowed not only more time with my kids, but time to reflect and really think about what I could do next. I actually enjoyed working hard and making money, but now I was looking for something that would allow me the flexibility to be home with the kids and also keep me productive.

Blogging was a relatively new thing in 2008, and I started following a few creative blogs and loved getting updates. It soon dawned on me that this was something I could do, even if only for fun. I have always been very creative and really into decorating, designing, and entertaining. I love photography and design and figured a blog would be a fun outlet to share anything creative that I was doing. In five minutes, I came up with a name for my blog, *The TomKat Studio*, based on the names of my two children, Tommy and Kate. Since my children had been the inspiration for my new start, it seemed only logical to name this new little adventure after them. An empty room in our house soon became my "studio." I signed up for a free blog platform and started sharing.

I never thought my passion and creativity would ever become a career, and though I started the blog on a whim, maybe deep down I knew (or hoped) it might become something more. It's crazy that what I felt was "starting over" has become a huge success. The TomKat Studio has been featured by Martha Stewart, HGTV, DIY Network and numerous national publications. I work with my amazing team on freelance projects for huge brands like Coca-Cola, Barbie, Pottery Barn Kids, and Hershey's. I still blog regularly and have built a social media following of over 300,000 followers.

The best part? I get to do what I love every single day, while being home with my family. I seriously couldn't be happier. And ironically, as the housing market recovered, we slowly started flipping houses again.

What I thought was the end of the road was simply a change in direction toward my passion and natural talents—a direction that gave my life better balance and more happiness . . . and now I can open the door when my kids come knocking.

◎ ◎ ◎ ◎

When Kim flipped one house too many, she could have flipped out. But instead, she realized this was simply where she was, not *who* she was as a businesswomen, wife, and mother. She was humble enough to walk away, quit chasing, and create a work life that was more in balance with her family's needs. Ironically, she fell into an even more successful profession (and eventually impacted more people) while still honoring her family's needs first.

Humility allows you to work through challenging seasons with grace and your head up, looking for the next opportunity.

THE ISLAND LIFE

by Kimmy Brooke

The windows were open, with the trade winds offering a fresh cool breeze as I began to prepare dinner. I could see Diamond Head out the back window. In front of me, the sun was setting over the open ocean, saying farewell to the day in a way that only Hawaii could. That night, we were starting with a Caesar salad, his favorite. I picked out the romaine lettuce myself and chopped it just the way he liked it. I made the dressing from scratch. I could hear the waves crashing along the shore. The salt air filled my senses and fueled me. This was paradise. I was living the dream—and I couldn't believe this was really my life.

"Is it ready yet?" said the familiar voice from behind me.

I quickly stood at attention and was reminded that this wasn't my life at all. I was just an employee in someone else's life. My husband and I had been hired by a family to tend to all their needs. They had homes in exotic places all over the world; Hawaii was just one of them. This was one of my favorites—20,000 square feet of perfection. My favorite part was the infinity pool. When the family was out of town, I would swim laps each evening at sunset to rinse away a hard day's work.

At the age of thirty-five, my greatest accomplishment to date had been the birth of my daughter. Other than that, I didn't have much to show for my life—or much else to speak of. Though I had a college degree and was licensed as a massage therapist, we struggled as a family to get ahead. Most days, it felt like we were always behind the eight ball. I was spending my days cleaning, polishing, and caring for the accomplishments of others. I served with humility, but in my heart I wanted more.

Though we were so grateful for the work, there was always a voice inside me screaming, *You are made for greater things! This is NOT your calling. You can do so much more.* Deep down, I knew that something bigger, something more powerful, something somewhere was waiting.

Just work hard, I told myself. *Be of service. But push forward. Keep looking for it, and when the time is right, the opportunity will appear.*

Even when life threw challenges at me—financial trouble, a divorce, a bitter season, a victim season, and even an angry season—I kept working hard and seeking that greatness within me. I knew I needed to be an example for my daughter and write a better ending to our family story.

One day, I saw a friend post details on a weekend workshop he had taken. I'd noticed that he was happier, more confident, and more secure, so it piqued my curiosity. I wanted to feel that way.

Sign me up! I said to myself.

I spent the weekend learning to look at my life through different goggles. I learned to work on me and my dreams. And more importantly, I learned how to map out a detailed plan for a better future.

I began to feel more powerful. I began to feel for the first time in ages a sense of excitement for the possibilities in life that awaited me. And once again, that voice—that loud, unknown voice—spoke to me and said, *You are meant for greatness!*

I not only listened that weekend, I followed through. I knew that I was made for more than living someone else's dream life. It was time for me to go get my own.

I felt free and ready to take on the world. I realized that I am fully in control of my life. I get to choose how my life turns out. I get to choose how I feel. And most importantly, for the first time possibly ever, I believed in me!

I became an entrepreneur. I was willing to do what it took—serve in any way needed—to provide me and my daughter a better life . . . a life where we had choices versus chains. It wasn't easy and involved many difficult challenges and choices. Though it hurt my heart, I was traveling constantly and had to put her in boarding school in ninth grade. In her eyes, I was shipping her off, but I saw it differently. In my eyes, I did what was necessary to provide a better life for my daughter and me.

But with the sacrifices came the rewards.

Eventually, I was able to bring her on trips with me and show her the world: Japan, Australia, Indonesia, Malaysia, Singapore, Canada, and all throughout the United States.

As a single mom, I was able to pay for her college education with cash versus student loans. And while our life was not like that of a "normal" family, the time we spent together was quality, focused, and the experiences through ups and downs have brought us closer than I ever thought possible.

But most importantly, I was able to show her that anyone can triumph through hard work, dedication, and deciding what you want. I taught her that if you humbly serve every opportunity that comes your way, good things will happen.

I also taught her the lifelong commitment of being of service to others. Today, we collaborate with fifty other women in my industry to support an eighteen-month learning program for women in Guatemala. It helps abused and uneducated women become microentrepreneurs—producing products that they can sell to help feed their families. Not only does it educate the women and lower the rate of spousal abuse for these families, but the women pass on this education to their own children—and others—through a requirement for them to give back and teach others when they graduate after eighteen months.

Over my lifetime, I've been grateful for every bump, bruise and scratch—as well as for all the opportunities where I've been able to serve—that have gotten me to where I am today. I'm nearly fifty now, and I just purchased my dream home. And as I prepare Caesar salad—with the Hawaiian landscape out the back window and the waves crashing on the lanai in front of me—I am living my dream . . . not someone else's.

How about you? Are you humble . . . *sincerely* humble? Or are you falsely humble . . . saying and doing things to appear humble to others? Take a look at these tips to help you pursue true humility:

ATTACH YOURSELF TO A CAUSE GREATER THAN YOU. Some of the most famously successful people of our time are also the most quietly philanthropic. They're not seeking praise. They just have a heart for helping others. When you're focused on helping others, there's really no room to be arrogant about your own accomplishments. That's why we recommend attaching yourself to a cause greater than yourself. It keeps you humble.

ASSEMBLE YOUR "TRUTH CREW." One way to always stay humble is to listen to people you trust. Look around your inner circle of friends and family. Who do you trust enough to tell you the truth? Whose assessments are you willing to listen to? Approach them separately about being part of your Truth Crew—calling you out when you go sideways or act out of arrogance and ego.

A side benefit of a truth crew is they can also shield you from censure by outsiders who barely know you—and who couldn't possibly know enough about you to offer valid criticism. You've seen the type: negative women who meet a successful businesswoman and automatically assume she's a bad mom. Or college girls who see an attractive young woman, star athlete, or top competitor and assume she's high-maintenance. Your truth crew can be there for you, keeping it real when your critics have their claws out.

PRACTICE SELFLESSNESS: WHAT COULD YOU DO FOR NOTHING IN RETURN? In our unbalanced culture today, it seems that everyone is out to gain some advantage for themselves. But if you're humble, you realize *instead* that the path to a better world is when we all put someone else's needs first with no expectation of anything in return. We shine as a community when we come together (with our different skills and abilities) to lift up others.

WISDOM

"We need to accept that we won't always make the
right decisions, that we'll screw up royally sometimes—
understanding that failure is not the opposite
of success, it's part of success."

—Arianna Huffington | @ariannahuff
Founder of The Huffington Post
and CEO of Thrive Global

Wisdom comes from many places: your own experiences, people you know, and successful people you would like to follow. Listening to all three will help you grow in Oola.

But listening is always the challenge, isn't it? Listening to wise counsel. Listening to your own intuition. And *not* making the same mistake twice.

When we speak with women, we're often shocked by the stories of smart, successful women who *didn't* listen to themselves and learn from their past mistakes. They keep making the same mistakes over and over again.

"I've been in eight bad relationships," we'll hear. "And I'm in the ninth one right now."

Of course, nobody says it quite that way, but you can tell from the conversation that bad relationships are this woman's forté. Making money, then losing it repeatedly, is also a common theme—as is yo-yo dieting, impulse buying, and one failed get-rich-quick scheme after another. Enough!

Look, we're not here to beat you up about past mistakes—we've made more than we can count. You got this far with a combination of smart decisions—and not-so-smart decisions. Wisdom comes from both. In fact, both are part of the human condition.

But to use wisdom as an accelerator to get to Oola, you need to review your *past* outcomes every time you make an important *new* decision. Listen to your intuition and your gut instinct—that handy mental acuity you develop by making good and bad decisions over time. If you're about to quit your job, get a new dog, hire that contractor, or sink your last $1,000 into yet another friend's business venture, well hey, how'd that work out for you last time?

◎ ◎ ◎ ◎

SOMETIMES A DOOR CLOSES

by Sharon Lechter

n 2007, I was at the height of my financial success and should have felt great, on top of the world in fact . . . but I was miserable inside. Each morning, I would ask myself, *Are we still making a positive difference in peoples' lives?* And because I could still say "yes," I chose to stay in a business relationship that was destructive to me, both spiritually and emotionally, because the business was still making a positive difference for *other* peoples' lives. It was a daily battle to keep the business on that positive course while maintaining the rigorous quality control that had successfully built the Rich Dad brand up to that point. What was good for others was killing me.

My life's mission was to teach financial literacy and provide the education and tools to help people take charge of their personal financial lives. As co-author of *Rich Dad Poor Dad* and co-founder of the Rich Dad Organization, I thought I had found my life's work, my legacy. Building the company as CEO over a ten-year period was at first very exciting because we saw people turning their lives around financially and building financial foundations for themselves and their families. Our first of fifteen books, *Rich Dad Poor Dad* reached number one on the *New York Times* Best Seller List and stayed there for over seven years. I was involved in expanding the business by negotiating multimillion-dollar deals for publishing, infomercials, coaching services, and regional seminars. I loved what I was doing and we were truly making a positive impact around the world.

While originally aligned with my partners on the direction of the company, we started growing apart. They say success brings out more of who you truly are . . . and I found it to be true in our case. After ten years of working together, our personal goals and missions had changed and were no longer congruent.

In March 2007, I made the decision to leave the Rich Dad Company at the height of our success. I have never regretted the decision to leave. No amount of success is worth putting your health or your principles at risk. I learned a costly lesson about the importance of taking care of myself. I am extremely proud of what we created in those first ten years at Rich Dad, but am even more proud of myself for deciding to leave when I did—even in the face of not knowing what the future would hold for me.

While I never regretted the decision to leave, there were many days when I felt lost and a little sorry for myself. We were well set financially, but I was not quite sure what to do next. I would second-guess certain decisions I had made along the way; my self-confidence was shaken. Then a few months later the phone rang, and my caller ID read "White House." I was asked to be on the first-ever President's Advisory Council for Financial Literacy, serving first President Bush and then President Obama. It was such an incredible honor.

I would not have received that phone call had I still been at Rich Dad.

I realized that you have to close certain doors in your life before others can, or will, open.

A couple of months later, I received another phone call. This time it was from Don Green, CEO of the Napoleon Hill Foundation, asking me to co-author the first of what has become a series of books, including *Think and Grow Rich for Women.*

I would *not* have received that phone call from Don Green had I still been at Rich Dad.

I realized there was a bigger plan unfolding for me. What I had seen as my life's work at Rich Dad, my legacy, was in actuality, just the first step in my journey in creating my life's work.

Sometimes you have to close one door for other doors of opportunity to open.

Leaving a profitable business, making the decision to stand in your own space, and staying true to yourself is a huge undertaking, both spiritually and financially. It can instigate fear even in the most experienced individuals.

This time period in my life had me facing the greatest height of success, combined with the greatest lows of personal stress and business drama. I truly felt that the worst was over, however there was a much bigger trauma waiting for me.

In December 2012, I lost my youngest son. There truly is no greater pain. There is no greater dose of reality for understanding what is important in life. It is not the financial success. It is not the accolades. It is not living for the future. It was as if time stopped and stood still.

It was as if a door in my life had been slammed shut.

The very essence of my life was in question. *Why am I here? Why my son? What more is there to life?*

What seemed like major issues were no longer major. What seemed like the most stressful situations no longer mattered at all. The anger at certain individuals who had caused me pain paled in comparison to the pain I felt from losing my son.

It took a long time for me to "feel" again. The numbness was insurmountable. I would put on a strong façade and continue my work, but the emptiness inside was profound.

Then one day, a friend introduced me to the Prayer of Jabez:

Oh, that You would bless me indeed,
and enlarge my territory,
that Your hand would be with me,
and that You would keep me from evil, that I may not cause pain!

—I Chronicles 4:10 (NKJV)

I started reciting the Prayer of Jabez several times a day, before each meeting, interview, or speech. Giving up control to a higher power and asking that the words be provided to and through me so that I could make the greatest impact. Having faith, whatever your belief system, helps you through difficult times.

Instead of just writing books that would be widely distributed or giving speeches to hundreds of people at a time, my husband and I began serving and mentoring individual entrepreneurs looking to take their businesses to the next level. The emptiness in our hearts from losing our son will always be there, but our hearts began to fill with love and gratitude for the work we were and are still doing with those we mentor.

My journey has shown me the highest highs and the lowest lows. I have chosen to close doors and have also faced doors that have been closed on me. Each time forced me to face the future, to make a choice: do I continue, or give in to my circumstances and give up on the future?

It has not been easy, but all of my life experiences, both good and bad, have come together to create who I am today. I have learned how precious our time on Earth is. When asked what the meaning of life is, I am reminded of my father's words to me each night as a child. "Have you added value to someone's life today?"

Each and every day provides us with the opportunity to choose how we live our lives. Living the life of your dreams is entirely up to you.

◎ ◎ ◎ ◎

Life is a great teacher. If you listen, your experiences can direct your path. If you're willing to learn, you may be able to avoid pain along the way. And if you're open, the opportunities available to you may be bigger than anything you could have imagined.

Wisdom can also be learned from others. So what can be learned from a lifetime of listening, learning, and being open to more?

LOSING MY MARBLES

by Charlotte Amdahl

have no idea where the years have gone. All the clichés I once rolled my eyes at are now flashing before me: "life is short," "don't blink," "age is just a number," and "you're only as old as you feel."

Driving on a quiet desert road on the way to a birthday party, I was thinking about "you're only as old as you feel." Because when asked how I'm doing, I'm quick to reply "Life is good!" I don't want to trouble my kids or others with my stuff. They have busy lives and stuff of their own to deal with. But if I am honest, the signs of a full life are there. I move a little slower, my vision is not as sharp, technology feels over my head, things ache that shouldn't, I watch more than I participate, my mind is not as quick, and given the choice to sit or move . . . sitting seems like the right choice.

As we're driving, I look over at the man next to me. It's his birthday we're celebrating today. We are heading to my son's house forty minutes up the road. Coincidently, it is our youngest son's birthday today as well. Celebrating them together is a tradition in our family. As I look at him, through the weathered skin and frail frame, I still see the caring blue eyes and strong man who stole my heart in high school, rescued me from a small farming community, and took me to the exciting big city of 40,000 people. Rochester, Minnesota, was only sixty miles from the farm where we grew up but it felt a world away.

It felt like an adventure. We had so much we wanted to accomplish. We built a life together. We pursued our dreams together. And after fifty-nine years of marriage, we have lived a lot of life together.

As we arrive at the birthday party and I get out of the car and open the back hatch, I reach for his wheelchair and think, *When did this happen?* Don't get me wrong, we have an amazing life, and we have so much to be grateful for. But today, as I struggle to get a wheelchair out of the back of an undersized SUV, it seems like only yesterday I was struggling to keep four kids settled in the back of an oversized station wagon. It seems like only yesterday I was celebrating with my birthday boys, one with thirty-five candles and the other with seven, and watching their matching blue eyes light up over a mutual love for pizza and cake.

Today at the party, I have to take my time to get my man settled in his new wheels. His legs work, but they are too weak to navigate the short sidewalk up to the house. His lungs work, too, but not well enough to process the effort it would take to make the twenty-five steps to the front door. His strong will and pride hates this, but he knows it's what we need to do to spend time with those we love the most.

As my son and his family greet us at the door, all the effort is instantly worth it. The grandkids greet us with big smiles and even bigger hugs. They all start talking at once, getting us caught up on everything from what is going on in school, to pets, and even trying to teach us Snapchat. Their energy gives us energy. Their smiles make us smile.

Walking by my son's office, I noticed something odd: a display of marbles. He has two clear glass jars of marbles on a shelf, with a single marble in the middle prominently on display for everyone to see.

The reason I think this is odd is that he didn't even *like* marbles as a kid. I remember him loving Legos and baseball cards, but marbles? I asked him about the marbles. He began talking almost more quickly than I could hear. He enthusiastically shared that his display of marbles has meaning; that each marble represents one year. On average, men in America start with seventy-six marbles and women with eighty-one. The jar on the right represents years lived, and the jar on the left represents years remaining, and the marble in the middle represents this year—the year he is living today. Every year on his birthday he moves one marble from left to right. The display is there to remind him that life is short, life is precious, and to live fully and with intent—to spend each moment on things that matter.

In his case, that is fine, but if I reflect upon my own life, my jar on the left is nearly empty, with just three marbles remaining.

I think about the jar on the right, the one that represents the years lived. There are amazing memories there. Raising four kids, being a working mom, being a stay-at-home mom, fifty-nine years of marriage, twelve grandkids, seven great-grandkids, travel, experiences, growing up on the farm, summer weeks at the lake, starting a business, retiring in Arizona, and all the adventures in between. There is also some pain in that jar. Financial stress, surviving breast cancer, marriage challenges, kids driving me crazy, health scares, losing loved ones . . . just to name a few.

I think about the jar on the left. The one with three marbles in it. Although I know only God knows my time, this does make me think. What do I want to do in life . . . and what am I waiting for?

And I think about the single marble, prominently on display in the middle, the one that represents this year, this moment. Over time, I have learned to live this marble differently. What has become clear and has changed over time is that what I focus on and value now is so much different than when I was younger.

I am no longer concerned with being the perfect family, building a career, becoming a millionaire, what the neighbors are up to, the latest fad diet, buying a bigger house, or even traveling the world. I am reaching less and hugging more. I now value being present and loving people where they are and for who they are and being grateful for the moments they are in front of me. The boys stopping in for a visit after a round of golf, or the girls flying in to spend a few days to escape the Minnesota winter, the grandkids popping in unexpectedly, a random phone call to catch up with my siblings or old friends, or welcoming a great-grandchild into the world . . . these moments are what I value most.

This is what matters and this is how I am going to spend the marble in the middle, and the precious few I have left. I am spending my time loving others, continuing to learn to love myself, and showing love to all I those I meet. And I am going to eat cake at the birthday party today. Life is too short to deny myself cake at a party. My son, the OolaGuru, says this all the time, too: "It's all about balance."

With age comes wisdom, but it's also possible to gain wisdom at any age. Are you, too, present enough to let life's wisdom speak to you? Here are a few approaches for allowing wisdom to enter into your life.

GAIN WISDOM FROM LIFE EXPERIENCES. You don't gain wisdom from playing small, so commit to living large and pursuing new opportunities. Be calculated, but take risks. At the same time, be real. You'll make mistakes. But if your mistakes seem to be repeating themselves, ask, "Where do I keep screwing up—and where can I gain wisdom from past experiences?"

Use the confidence gained from your wins to push forward, and the knowledge learned from your losses to course-correct. With each experience your wisdom database grows.

SEEK WISDOM FROM PEOPLE WHO'VE ACHIEVED WHAT YOU WANT. Accessing the right kind of wisdom for the right kinds of decisions is the key to accelerating your way to Oola. But you also have to be sure that the people you're listening to have *actually achieved results*—not just formed opinions.

While it may seem obvious, you'd be surprised how many women ask their broke neighbor for financial advice, or seek marriage advice from someone who's currently not speaking to their spouse and been divorced three times. And if you own a business and are looking for a mentor to guide you through your growth phase or a particularly tricky transaction, this point will be even more important.

Be judicious. Check credentials. Make sure the expert you're listening to has already succeeded in the *specific* area where *you* want to excel.

In the same way, be careful about getting advice from people who make money from selling their advice—particularly in the area of financial products, nutrition, and weight loss. Will they gain financially by steering you to a specific product versus exploring what's best for your needs? Check it out. Then check *them* out. You must choose wisely when seeking wisdom from others.

SPEND TIME IN PROPORTION TO THE DECISION BEING MADE. Deciding to buy a pack of gum or bottle of water takes just seconds, while purchasing a home, deciding to get married, or making a change in your career path requires serious time and dedicated analysis.

Make certain that the time you spend making the decision is directly proportional to the impact of the decision being made. Make small decisions quickly, but give big decisions the time they need.

3 SIMPLE STEPS TO THE **OOLA**LIFE

"No deposit, no return. We never get out of things more than we put into them."

— Gretchen Rubin | @gretchenrubin
Author of *Better Than Before*

Getting to your OolaLife takes action. Over the past twenty-one chapters, our intent has been to educate you about the 7 F's—and inspire you to overcome OolaBlockers and fully utilize the OolaAccelerators. Now the rubber meets the road.

It's time to make plans and get in motion. Over the next three chapters, we'll do that together—creating a workable plan to build the life you dream of and deserve.

There are three simple steps.

Step One, you need to check in with yourself: where are you right now in your life and where could you do better? Chapter 24—The OolaWheel—will help you with this reality check.

Step Two, you'll figure out where you want to go. What are the goals and dreams you have for your life? You'll lay out an OolaPlan that is unique to you.

Finally, in Step Three, you'll learn about the OolaPath—and how to take the daily actions you need to get you to your goals. It's time to get serious.

CHAPTER 24

Step One:
The **Oola**Wheel

Where Are You Today?

> *"Self-awareness is the ability to take
> an honest look at your life without any attachment
> to it being right or wrong, good or bad."*
>
> — Debbie Ford
> *New York Times bestselling author of nine books
> on personal transformation and human potential*

As the bright California sun sparkled on the warm sand of Newport Beach, Eric Smith reflected on his life. Without a doubt, the past year had been the most challenging he had lived so far. He'd lost his entire family in a series of tragic events. His father had died just the month before. And out of depression or desperation or both, he'd driven his 2004 Toyota Avalon across the country from Florida to California. His goal wasn't a place, but a pursuit.

He was lost and needed to find himself. Having traveled the 2,700 miles from Ft. Lauderdale to Los Angeles, he still was without an answer.

But that day on the beach, things were about to change . . . for good.

Looking down, he saw a copy of *Oola: Find Balance in an Unbalanced World*—someone's dog-eared copy stuck in the sand after a day of summer reading. Turning its pages, Eric read insights and stories he'd never been open to hearing before. It said he was created for a purpose—a unique calling on his life that no one else was equally equipped to do . . . that he needed to find gratitude in all things, both the good and the bad. It also said he needed a plan if he wanted to move forward and begin living Oola—and that plan began with a first step.

It's about time I stopped feeling lost, Eric thought. *So what do I have to do?*

Re-energized to make his future a top priority, Eric used the road trip back home to Florida to get real with where he was in all 7 areas of his life. Instead of being stressed and overwhelmed, he felt hope for the first time in as long as he could remember.

Grateful to have discovered the book in the sand that day, Eric knew this copy was meant to inspire someone else to begin living their OolaLife. He wrote a note inside his tattered copy of *Oola* about how its message had changed his life—praying that it would fall into the hands of someone in need. And he left it in a bag on a sandy beach in Ft. Lauderdale.

It could have been any book I found that day, he later wrote to us, *but for some reason it was this book. I like to think it was destiny.*

IT'S **IMPOSSIBLE** TO GET WHERE YOU'RE GOING WITHOUT **KNOWING** WHERE YOU ARE NOW

When you use your smartphone's maps app to get directions, the first thing that shows up is where *you* are at this moment—represented by a little blue dot. Plug in your destination, and your smartphone will use GPS technology to give you step-by-step, mile-by-mile directions from your current location to your desired endpoint. Before you can go anywhere, you need to know exactly where you are right now.

It never asks you about your past and doesn't care what mistakes you've made. It won't even factor in current challenges you might be facing. It simply shows you the fastest route from where you are now to where you want to go.

Well, what if *your own life plan* was that simple? What if, just like GPS, you didn't judge yourself, take yourself down distracting side roads, or factor in time-consuming stuff? You would just chart your course without bringing in a lot of outside factors to stop you. In fact, if you were using GPS, you wouldn't chart your own course *any other way.*

STARTING TO BUILD YOUR **OOLALIFE**: HOW DO **YOU** ROLL?

If you've ever ridden a bicycle, you know the wheels are the most important component. To keep the wheel strong, spokes radiate from the hub, and the valve in the tire helps you keep it full of air. Without the spokes, hub and valve, the wheel—and therefore, the bicycle—would eventually stop rolling and come to a stop.

Life is a lot like that wheel.

THE **SPOKES**

On the OolaWheel, there are seven spokes—each representing one category (or "F") of Oola. When the spokes are balanced, the wheel just *works*. It moves forward easily.

THE **HUB**

The hub of the wheel is the key—it's the base, the foundation, the core from which everything else emanates. Without a solid and secure hub, even with perfectly balanced spokes, your wheel will ultimately fail.

If you're cruising along, for instance, and a crisis hits your finances, you could pull the *Finance* spoke off your wheel and your bicycle would still roll. It'd be clunky, for sure, but the other spokes would hold it together and the wheel would still work. Add a divorce related to that financial stress—taking away another spoke—and yep, your bike would still go.

As long as you have a solid hub, you could lose *almost everything* and your wheel would still roll. It would be painful, clunky, and slow. But you would still move forward.

What's your hub? This is your question to ponder. What's the foundation on which your life is built? What's your anchor?

THE **VALVE**

Your unique value system acts like the *valve* of your wheel. What inspires you? Which F of Oola comes naturally to you and motivates you? This is what makes up your highest values. For some people, it's Finance. For others, it may be Family or their career (Field). Whatever it is for you, you're gifted in this area and you don't have to be asked or encouraged to pursue it.

Equally, we all have things in our life we naturally avoid. These are your low values. For the OolaSeeker, it's finance—he hates spreadsheets and budgets. The OolaGuru, on the other hand, finds the lowest value in Fun. Frankly, he would much rather be working (Field).

The intent is to use your high values to "pump up" key areas in life that you tend to ignore or avoid. For example, if your highest value is your kids (Family) and your lowest value is Fitness, think through how working on your fitness and overall health will benefit your family. Maybe you'll set a good example for them. Maybe you'll be able to participate in activities instead of standing on the sidelines. And maybe by taking better care of yourself, you'll be around long enough to see your grandkids have kids of their own.

LOOKING AT YOUR OWN **7 F'S OF OOLA**

To get a picture of where your life is now, complete the series of questionnaires starting on the next page—one for each of the 7 key areas of life. They're designed to help you "score" yourself on where you are now. Are you killin' it in some areas but completely messed up in others?

You can also find an interactive OolaWheel and a printable worksheet containing the OolaWheel at *www.oolalife.com/Step1*. Let's get started.

Simply rate the following on a **scale from 1 to 10**: 1 being low/bad/least true and 10 being high/good/most true. Write your number in the blank for each of the 10 questions. Then, at the bottom of the page, add up the total for all 10 questions and divide by 10. Put a dot on the spoke for FITNESS on your OolaWheel on page 317.

OOLAFITNESS

1) I would rate my current health .... ____

2) How close am I to my ideal weight? .... ____

3) I would rate my overall mental health .... ____

4) I do at least 3 cardio/resistance sessions per week. .... ____

5) How hard do I push myself during exercise? .... ____

6) I am active outside of exercise... ____

7) I practice relaxation daily. .... ____

8) I love my life and have little stress. .... ____

9) My meals are nutrient rich and proper calories for my body. ...... ____

10) I eat a balanced diet and avoid processed and fast food............. ____

TOTAL SCORE: _____ **/ 10 =** [   ]

(Circle this number on page 317)

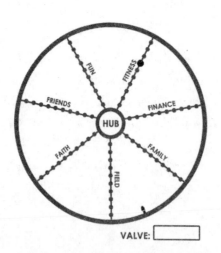

VALVE: [   ]

Simply rate the following on a **scale from 1 to 10**: 1 being low/bad/least true and 10 being high/good/most true. Write your number in the blank for each of the 10 questions. Then, at the bottom of the page, add up the total for all 10 questions and divide by 10. Put a dot on the spoke for FINANCE on your OolaWheel on page 317.

OOLAFINANCE

1) I would rate my current personal finances .... ____

2) I am saving at least 10% of every dollar I make for nonretirement purchases (car, trip, down payment, etc.). .... ____

3) I am completely debt free (minus my mortgage). .... ____

4) My monthly income exceeds my monthly expenses. .... ____

5) I am investing at least 15% for retirement. .... ____

6) I have an emergency account equaling at least 7 months of expenses. .... ____

7) I have the proper insurance (health, term life, property, etc.)....... ____

8) I give my money generously and with no expectation of anything in return. .... ____

9) I have a complete and updated will. .... ____

10) I have a solid budget and stick to it every month. .... ____

TOTAL SCORE: _____ **/ 10 =** [ ]

(Circle this number on page 317)

VALVE: [ ]

Simply rate the following on a **scale from 1 to 10**: 1 being low/bad/least true and 10 being high/good/most true. Write your number in the blank for each of the 10 questions. Then, at the bottom of the page, add up the total for all 10 questions and divide by 10. Put a dot on the spoke for FAMILY on your OolaWheel on page 317.

OOLAFAMILY

1) I would rate my current family situation .... ____

2) We eat at least one meal per day together as a family. .... ____

3) My immediate and extended family is functional........................... ____

4) Thinking of family makes me feel happy. .... ____

5) I am honest with my family members. .... ____

6) I work hard at being a better family member. .... ____

7) I set aside personal time with my family—without phones. .... ____

8) My family is loving, patient, supportive, and respectful................ ____

9) I hold no hurt feelings toward any family members. .... ____

10) I feel I spend the enough time with my family to meet their needs.. ____

TOTAL SCORE: _____ **/ 10 =** [   ]

(Circle this number on page 317)

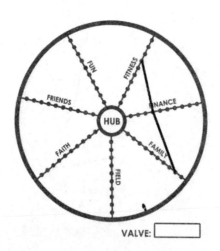

VALVE: [   ]

Simply rate the following on a **scale from 1 to 10**: 1 being low/bad/least true and 10 being high/good/most true. Write your number in the blank for each of the 10 questions. Then, at the bottom of the page, add up the total for all 10 questions and divide by 10. Put a dot on the spoke for FIELD on your OolaWheel on page 317.

OOLAFIELD

1) I would rate my current overall job satisfaction............................ ——

2) My job financially meets my needs. .... ——

3) I love my job. .... ——

4) I feel as if I am doing what I was created to do............................... ——

5) I have solid goals for my field. .... ——

6) My current job doesn't interfere with my family and
   personal time. .... ——

7) My current job makes the world a better place. .... ——

8) My job utilizes my natural gifts and abilities...................................... ——

9) My current job can support my long-term financial goals. .... ——

10) My job offers the opportunity to grow personally,
    professionally, and financially... ——

TOTAL SCORE: _____ **/ 10 =** [   ]

(Circle this number on page 317)

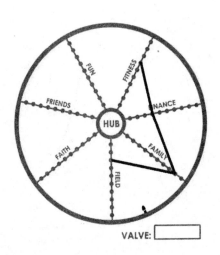

VALVE: [   ]

Simply rate the following on a **scale from 1 to 10**: 1 being low/bad/least true and 10 being high/good/most true. Write your number in the blank for each of the 10 questions. Then, at the bottom of the page, add up the total for all 10 questions and divide by 10. Put a dot on the spoke for FAITH on your OolaWheel on page 317.

OOLAFAITH

1) I would rate my faith .... ____

2) I feel connected to a higher purpose. .... ____

3) I am plugged into a faith community to continue to learn/grow. .... ____

4) I spend at least 20 minutes a day in meditation and/or prayer. ..... ____

5) My beliefs and the way I live my life are congruent. .... ____

6) I use my faith to help resolve conflict and issues in my life. .... ____

7) I reflect on my faith often thoughout the day. .... ____

8) I forgive easily. .... ____

9) I rely on my faith to guide my choices and decisions. .... ____

10) I feel comfortable sharing and teaching my faith to others. .... ____

TOTAL SCORE: _____ **/ 10 =** ▢

(Circle this number on page 317)

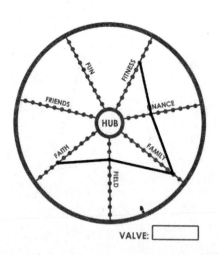

VALVE: ▢

Simply rate the following on a **scale from 1 to 10**: 1 being low/bad/least true and 10 being high/good/most true. Write your number in the blank for each of the 10 questions. Then, at the bottom of the page, add up the total for all 10 questions and divide by 10. Put a dot on the spoke for FRIENDS on your OolaWheel on page 317.

OOLAFRIENDS

1) I would rate my social network of friends .... ____

2) I have unconditionally loving, supportive, and empowering friends. .... ____

3) I am satisfied with the number of friendships in my life. .... ____

4) I am a good example/mentor for my friends. .... ____

5) My friends support my dreams and are good examples/ mentors for me. .... ____

6) When I think of my 3 closest friends, I have no stress. .... ____

7) I openly communicate and trust my friends. .... ____

8) I have friends who are good mentors in all 7 F's of Oola. .... ____

9) I have no hard feeling or ill will toward my present friendships.... ____

10) I am not judgmental toward my friends. .... ____

TOTAL SCORE: _____ **/ 10 =** [   ]

(Circle this number on page 317)

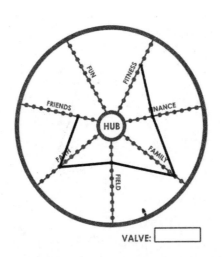

VALVE: [   ]

Simply rate the following on a **scale from 1 to 10**: 1 being low/bad/least true and 10 being high/good/most true. Write your number in the blank for each of the 10 questions. Then, at the bottom of the page, add up the total for all 10 questions and divide by 10. Put a dot on the spoke for FUN on your OolaWheel on page 317.

OOLAFUN

1) I would rate my fun in life.. ____

2) I enjoy and am having fun in life... ____

3) I try new things often. .... ____

4) I have fun and invest time pursuing my personal passion
   (i.e. hobby, interest)... ____

5) I have fun outside of work at least 3 times per week...................... ____

6) I check off at least one "bucket list" item each year....:................ ____

7) I am a fun person to be around. .... ____

8) Fun rarely interferes with my responsibilities. .... ____

9) People would say that I am a fun person. .... ____

10) I easily find free fun in simple everyday life. .... ____

TOTAL SCORE: _____ **/ 10 =**

(Circle this number on page 317)

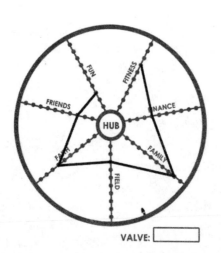

VALVE:

COMPLETE THE OOLAWHEEL

Now that you've completed the questionnaires, transfer your scores from pages 310–316 to the OolaWheel and connect the dots. If your connect-the-dots circle is smooth, it shows you're balanced. But if it's jagged and spiked, it will identify those one or two areas where you're off the charts and out of balance. If you've been thinking lately, *I'm feeling stressed and out of balance . . . I'm not rolling very well,* the OolaWheel exercise will show you why.

Follow these steps for completing your OolaWheel.

Step 1: Identify your Hub and write it in the Hub of the wheel.

Step 2: Identify your highest value and write this in the valve of the diagram.

Step 3: Place a dot on each spoke of the diagram. This is where you rated yourself on each questionnaire. If you scored a "1" in any area, for instance, you would mark the *first dot* closest to the hub. If you scored a "5," your dot would be about halfway out.

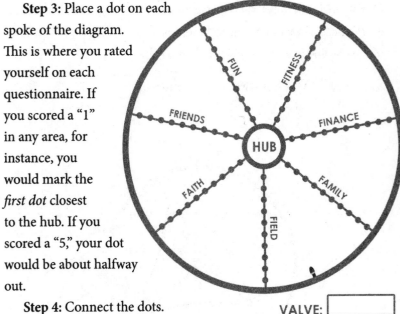

Step 4: Connect the dots.

Step 5: How do you roll? Where do you need to improve first?

VALVE:

HOW DOES **YOUR OOLA**WHEEL LOOK?
WHAT DO YOU **NEED** WORK ON FIRST?

Here's where the OolaWheel is important: identifying where you're the most out of balance will cue you up on where to start. If your finances are messy and they're impacting the other areas of your life, plus keeping your wheel from being in balance, you'll want to clean up those messes before moving ahead on the other six F's of Oola.

In the next chapter, you'll be creating a customized plan to bring all 7 areas into alignment. Now that you know where you are, it's time to formulate a plan for where you want to go. Let's move on to Step Two: The OolaPlan . . .

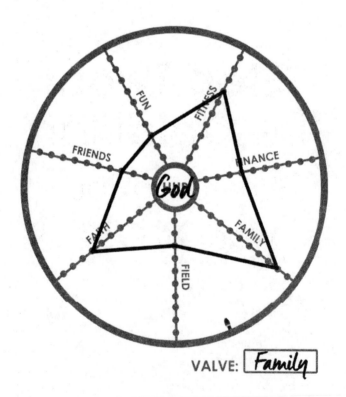

VALVE: Family

Step Two:
The **Oola**Plan

Where Do You
Want to Go?

"Define success on your own terms, achieve it by your own rules, and build a life you're proud to live."

— Anne Sweeney | @Anne_Sweeney
Former president of ABC Cable Networks Group
and The Disney Channel Worldwide

What's my OolaOne? thought Kate Notaro. *What's the one thing that—if I could change it—would improve every area of my life?*

Reading the original *Oola* book and later meeting the OolaGuys as they were collecting dreams on the OolaBus in Buffalo, New York, Kate knew the answer instantly: quit smoking.

She'd been a smoker for over twenty years, but at that moment, she decided to quit for good . . . no excuses. After the first few months of being smoke-free, it dawned on her how much money her family was saving. She had more free time and felt 100 percent better.

Soon, others began to take notice, and—inspired by Kate's success—two friends decided to quit also. But when Kate's *family* started noticing the positive changes in her (both physical and mental); that's where their Oola really took off. Kate's daughter Madison set a goal and crushed it with a 4.2 GPA while taking honors classes and playing volleyball. And her thirteen-year-old son Alex achieved the goal he put on the OolaBus of losing thirty pounds and made the soccer team over several more talented players. He even made the swim team, along with gaining a new sense of confidence.

Inspired by the positive changes in their family, they decided to fly to Vegas and attend OolaPalooza. Kate and her husband Tony shared one of the most powerful experiences ever as they made joint plans for their lives and their marriage. They wrote some difficult goals, but returned home armed with a newfound motivation to participate in their first 5K run, get reconnected to a church family, cut sugar from their diet, and pay off $16,000 in credit card debt.

Kate even recommitted to leaning into her relationship with Tony, overcoming fear and resentment that still lingered from an abusive first marriage.

What could you accomplish by setting one bold and daring goal? Let's start by learning to set goals the Oola way . . .

GOALS ARE **MILESTONES** TO YOUR **DREAMS**

Most of us have dreams. They help us visualize the perfect life complete with the kind of people, things, and accomplishments we want to have. Dreams are huge, exciting, and free of fear, self-doubt, and other limiting beliefs. *If I knew it would really happen,* we think, *what would I want in my life?* Dreams don't require you to know the "how"—they only require you to know "what."

Unfortunately, when it comes to bringing those dreams to reality, most people confuse dreams with *goals.* Goals are the milestones—the little steps you need to complete on the way to achieving your dreams. Goals are action steps, planned then accomplished. They're the baby steps you must follow—day by day—to get to your dream lifestyle.

ARE YOU **SMART** ABOUT YOUR GOALS? OR ARE YOU **LYING** TO YOURSELF?

A good way to write your goals is to follow the S.M.A.R.T. formula created in 1981 by George Doran, writing for *Management Review* magazine. "There's a S.M.A.R.T. way to write goals and objectives," the article began—and we agree. Here are the characteristics *your goals* should include:

SPECIFIC—The goal should contain actual numbers, amounts, sizes, or other well-defined terms you want to reach. It would be understandable and clear to anyone else, and is memorable to you.

MEASURABLE—When your goal includes the specifics above, you can actually measure whether you're close to achieving it or still far away. You can keep score and track your progress. But most importantly, only if it's measurable will you be able to determine when you've achieved your goal.

ACCOUNTABLE—When a goal is specific and measurable, you can be held accountable to it. Find someone who loves and supports you and who will keep you accountable to the goals you have set for your life. For us, this was our small group of guys in Vegas. For you, it may be friends, neighbors, co-workers, or supportive family members. Find a group that loves you well enough to be tough with you and keep you on task so you don't drift from the goals and dreams you've set for your life.

If you've ever said, *I'm gonna start a diet on Monday. I'm gonna turn off my phone on Sundays. I'm gonna pay off my biggest credit card by New Year's*—then didn't—you need an accountability crew.

REALISTIC—Where dreams are huge, intangible, and often feel unrealistic, goals need to be set in a way that they are doable with the resources, knowledge, time, and money you have available—*or those you could acquire.* This is an important distinction since most people stop pursuing their goals because they don't have the necessary resources *now.* The one thing you *do have,* however, is determination, passion, and the ability to collaborate with others who can guide you, inform you, invest in you, and otherwise help you reach you goal.

TIME-BASED—Perhaps the most important characteristic of a goal is that it includes a *date and time* by which you'll achieve the objective. *By January 1, 2019,* you might write, *I will have completely paid off my $68,000 in student loans.* Do your homework; research the process; ask experts who might know—only then can you realistically determine this time frame. Be sure to give yourself *enough* time to realistically achieve the goal, but not so much that your pursuit of the goal fills all available time. Projects tend to expand into the time allotted. Don't let them.

21–7–1:
FINDING YOUR OOLAONE

We're fans of Warren Buffet, the billionaire investor and unassuming philanthropist from Omaha, Nebraska. When making goals, he recommends writing down the top twenty things you want to do in life—then crossing out all but the top three . . . *then pursuing those.*

We agree.

If you wrote down ten things under each of the 7 F's of Oola, you'd have a whopping seventy goals to accomplish. That's a formula for overwhelm. Instead, choose your Top 7—not necessarily one per category, but the seven goals that will give your life more balance (*and are in line with the biggest dreams you have for your life*). Do this and you'll be working steadily to create balance in all seven areas. Once you've built momentum and a strong belief in yourself, then look at the other goals and take them on.

Of course, if you really want to up-level your life quickly and with the greatest impact, we challenge you to narrow your focus from seven to just one big, audacious goal that would truly change your life. It may not be the one you *want* to do, but it's the one you know deep inside you *need* to do. Is it finding a higher paying job or finishing your MBA? Is it losing weight and preventing future health challenges? How about confronting that addiction? Would becoming debt-free change life as you know it? What's your *one thing* . . . your OolaOne?

GRAB A SHARPIE AND
START WRITING YOUR **GOALS**

On the Oola "stickers" printed on the following pages,** we invite you to start writing your top Oola goals. Practice how to properly set goals in a way that you can achieve them by writing three for each of the 7 F's of Oola (for a total of twenty-one goals). Use the SMART format mentioned earlier. Then, narrow down the twenty-one goals to your most important seven goals—the seven that will give your life more balance and which are in line with your biggest dreams. Then pick your OolaOne: the one single goal that, when accomplished, holds the power to spark the change that can transform your entire life.

Once you've done that, pull the stickable sticker from this book, write your OolaOne goal, and "make it stick" by tracking down the OolaBus on social media and personally adding your dream to the tens of thousands of others we have collected on our journey.

Now, let's get started!

** Or download them for free at *www.oolalife.com/*

21 GOALS

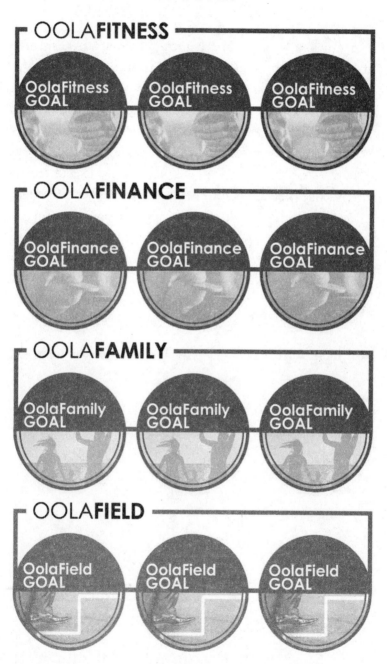

21 GOALS (continued)

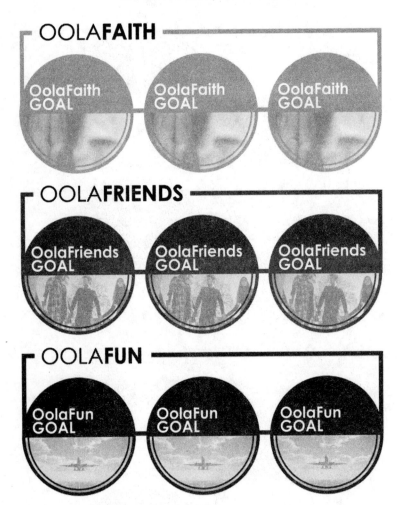

OOLA**FAITH**

OolaFaith GOAL

OolaFaith GOAL

OolaFaith GOAL

OOLA**FRIENDS**

OolaFriends GOAL

OolaFriends GOAL

OolaFriends GOAL

OOLA**FUN**

OolaFun GOAL

OolaFun GOAL

OolaFun GOAL

TOP 7

OOLA**ONE**

Step Three:
The **Oola**Path

How Are You Going to Get There?

"So often people are working hard at the wrong thing. Working on the right thing is probably more important than working hard."

— Caterina Fake | @caterina
Co-founder of the website Flickr,
acquired by Yahoo! for $35 million

f you've ever sat down with the recognized leader in your field or the top-selling agent in your industry or the foremost philanthropist in your category, you can probably guess what was going through our minds the first time we met Jack Canfield, the originator of the *Chicken Soup for the Soul* book series.

We had quietly stalked him for months—researching him, finding out who his key people are, and tracking the history of his career. We wanted advice in how to scale the Oola message and change the world with this word by creating more *Oola* books and building a lifestyle brand. We decided to follow our own advice, dream big and start with the most published non-fiction author of all time.

What does it take to publish over 220 books and have 550 million copies in print in 49 languages? What does it take to land on the *New York Times* Best Seller List 40 times—with eleven books at #1 and a record-setting seven books on the list *at the same time?* How could we go from hosting OolaPalooza events in the United States to training millions of people in 108 countries?

When you sit down with someone of Jack Canfield's caliber, you go prepared. But you also keep things simple.

After connecting with Jack's longtime business partner, Patty Aubery, we scored a meeting and went with a 3x5 notecard of the *specific* outcomes we hoped for: details on how to take our message to scale, strategies for how they sold so many books—even advice on how to keep our own lives in balance as the Oola brand grew. If we could also score some small follow-up commitments from Jack, we thought, well that would be even better.

As the conversation began and Jack pulled a 3x5 card from his pocket to jot down some contacts he wanted to send us, we gave each other the side-eye. *A 3x5 notecard,* we silently voiced to one another. *Yeah, we're in the right place.*

WHY A 3X5 NOTECARD?

For us, using 3x5 notecards goes back to 1997 when we first met with our crew to set goals at the Hard Rock Hotel in Las Vegas. The music was loud, the lighting was bad, and we definitely didn't want to be the guys sitting there with our laptops open. We wrote on the notecards not only where we were in each of the 7 key areas of life, but also where we wanted to go—and most importantly, *those action steps we would take* to make our dreams become a reality.

To this day, we still use notecards and recommend that you do the same. There's something special about contemplating the specific actions you need to take to achieve your dreams, then writing them in your own handwriting, and feeling the sense of accomplishment by crossing off each task once it's completed. There is power in this process, and also beauty in its simplicity.

DAILY ACTION: 3X5 NOTECARD

In the busyness of this unbalanced world, it's easy for your dreams to get lost in the clutter of day-to-day life. So one way to make sure they stay top priority is, every night before you go to bed, grab a 3x5 notecard and write down at least three action steps you'll take the next day that will move you closer to one (or more) of the Top 7 goals you set on your OolaPlan.

The notecard can include the daily stuff, too—groceries, dry cleaning, picking up the kids from practice—but make sure that *at least three* items on your list are action steps that will move you closer to your OolaLife. Draw a line down the middle, if needed, to separate the junk errands from your real-life goals.

Do Step Three: The OolaPath every day and in one year, you will have taken more than 1,000 action steps toward your OolaLife—while most people we meet haven't taken *any steps* toward their dreams in years. Let's get started!

LIVE**OOLA**

- Groceries
- Laundry
- Pick up kids
- Wash the car

- 2 mile run
- Create budget
- Date night

BE GRATEFUL, HAVE FAITH, AND GO GET YOUR OOLALIFE.

LIVE**OOLA**

BE GRATEFUL, HAVE FAITH, AND GO GET YOUR OOLALIFE.

DON'T **LOSE** YOUR **DREAMS** TO THE GRAVEL

At our last OolaPalooza, we tried to recreate a lesson that the OolaGuru saw recently at his church. On the night before our event, we found ourselves at a Hobby Lobby store in rural Kansas City purchasing a large glass vase, seven fake oranges, and two bags of gravel. Without rehearsing, we hopped on stage the next day and began filling the vase with a combination of oranges and gravel to teach a valuable lesson. While the process was supposed to be dramatic, it ended up being hysterical when the OolaSeeker chased rolling oranges across the stage and the OolaGuru struggled to remove his hand after getting it stuck in the vase.

As the crowd roared with laughter, we realized the lesson came across just the same: if you fill the vase with the gravel first, then try to add the seven oranges, you'll never fit everything in. But if you start by adding the oranges first, then slowly pour in the gravel, letting it filter down around the oranges—miraculously it all fits.

The point of this stage fail is that the gravel represents the day-to-day clutter of our lives: running errands, kid stuff, soccer practice, emails, shopping, vet appointments, cleaning house, making meals, social media . . . life. The seven oranges, on the other hand, represent the seven key areas of life—your 7 F's of Oola.

If you take care of your major goals first, then fit the little things around them, miraculously it all gets accomplished.

In the same way, the journey to your OolaLife is a three-step journey, so don't stop at just two. Take action by putting your oranges in first. Spend time every night writing down three or more action items that are deliberately intended to bring about the goals you have for your life. Only then should you let the gravel fill in the spaces that remain.

Simply planning and taking your first action steps toward the OolaLife is often what will stop the insanity and make you feel more in control. It's like a pattern interrupt. You're taking charge of your future.

But don't just stop with planning. The purpose of this book is to encourage and inspire you to *pursue* a better life—one with less stress. A life that is balanced and growing: the life you dream of and deserve. The OolaLife.

After meeting and working with thousands of Oola Women, we can assure you, from experience, that just making these decisions will give you a sense of accomplishment and make you feel like you're halfway there.

Now's the time to ensure you do what's necessary to go the remaining distance. Start taking action today.

CONCLUSION

ONCE YOU START, THERE'S NO GOING BACK TO **"ORDINARY"**

Your life was designed to be unique, compelling . . . exceptional. With the three simple steps to your OolaLife, it can be.

But one bonus outcome you may not have considered before is how much *just the pursuit* of greatness will change you as a person. You'll learn new skills, meet new contacts, and gain new wisdom. No one can take away *who you become* as a result of pursuing your goals.

Once you become a more connected entrepreneur, a more engaged mom, a more accomplished career professional . . . there's no going back to ordinary. And think about those around you. Because you're becoming a better individual, your family, friends, coworkers, and others you interact with will naturally become inspired to improve, too—a phenomenon that will slowly change your community and ultimately transform the world. If you've ever thought, *I'm just one person. What could I possibly do?* Realize that getting to #Oola is how *together* we can change the world with a word.

NOW IT'S TIME TO **WRITE** YOUR **OWN** OOLA STORY

Remember that this book contains *other* women's stories. Its principles are the product of *our* path and our experiences. Now it's time to write your own story and begin creating a new body of knowledge for yourself. Your Oola is your Oola. Your starting place and the goals and dreams you've set are uniquely your own. Boldly be yourself, take action every day and go after them (even if it means buying a goat). ;-)

Don't pursue happiness, pursue Oola. If you commit to that alone, you'll meet happy many times along the way.

STAY **CONNECTED** TO OOLA BY **JOINING** US IN A BIGGER VISION

The Oola movement is growing daily—a community of people who love and support each other as we actively pursue a better life. You'll meet countless other women—through our blog stories, interviews, and social media posts. So get involved! Sign up for the free 21-Day Oola for Women Challenge at *www.oolalife.com/women*. You'll find daily inspiration and learn more about the women you met in the stories in this book.

Grab us at an upcoming OolaPalooza event. Or stay connected with us at *www.oolalife.com* or on social media @oolalife and @oolaseeker and @oolaguru.

We're always humbled and grateful to meet readers who took the time to immerse themselves in this book and who are willing to be vulnerable and honest about where they can do better. We applaud you for being courageous enough to take the first step in making positive changes in your life. Together, we can change the world with a word: #Oola

Be grateful, have faith, and go get your OolaLife.

ABOUT THE AUTHORS

DAVE BRAUN (Salt Lake City, Utah) and **TROY AMDAHL** (Phoenix, Arizona)—aka the OolaGuys—are co-authors of the international bestselling book *Oola: Find Balance in an Unbalanced World.*

Dave (OolaSeeker) and Troy (OolaGuru) are renowned experts in goal-setting and creating a proper work-life balance. They frequently criss-cross the country in a 1970 VW Surf Bus, speaking to people, collecting their dreams on stickers that cover the bus, and helping them find balance and growth in the 7 key areas of life—the 7 F's of Oola. By revealing how to remove the stress related to a life out of balance, they unlock the greatness that is inside all of us. A better "YOU" makes a better family, a better community, and ultimately a better world. The OolaGuys are committed to changing the world with this word, and with their simple yet life-changing message.

ACKNOWLEDGMENTS

L ike most other achievements in life, a book is the result of the dedicated efforts of many people. We want to extend a big Oola thank you to:

Janet Switzer, the *New York Times* bestselling coauthor of *The Success Principles,* and a woman whose work in the personal development industry spans 25 years, 30 languages and over 100 countries. Your expertise and guidance made this book possible. From helping us shape the *Oola for Women* manuscript, to navigating the publishing process with us, to helping us write a #1 bestselling book, you are an absolute professional. Thank you for your smart insights and long hours spent in the conception and planning of *Oola for Women;* the easy-breezy interviews that captured our ideas, stories and training content; and the writing of chapters and tutorials that articulated our teachings. What a class act. We're so grateful for you.

Christian Blonshine and Peter Vegso, our publishers at Health Communications, Inc. You are more than publishers, you are family. You saw our vision for the Oola brand and guided us from start to finish with savvy advice and an open mind. Thank you for becoming a champion for the Oola lifestyle and worldwide potential—and for creating rousing support for *Oola for Women* with your amazing sales team. We're so thankful you've joined us on this journey!

Patty Aubery, president of the Jack Canfield companies and *New York Times* bestselling coauthor of *Chicken Soul for the Christian Soul*. We're so grateful for your wisdom, enthusiasm, and insights as we've built the Oola publishing brand. Thank you for jumping in with advice, connections, expertise, and keen business sense derived from nearly 30 years at the top of this industry. Your guidance and friendship has been an amazing gift to us.

Christine Belleris, our brilliant and supportive editor at HCI Books. Thank you for your passion and unflagging energy for the *Oola* book series, and for your review and advice on the manuscript. You rock. We loved working with you.

Kim Weiss, book publicist extraordinaire, and Meryl Moss and the team at Meryl Moss Media. Thanks so much for bringing your special brand of enthusiasm and expertise to the *Oola* book promotional tour.

Anthony Clausi, who proofread the manuscript. You have a keen eye and impressive attention to detail. Thanks for a fantastic job. Lawna Patterson Oldfield, who designed the book's interior pages. Great job and many thanks.

Svetlana Uscumlic, who designed the book cover and jacket. We love it!

Ryan Longnecker, who shot the cover photo. Hope you had as much fun that day as we did. If the OolaBus had a personality, hey, you captured it!

Larissa Hise Henoch, Lori Golden, Allison Janse, Ian Briggs, Dawn Grove, Gina Johnson, and all the other professionals at Health Communications, Inc., who were instrumental in designing, typesetting, digitizing and producing this book—then getting it out to readers everywhere. You are so good at what you do.

Max Amdahl, Chaly Jones, and Team Oola who worked tirelessly on advance promotion of this book and continue today—with relentless effort—to expand the reach of the Oola message through countless channels and markets. Couldn't do it without you all—we're honored to be working with you.

To our families, for being the reason why life balance and living in Oola is so important to us. We love you, we love you, we love you.

And finally, thanks especially to our forty-two contributing writers who shared their lives throughout the pages of this book. Thanks also to the countless thousands of participants at OolaPalooza and other events over the past three years for sharing their goals, challenges and victories with us. Your passion to change your lives is what inspires us every day. Thanks for stepping out of your comfort zone and being role models for other women. Your heart and soul are woven throughout the pages of this book. With your love and support, we are more confident than ever that, together, we can change the world with a word: #Oola

The Oola Wheel

WHERE ARE YOU TODAY?

FITNESS	7.33
FINANCE	6.33
FAMILY	7.67
FIELD	4.00
FAITH	9.33
FRIENDS	5.67
FUN	10.00

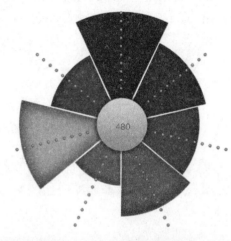

480

Your OolaScore 480

OolaSeeker's OolaScore 5 7 7
OolaGuru's OolaScore 7 1 2

By answering three simple questions in the 7 key areas of life, you will establish a starting point. This FREE and simple test will quickly expose where your life is out of balance and stressed.

FREE LIFE BALANCE TEST:

WWW.OOLALIFE.COM/STEP1

CONTINUE YOUR JOURNEY TO YOUR
OOLALIFE WITH THE **FREE 21-DAY**

#OolaforWomen
CHALLENGE

Sign-up link:

WWW.OOLALIFE.COM/WOMEN

Stay Connected

@OolaLife @OolaGuru @OolaSeeker

*"THE BEST PART OF THE JOURNEY IS THE
PEOPLE WHO WALK IT WITH YOU."*

OOLAPALOOZA

50% EDUCATIONAL | 50% ENTERTAINING | 100% LIFE-CHANGING

Life out of balance? Seeking the life and business of your dreams? The time is NOW. Join us for our favorite event of the year! We get to dream with you, set goals together, support each other, and keep each other accountable. This is what we have done together for over 17 years and now we get to do it with you. We will reveal not only how to succeed in business, but also how to achieve your full potential in all 7 key areas of life.

Learn more & sign up:

WWW.OOLALIFE.COM/OOLAPALOOZA

Want the OolaGuys to speak at your event?
EMAIL **EVENTS@OOLALIFE.COM**

RECEIVE 10% OFF YOUR
first purchase
FROM THE OOLASTORE

PROMO CODE: **OOLAWOMEN**

WWW.OOLALIFE.COM/STORE

TOGETHER

WE CAN CHANGE THE WORLD
WITH A WORD #*Oola*

READ ALL THE BOOKS IN THE OOLA SERIES:

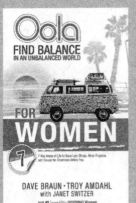

WILL THE NEXT OOLA BOOK INCLUDE YOUR STORY?

What do Oola readers find most memorable about our books? It's the heartfelt stories from ordinary people just like you who are trying to make the most out of this crazy journey called "life." Do you have a short personal story that you think imparts the lessons of living Oola? If so, share it with us for the chance to be featured in one of our upcoming books. Submit it at the site below.

WWW.OOLALIFE.COM/STORY